ALCOHOLISM

Other Books in the Current Controversies Series:

ALCOHOLISM

David L. Bender, *Publisher*
Bruno Leone, *Executive Editor*

Bonnie Szumski, *Managing Editor*
Katie de Koster, *Senior Editor*

Carol Wekesser, *Book Editor*

CURRENT CONTROVERSIES

Cover photo: © O'Brien & Mayor Photography/FPG

Library of Congress Cataloging-in-Publication Data

Alcoholism / book editor, Carol Wekesser
    p. cm. — (Current controversies)
    Includes bibliographical references and index.
    Summary: A collection of articles debating the seriousness of alcoholism, its causes, treatment, and its effects on families.
    ISBN 1-56510-074-3 (lib.) — ISBN 1-56510-073-5 (pbk.)
    1. Alcoholism—United States. 2. Alcoholism—Treatment—United States. [1. Alcoholism.] I. Wekesser, Carol, 1963-   . II. Series.
HV5066.A42   1994
362.29'2'0973—dc20
                                               93-22396
                                                   CIP
                                                   AC

Printed on
recycled paper

© Copyright 1994 by Greenhaven Press, Inc., PO Box 289009, San Diego, CA 92198-9009
Printed in the U.S.A.

Contents

Chapter 2: Is Alcoholics Anonymous the Most Effective Treatment for Alcoholism?

Yes: Alcoholics Anonymous Is the Most Effective Treatment for Alcoholism

No: Alcoholics Anonymous Is Not the Most Effective Treatment for Alcoholism

Chapter 3: Do Alcohol Advertisements Encourage Alcohol Abuse?

Yes: Alcohol Advertisements Encourage Alcohol Abuse

No: Alcohol Advertisements Do Not Encourage Alcohol Abuse

Chapter 4: Do Adult Children of Alcoholics Benefit from Recovery Groups?

Yes: Adult Children of Alcoholics Need Recovery Groups

Recovery groups provide adult children of alcoholics with a forum to express their childhood anger. Such groups should be used as stepping-stones to help ACOAs accept the problems of their childhoods and go beyond these problems to build emotionally healthy lives.

No: Recovery Groups for Adult Children of Alcoholics Are Problematic

Chapter 5: How Should Alcoholism Be Treated?

Foreword

By definition, controversies are "discussions of questions in which opposing opinions clash" (Webster's Twentieth Century Dictionary Unabridged). Few would deny that controversies are a pervasive part of the human condition and exist on virtually every level of human enterprise. Controversies transpire between individuals and among groups, within nations and between nations. Controversies supply the grist necessary for progress by providing challenges and challengers to the status quo. They also create atmospheres where strife and warfare can flourish. A world without controversies would be a peaceful world; but it also would be, by and large, static and prosaic.

The Series' Purpose

The purpose of the Current Controversies series is to explore many of the social, political, and economic controversies dominating the national and international scenes today. Titles selected for inclusion in the series are highly focused and specific. For example, from the larger category of criminal justice, Current Controversies deals with specific topics such as police brutality, gun control, white collar crime, and others. The debates in Current Controversies also are presented in a useful, timeless fashion. Articles and book excerpts included in each title are selected if they contribute valuable, long-range ideas to the overall debate. And wherever possible, current information is enhanced with historical documents and other relevant materials. Thus, while individual titles are current in focus, every effort is made to ensure that they will not become quickly outdated. Books in the Current Controversies series will remain important resources for librarians, teachers, and students for many years.

In addition to keeping the titles focused and specific, great care is taken in the editorial format of each book in the series. Book introductions and chapter prefaces are offered to provide background material for readers. Chapters are organized around several key questions that are answered with diverse opinions representing all points on the political spectrum. Materials in each chapter include opinions in which authors clearly disagree as well as alternative opinions in which authors may agree on a broader issue but disagree on the possible solutions. In this way, the content of each volume in Current Controversies mirrors

11

the mosaic of opinions encountered in society. Readers will quickly realize that there are many viable answers to these complex issues. By questioning each author's conclusions, students and casual readers can begin to develop the critical thinking skills so important to evaluating opinionated material.

Current Controversies is also ideal for controlled research. Each anthology in the series is composed of primary sources taken from a wide gamut of informational categories including periodicals, newspapers, books, United States and foreign government documents, and the publications of private and public organizations. Readers will find factual support for reports, debates, and research papers covering all areas of important issues. In addition, an annotated table of contents, an index, a book and periodical bibliography, and a list of organizations to contact are included in each book to expedite further research.

Perhaps more than ever before in history, people are confronted with diverse and contradictory information. During the Persian Gulf War, for example, the public was not only treated to minute-to-minute coverage of the war, it was also inundated with critiques of the coverage and countless analyses of the factors motivating U.S. involvement. Being able to sort through the plethora of opinions accompanying today's major issues, and to draw one's own conclusions, can be a complicated and frustrating struggle. It is the editors' hope that Current Controversies will help readers with this struggle.

"Alcoholism causes more harm than all other drugs combined. Yet while Americans are willing to wage a war on illegal drugs, they are less willing to combat the nation's love affair with alcohol."

Introduction

Many Americans drink alcoholic beverages. They toast birthdays, weddings, and other family rituals with wine, and swig beer and sip cocktails at holiday parties and weekend outings. In 1987, the average American drank the equivalent of 56 gallons of beer, and in 1988, Americans spent nearly $88 billion on alcohol.

But this love of alcohol sometimes comes at a high price. Since the nation's founding, alcohol abuse has destroyed lives and ruined families. An average of three hundred people die each day from alcohol-related causes, and alcohol is tied to one-fifth of the nation's suicides and more than half of its violent crimes. Alcoholism—the addiction to alcohol—is responsible for much of this misery. Through the years, authorities have enacted a variety of restrictions to balance Americans' love of alcohol with the harm it causes.

Although the word "alcoholism" was only coined in 1860, Americans have long known the pain alcohol can cause. Colonial authorities, concerned that the colonists on average drank a pint or a quart of beer or cider at a time, punished public drunkenness with the stocks or flogging. Even with such severe punishments drinking was so popular that laborers would stop several times each day to drink. (Most expected the employer to provide the beer or rum.) The colonists largely ignored a 1645 law that outlawed drinking more than a half-pint. This inability to control alcohol abuse clearly frustrated the courts, and in 1648 Massachusetts deputies admitted that drunkenness was rampant despite the "wholesome laws provided and punished."

As the popularity of alcohol increased throughout the eighteenth century, so did concerns about alcoholism. In 1784 American physician Benjamin Rush published *An Inquiry into the Effects of Ardent Spirits upon the Human Body and Mind*, in which he identified alcohol addiction as a disease causing liver failure, epilepsy, gout, and madness, among other afflictions. The rising popularity of distilled spirits especially concerned Rush and others, for this "hard liquor" enabled drinkers to become intoxicated more quickly.

Most Americans did not heed Rush's warnings. By 1820, the average American was drinking enough alcohol to equal about *seventy* gallons of beer annually. Alarmed physicians continued to cite the health hazards of excessive drinking. Social critics theorized that alcohol abuse contributed to poverty. These concerns led to increased support for the temperance movement, which advocated the elimination of alcohol consumption. Average alcohol consumption decreased by more than half after the first temperance crusade in the late 1820s. This movement grew, and by 1855 thirteen states had prohibited the sale of alcohol. As later leaders would learn, however, prohibition laws are easier to pass than to enforce. With the outbreak of the Civil War came an outbreak of alcohol consumption and abuse, and a suspension of the temperance movement.

The prohibitionists were not vanquished, however. After the war they regrouped and once again preached temperance. This time the movement gained enormous strength from social reformers, who saw how male alcoholics harmed their wives and children: alcoholics are more likely to be abusive, and have more difficulty staying employed. Decades of marching and speaking by the Woman's Christian Temperance Union (WCTU), the Anti-Saloon League, and other groups finally led to the passage of the Eighteenth Amendment in 1919, which prohibited the manufacture, sale, transportation, import, and export of alcohol. Those who abhorred the harms of alcohol could claim victory.

But Prohibition was a failure. Americans ignored it and authorities could not enforce it. Americans still demanded alcohol despite the health and social problems associated with it. Many recent immigrants came from nations where beer, wine, or other alcoholic beverages were important in cultural traditions, and they were unwilling to give up these traditions. Other Americans simply enjoyed drinking socially. Authorities also found that alcoholics would find and drink alcohol in any form, regardless of the law. After Congress repealed Prohibition in 1933, authorities began to focus on other measures to control alcoholism, including programs such as Alcoholics Anonymous, inpatient treatment in hospitals and clinics, and psychological counseling.

Today, America's love/hate relationship with alcohol continues. For example, while Surgeon General Antonia C. Novello in 1992 decried alcohol abuse among underage Americans, alcohol advertisers continued to portray young people partying with beer and wine coolers. Alcoholism causes more harm than all other drugs combined. Yet while Americans are willing to wage a war on illegal drugs, they are less willing to combat the nation's love affair with alcohol. As James B. Jacobs of New York University states:

> Americans have been exhorted to drink moderately since the beginning of the Republic, and such exhortations are common today. The media are filled with warnings against excessive drinking, especially drinking and driving. Still, human nature and a cultural and social system that promotes alcohol consumption make it unlikely that . . . public education can reduce the amount of excessive and pathological drinking. If, as a society, we want the pleasures and benefits of abundant alcoholic beverages, it seems we must also absorb a very heavy cost.

Alcoholism

Alcoholism: Current Controversies explores why so many Americans seek "the pleasures and benefits of abundant alcoholic beverages," and what factors cause some to become alcoholic. The contributors offer ideas that could help America and its affection for alcohol and reduce the many social and health problems related to this addiction.

Chapter 1

Is Alcoholism a Disease?

Chapter Preface

In his 1960 book *The Disease Concept of Alcoholism*, researcher E.M. Jellinek theorized that alcoholism is a disease, with specific causes, a predictable progression, and diagnosable symptoms. Today, many physicians, therapists, and others who treat alcoholism agree that it is a chronic disease with an unknown biological or genetic cause. Most researchers believe individuals are born with a predisposition to alcoholism, and that other factors—personality, family life, social surroundings—push the potential alcoholic into alcoholism.

Those who believe alcoholism is a disease tend to view alcoholics as victims of a medical condition. Consequently, while they acknowledge that the alcoholic's behavior contributes to the addiction, such researchers usually focus on finding chemical, biological, or genetic cures for the addiction rather than on punishing the alcoholic or treating him or her solely with psychological therapy. As researcher Kenneth Blum states, "The solution to the problem of alcoholism cannot be found in the ballot box [as in Prohibition], or in the policeman's club or gun. It can be found only in the laboratory where the disease process can be explored."

Despite the widespread acceptance of alcoholism as a disease, however, there are still many who dispute this theory and who believe that it interferes with the alcoholic's ability to recover. Herbert Fingarette, a leading researcher on alcoholism and addiction and the author of *Heavy Drinking: The Myth of Alcoholism as a Disease*, states:

> Many heavy drinkers view the labels "diseased" and "alcoholic" as stigmatizing, and so they reject help under such terms. Furthermore, the notion that this disease causes people to lose the ability to control their drinking may discourage a heavy drinker from trying to stop in the (false) belief that it's hopeless.

Alcoholism cannot be a disease, Fingarette concludes, because it does not have a predictable progression (not all people who abuse alcohol become alcoholics, and not all alcoholics inevitably die from their addiction) and because the causes of alcoholism vary from alcoholic to alcoholic (emotional traumas cause some people to drink, while others drink to socialize).

Finally, many recovered alcoholics and therapists assert that whether alcoholism is a disease or not is irrelevant. Either way, the alcoholic's behavior must change, and this is what treatment should focus on. As researcher George Vaillant of Dartmouth University states, alcoholism "will require great responsibility from the patient. In alcoholism, as in much of medicine, we dress the wound; the individual's own resources heal it."

How one defines alcoholism—as a disease or simply as a destructive behavior—affects how one believes society should deal with alcoholics. The following chapter discusses whether the widespread perception of alcoholism as a disease is accurate and beneficial to alcoholics and society.

Alcoholism Is a Genetically Inherited Disease

by Kenneth Blum with James E. Payne

About the authors: *Kenneth Blum, an internationally recognized authority on psychopharmacology and substance abuse, is professor of pharmacology, chief of the Division of Addictive Diseases, and director of the Laboratory of Pharmacologies at the University of Texas Health Science Center in San Antonio. He is especially recognized for discovering a gene that might be associated with alcoholism. James E. Payne is a writer and former editor who heads the National Foundation for Addictive Diseases.*

To the normal individual, alcohol is a pleasant indulgence. It eases tension, releases inhibitions, promotes conviviality, and generates temporary feelings of well-being. Occasional overindulgence may lead to foolish or destructive behavior, but if used in moderation alcohol does not appear to injure health, or lead to habitual excessive drinking. (However, women should not drink during pregnancy to avoid possible danger to the developing fetus.) A summation of the normal person's attitude would be: "I enjoy drinking, but I can drink or leave it alone, and I don't understand why other people can't do the same."

The destructive potential of alcohol is apparent, however, even in this normal individual. When alcohol in sufficient quantity reaches the cerebral cortex, speech is slurred and thinking becomes confused. When the cerebellum is reached, balance and coordination are affected; the individual staggers and has trouble holding a match or cup. If the limbic system becomes involved, emotions are likely to be exaggerated, and boisterous or aggressive behavior, even violent behavior, may result. Judgment is clouded, and the individual tends to act in a primitive, unthinking manner.

Alcohol as a Necessity

If the normal person drinks until intoxicated, the ability to handle complex tasks is impaired, speech becomes even more slurred, and a loss of balance may make walking difficult or impossible. Speed and distance judgments are faulty, and accidental injury becomes a high probability.

To the alcoholic, who lives daily with a high level of anxiety and strong feelings of inadequacy and low self-esteem, and who may experience destructive pressures of anger or hostility, or the debilitating "low" of depression, alcohol seems not an indulgence but a necessity. The negative feelings are a

> *"To the alcoholic, . . . alcohol seems not an indulgence but a necessity."*

constant source of emotional pain, a pain so powerful it cannot be ignored, and so unendurable it must be suppressed; an unending legacy of pain. Alcohol temporarily masks these feelings or reduces their intensity. That is why this chemical, in the early stages of alcoholism, seems such a welcome friend. For a little while it makes the pain go away.

Physicians have long theorized that alcoholism is a disease; now scientists are learning that the behavioral as well as the physical problems associated with alcoholism are all part of a disease syndrome. It is the *disease* that makes life unbearable for the alcoholic and the members of the alcoholic's family.

The early symptoms of the disease of alcoholism, even before drinking begins, are often intense forms of restlessness, anxiety, stubbornness, and anger that drive the alcoholic into self-destructive, asocial, or antisocial behavior. Alcohol sets the trap by demonstrating that it can ease the pressure temporarily, and provide brief feelings of pleasure and well-being.

As the alcoholic takes the bait and begins drinking more and more, the nature of the trap becomes evident. When the initial "high" wears off, there is an increase in anxiety, hostility, or depression, and more alcohol must be consumed to regain the good feeling. As drinking continues over time, relationships with family, friends, and co-workers become progressively more difficult; body functions are damaged; mind functions such as memory and reasoning are disturbed or diminished; and a powerful craving for more alcohol is generated.

The Progression of the Disease

Once the trap has snapped shut, even though the alcoholic may realize the danger, the short-term rewards are so great and the urge is so powerful that the drinking habit has to be protected, and its adverse effects denied. At the same time, the alcoholic cannot escape the realization that he/she is different from normal people, is in trouble, and has lost control. Feelings of failure, irritability, or anger give rise to shame and guilt and they, too, must be denied. The overwhelming conviction is that alcohol cannot be given up.

Other psychological symptoms now begin to appear, and become more apparent as the disease progresses. Memory, reasoning, and judgment become increasingly faulty. Impulsiveness, irritability, and arrogance, even megalomania, may alternate with a growing need for sympathy and understanding. There may be a loss of inhibitions, leading to bizarre behavior and violations of personal ethics; reality may become hazy, giving way to a rich fantasy life sometimes accompanied by aggressive sexual behavior. Heavy drinking bouts may be followed by blackouts that leave no memory of events, or a distorted memory that ignores unpleasant happenings.

A complicating factor is that, as the alcoholic's own shortcomings multiply, the effort to shift the blame to others intensifies. This effort often leads to highly manipulative behavior and a disregard for truth.

Overall, the alcoholic is likely to experience a developing sense of panic, interspersed with irritability, quick outbursts of rage, or periods of deep depression. Such behavior, and the consequent adverse reaction of family, co-workers, and friends, inevitably leads to growing loneliness, and feelings of guilt or remorse that find expression in an all-pervading sadness.

Indifference and Dependence

Shame may now drive the alcoholic to enlist the aid of family members in hiding alcohol-related personal and family problems from friends and co-workers; but underneath there is an increasing concentration on self. This apparent contradiction reflects a conflict between feelings of indifference toward others, and feelings of anxious dependence.

If depression or sadness persists, a preoccupation with suicide may develop. The seriousness of the intention in a particular individual is difficult to determine, but many alcoholics commit suicide, and many more attempt it—a higher proportion than in the normal population.

> *"It is the **disease** that makes life unbearable for the alcoholic and the members of the alcoholic's family."*

As heavy drinking becomes habitual, serious physiological effects begin to appear. The lining of the esophagus may become irritated, leading to swelling. Irritation of the stomach and intestines may cause severe gastritis or ulceration. Unexcreted uric acid may crystallize in body tissues and joints, producing swelling and soreness. Hypoglycemia may interfere with the supply of glucose needed to raise blood sugar levels. An excess of catecholamines may cause excessive perspiration, tremor, fast pulse, and continuing waves of anxiety.

As nutritional deficiencies increase, the alcoholic may experience a loss of sensation in legs, ankles, and feet, and perhaps in hands and arms. Eventually the deep reflexes in these areas may weaken. If Wernicke's syndrome develops, it may bring vision problems, mental confusion, and a clouding of consciousness. If Korsakoff's psychosis develops, the alcoholic may experience severe memory defects and disorientation.

The liver becomes heavily involved. In the healthy body, the liver synthesizes proteins from amino acids, helps to metabolize fats and carbohydrates, detoxifies potentially dangerous compounds, and metabolizes alcohol. However, its capabilities are limited. The healthy adult liver can only metabolize the equivalent of one can of beer per hour, and heavy drinking can overload the system.

An early effect is an increase in liver fat, a condition called hepatosis. More drinking may lead to hepatitis, a condition which causes the death of liver cells. If heavy drinking continues, cirrhosis may develop with a consequent scarring of liver tissue. Scarring decreases blood flow in the liver, interferes with its detoxification processes, and reduces its ability to produce proteins needed for the maintenance of the body.

Alcohol and Pregnancy

In pregnant women, heavy drinking can lead to the dangerous "fetal alcohol syndrome" as alcohol penetrates the placenta and reaches the unborn child. Continued exposure of the fetus to alcohol can lead to retardation as well as to structural and functional disorders such as incomplete hand development, defective eyelids, and brain abnormalities that cause impairment of both intellectual and motor abilities.

As heavy drinking continues in men or women, secondary physical deterioration may affect any cell, organ, function, or system in the body. Thus alcohol may become a factor in cancer, pneumonia, circulatory and heart ailments, and a wide variety of other physiological problems.

If the heavy drinker is suddenly deprived of alcohol, the withdrawal syndrome sets in: a response characterized by tremors, nausea, weakness, and a fast heart rate, followed by an increase in anxiety or hostility. If severe, withdrawal may be accompanied by delirium, clouding of consciousness, disorientation, seizures, and—in some instances—hallucinations. Breathing and pulse rate may become irregular, sleep is disturbed, tremors may recur, and the individual is likely to experience high levels of anxiety, frustration, irritability, or depression. Without careful treatment, this syndrome can lead to convulsions and death.

Probably the most frustrating effect of alcoholism for physicians, counselors, friends, and families is the phenomenon of *denial*. Convinced that alcohol is the only defense against his/her unbearable emotional pain and physiological need, the alcoholic regards any attempt to interfere with drinking as a personal attack that must be defeated at all costs. The lying, the evasions, the hiding of bottles, the broken promises, the attempts to shift blame, followed by pleas for patience and understanding—all are devices used to protect the drinking habit.

> *"As the alcoholic's own shortcomings multiply, the effort to shift the blame to others intensifies."*

As a part of the disease syndrome, the typical alcoholic displays many or most of the following characteristics:

• restlessness, impulsiveness, anxiety

- selfishness, self-centeredness, lack of consideration
- stubbornness, ill humor, irritability, anger, rage
- depression, self-destructiveness, contactlessness
- physical cruelty, brawling, child or husband/wife abuse
- arrogance that may lead either to aggression or to coldness and withdrawal
- aggressive sexuality, often accompanied by infidelity, which may give way to sexual disinterest or impotence
- lying, deceit, broken promises
- low self-esteem, shame, guilt, remorse
- reduced mental and physical function; eventually, blackouts
- susceptibility to other diseases
- denial that there is a drinking problem
- and always, loneliness.

Types of Alcoholics

The particular set of characteristics exhibited will vary from case to case, determined in considerable part by the type to which the alcoholic belongs. The types have been variously classified, and I will discuss some of these classifications later. But for present purposes I will consider just two general types:

1. Alcoholics who inherit a predisposition to compulsive drinking. There is evidence that their brain wave patterns and brain chemistry are abnormal, and they may have trouble performing certain cognitive tasks. My observation, and that of others, has been that these genetic alcoholics, once they begin drinking heavily, are rarely able to achieve sobriety without professional assistance; have difficulty remaining in treatment programs; and have a comparatively low recovery rate. If they achieve sobriety through an act of will, without treatment, they are likely to become "dry drunks"; that is, they remain sober, but retain many of the behavioral characteristics of the alcoholic.

> *"Many alcoholics commit suicide."*

2. Alcoholics who may not have a genetic anomaly, but develop a habit of excessive drinking as the result of long-continued stress or long-term social drinking. Whatever the superficial motivation, prolonged heavy drinking probably produces progressive changes in brain chemistry that lead to craving. If stress is removed, or if environmental conditions change so that drinking is not encouraged, these alcoholics respond well to treatment and their chances of recovery are favorable. They sometimes are able to stop drinking of their own volition, unaided.

In either case, the environment acts as the trigger, initiating the actual onset of the disease.

Prior to the beginning of scientific research into the causes and nature of alcoholism, these observational and anecdotal insights were the source of most of our knowledge about the disease. We knew how alcoholics looked and behaved when under the influence, but why they drank was a profound mystery. . . .

In 1977 T.-K. Li and his colleagues at the Indiana University School of Medicine developed the P (alcohol-preferring) and NP (nonpreferring) rat strains. The P rats met most of the requirements of an animal model of alcoholism. They voluntarily drank large quantities of an alcohol solution, and would actually work to obtain alcohol by pressing a lever.

> *"The environment acts as the trigger, initiating the actual onset of the disease."*

Eventually they became dependent on alcohol, developed a tolerance to it and, if it was withdrawn, experienced the withdrawal syndrome. These mouse and rat strains proved to be powerful tools for genetic research.

But there was a troublesome question: Can findings from research in mice or rats be generalized to humans? Because alcoholic animals can be bred, can we assume that genetic influences are important factors in human alcoholism?

Affirmative answers began to emerge as early as 1972 when M. A. Schuckit, D. W. Goodwin, and G. Winokur at Washington University School of Medicine in St. Louis studied a group of individuals reared apart from their biological parents among which either a biological parent or a surrogate parent had a drinking problem. The subjects were significantly more likely to have a drinking problem if their biological parent was considered alcoholic than if their surrogate parent was alcoholic. This association occurred irrespective of personal contact with the alcoholic biological parent. For each comparison of genetic and environmental factors, the genetic factor seemed to be more closely associated with the development of alcoholism.

In 1973, Goodwin, Winokur, and their colleagues at the Psykologisk Institut, Copenhagen, found further support for this thesis in a study based on a sample of 5,483 men in Denmark who had been adopted in early childhood. They found that the sons of alcoholics adopted by other families were over three times more likely to become alcoholics than were the adopted sons of nonalcoholics, and at an earlier age.

Additional confirmation came in 1978 when Michael Bohman at Umea University in Sweden compared rates of alcohol abuse in 2,324 adoptees and their biological parents. The sample included 1,125 men and 1,199 women, adopted before the age of three years. The parents included 2,261 mothers and 1,902 fathers. Bohman found that adopted sons of alcoholic fathers were three times more likely to become alcoholic than adopted sons of nonalcoholic fathers. Adopted sons of alcoholic mothers were twice as likely to become alcoholic as those whose mothers were nonalcoholic.

Searching for Answers

These earlier studies of sons of alcoholics were extended to include daughters in an important series of investigations of Swedish adoptees which was carried out by C. R. Cloninger and colleagues at the Washington University School of Medicine and at Umea.

They sought to answer four questions:

1. What characteristics of the biological parent influence the risk of alcohol abuse in the adoptees?
2. What characteristics of the adoptive parents influence the risk of alcohol abuse in the adoptees?
3. How do genetic and environmental factors interact in the development of alcohol abuse?
4. Is the genetic predisposition to alcoholism expressed in other psychopathological ways, depending on the environment experience and sex of the individual?

The investigators studied 862 men and 913 women of known parentage who had been adopted before the age of three by nonrelatives. A total of 35.3 percent of the adopted children had at least one biological parent known to abuse alcohol. A careful study was made of the subjects, categorized in terms of congenital background and postnatal home environment, and further divided into four subgroups according to their degree of alcoholism: none, mild, moderate, or severe. Characteristics of the biological parents were examined to identify those associated with a particular degree of alcoholism in the adoptees. To determine the effect of postnatal factors, the adoptive parents were also examined to identify influences that might be associated with particular degrees of alcoholism in the adoptees. Specific findings were:

> *"For each comparison of genetic and environmental factors, the genetic factor seemed to be more closely associated with the development of alcoholism."*

- 22.8 percent of the sons of alcoholic biological fathers were alcoholic, compared to 14.1 percent of the sons who did not have an alcoholic biological parent.
- 28.1 percent of the sons of alcoholic biological mothers were alcohol abusers, compared to 14.7 percent of sons who did not have an alcoholic biological parent.
- 10.8 percent of the daughters of alcoholic biological mothers were alcohol abusers, compared to 2.8 percent of daughters who did not have an alcoholic biological parent.
- Alcoholism in the *adoptive* parents was not a factor in whether or not adoptees would become alcoholic, indicating that home environment and imitation of elders was not a determining factor. . . .

All of the human genetic studies discussed above helped to establish a strong role for genetic predisposition and to clarify the role of environmental factors in activating that predisposition.

Alcoholism in Women May Be Inherited

by Kenneth Kendler et al.

About the author: *Kenneth Kendler is a physician affiliated with the department of psychiatry at the Medical College of Virginia in Richmond.*

Alcoholism in women represents a major, and increasing, public health problem. In men, twin and adoption studies have, with rare exceptions, suggested that genetic factors play an important role in the etiology of alcoholism. Furthermore, recent studies of samples who were overwhelmingly male suggest an association between alcoholism and the D_2 dopamine receptor gene.

The prevalence, age at onset, clinical features, course, and outcome of alcoholism differ substantially in men and women; therefore, risk factors for alcoholism in men cannot be assumed to apply to women. Compared to what has been learned from studies of alcoholism in men, our knowledge of the role of genetic factors in the etiology of alcoholism in women is sparse and contradictory. Of the three adoption and three twin studies that have examined this issue, three suggest that genetic factors are etiologically unimportant for alcoholism in women. Two studies suggest that, although significant, genes are less important as risk factors for alcoholism in women than in men. In one of these investigations, genetic factors were shown to be etiologically important in women only when alcoholism was narrowly defined. Only one study based on a small sample of female adoptees with alcoholism suggests that genetic factors play a major role in the etiology of alcoholism in women comparable with or greater than that observed in men.

The Role of Genetics

In this report, we extend previous research in this area by examining the role of genetic and environmental factors in the etiology of narrowly and broadly defined alcoholism in members of 1030 personally interviewed female-female twin pairs ascertained from the population-based Virginia Twin Registry.

Data for this report come from a study of genetic and environmental risk factors for common psychiatric disorders in white female-female twin pairs from the Virginia Twin Registry. The Virginia Twin Registry is a population-based register formed from a systematic review of all birth certificates from 1918 onward in the Commonwealth of Virginia. Current addresses of twins are obtained by matching to state records and from the co-twin or other relatives. . . .

> *"Alcoholism in women represents a major, and increasing, public health problem."*

The goal of this study was to clarify the role of genetic factors in the etiology of alcoholism in women. Our results, which are consistent across different definitions of illness, suggest that genetic factors play a major etiologic role in alcoholism in women. Furthermore, contrary to a recent report, our results suggest that the role of genetic factors in women is similar for both narrowly and broadly defined alcoholism.

These results are also inconsistent with those of previous twin and adoption studies, which suggest that genetic factors play at best a minor role in the etiology of alcoholism in women. Several methodological differences between this study and previous investigations might be responsible for these discrepant findings.

A Large Sample

First, the size of both our total sample (2060 individuals from 1030 complete female-female twin pairs) and that portion of the sample who are affected (185 women who met criteria for alcohol dependence and 357 who met broad criteria for alcoholism) is substantially greater than samples contained in previous studies. The three previous twin studies of alcoholism in women examined, respectively, 21, 55, and 87 pairs. The two adoption studies examined 49 adopted-away daughters of alcoholics, of whom 16 had broadly defined alcoholism, and a total adoption sample of 913 adopted women, of whom 31 had abused alcohol. Second, in all the previous adoption studies, proband twins or biologic parents with alcoholism were selected through psychiatric hospitalization or registration with temperance authorities. By contrast, in the present study, twins were selected through a population-based twin register independent of treatment status. Third, in three of the previous reports, assessment of alcoholism was made solely or largely by medical or governmental records or by self-report questionnaire. By contrast, in this study, all twins were personally evaluated by clinically experienced interviewers. Finally, the diagnostic approach to alcoholism varied widely across the studies.

The elucidation of the precise cause of the varying results from the completed twin and adoption studies of alcoholism in women must await further research. One plausible hypothesis is that the genetic loading for alcoholism in the modest proportion of women who seek treatment may not be typical of that found in the entire population of women with alcoholism. It is possible, for example, that patients seen in treatment settings may have been particularly influenced by social or familial environmental factors. In addition, conclusions about the heritability of alcoholism in women may differ substantially depending on the diagnostic criteria used and whether the diagnostic assessment is based on medical records or on structured personal interviews.

Although our population-based twin study examined only women, our heritability estimates for alcoholism in women are similar to those found by R.W. Pickens et al in the largest and methodologically strongest twin study of alcoholism in men conducted to date. Indirectly, our findings suggest that genetic factors are of similar etiologic importance for alcoholism in women and in men.

Estimates for the heritability of liability to alcoholism in women in this sample ranged from 50% to 61%, depending on the definition of illness. These findings suggest that the role of genetic factors in the etiology of alcoholism is substantial and that at least half of the total liability to alcoholism is a result of genetic factors. Our estimates for the heritability of liability to alcoholism are generally somewhat higher than those previously estimated from twin studies for coronary artery disease, stroke, peptic ulcer disease, and major depression; in the range of those previously reported for hypertension; and somewhat lower than those previously found for schizophrenia or bipolar illness.

> *"Genetic factors play a major etiologic role in alcoholism in women."*

Twin studies can also provide insight into the nature of environmental risk factors. For all three definitions of alcoholism, as well as for the multiple threshold model, no evidence was found for shared environmental risk factors. By contrast, individual-specific environmental risk factors (the kind not shared by an individual with her co-twin) appeared to play an important etiologic role in alcoholism. Our study suggests that 40% to 50% of the total variance in liability to alcoholism is due to environmental experiences that are not shared by both members of a twin pair. These results are not consistent with hypotheses that familial-environmental factors, such as social class, parental disciplinary practices, or parental drinking behavior, play a major etiologic role in alcoholism. . . .

Limitations

The results of this study should be interpreted in the context of three potentially significant methodological limitations. First, while based on a complete search of birth certificates from 1934 onward, our final study sample is unlikely to be completely representative of the entire twin population. Twins who moved out of state or did not return earlier questionnaires were less likely to be included in our sample. However, our results did suggest that the risk for alcoholism was unlikely to be strongly related to the probability of cooperation with the personal interview.

Second, our results should be interpreted in the context of the statistical power of this sample. In particular, in the presence of the substantial heritability found for alcoholism, familial-environmental influences that accounted for only a modest proportion of the total variance in liability would probably be undetectable. Therefore, we can appropriately conclude only that we were unable to detect major familial-environmental influences on the liability to alcoholism in women.

Finally, our assessments of alcoholism were performed at only one point in time. Previous studies with other psychiatric disorders have suggested that the reliability of such assessments is far from perfect. In our twin model, error of measurement in twin pairs is indistinguishable from individual-specific environment. Had we corrected for the unreliability of measurement or included interviews conducted at multiple time points, it is possible that we would have found the heritability of liability to alcoholism in women to be even higher than reported herein.

Contrary to the findings of most previous adoption and twin studies, our results support the hypothesis that in women, genetic factors play a major etiologic role in alcoholism. These findings are consistent with evidence that the association between alcoholism and the D_2 dopamine receptor locus may be of similar magnitude in both genders. As major efforts are now under way to elucidate the molecular basis of the genetic susceptibility to alcoholism, these results suggest that women, along with men, should be well represented in these investigations.

Experts Should Continue to Define Alcoholism as a Disease

by Robert M. Morse and Daniel K. Flavin

About the authors: *Robert M. Morse and Daniel K. Flavin are physicians affiliated with the National Council on Alcoholism and Drug Dependence, a national nonprofit organization that works to educate the public concerning alcohol and drug addiction.*

In 1972, the National Council on Alcoholism (NCA, now called the National Council on Alcoholism and Drug Dependence) published its seminal article entitled "Criteria for the Diagnosis of Alcoholism." This was followed in 1976 by the "Definition of Alcoholism," prepared by the Committee on Definitions of the National Council on Alcoholism and the American Medical Society on Alcoholism (now called the American Society of Addiction Medicine). This definition emphasized the progressive nature of alcoholism, the physical sequelae of alcohol use, and the phenomena of tolerance and withdrawal: "Alcoholism is a chronic, progressive, and potentially fatal disease. It is characterized by tolerance and physical dependency or pathologic organ changes, or both—all the direct or indirect consequences of the alcohol ingested." The authors of this definition also clarified and defined several concepts, including use of the terms *chronic and progressive, tolerance, physical dependency,* and *pathologic organ changes.*

Searching for Causes

Our knowledge in this area has not remained static, however, and many strides have been made toward understanding alcoholism since the creation of the National Institute on Alcohol Abuse and Alcoholism in 1970. Some of us have even become impatient for definitive answers to questions about the causes of and cures for alcoholism. Therefore, we must be reminded by E. Gordis of the "discovery curve." From basic research to clinical practice, the natural course of scientific discovery is a progressive and time-consuming process. One insight gradually leads to another so that, with thoughtful direction and steady support, progress continues. Thus, important contributions, such as the strong evidence for neurogenetic mechanisms in alcoholism or the modulation of alcohol intake by neurotransmitter (serotonin) inhibitors, have yet to pay off in terms of clinical usefulness. In addition to research advances, continuing efforts to develop a uniform, reliable classification sys-

> *"Alcoholism is a chronic, progressive, and potentially fatal disease."*

tem have led to a modification of terms and to clarifications of concepts used to describe alcohol-related problems and alcoholism. In this context, the 1976 definition emphasized the physiologic sequelae of alcohol use and failed to recognize the spectrum of biopsychosocial factors that influence the development of alcoholism and its manifestations.

The *Diagnostic and Statistical Manual of Mental Disorders, Third Edition, Revised* (*DSM-III-R*) of the American Psychiatric Association and the *International Classification of Diseases Ninth Revision* (*ICD-9*) of the World Health Organization have emphasized the concept of "alcohol dependence," introduced in 1976 by G. Edwards and M. M. Gross as "alcohol dependence syndrome," rather than the term *alcoholism*. At the time, Edwards and Gross noted that the diagnostic use of the term *alcoholism*, as then defined, was overinclusive and dependent on the mercurial, value-laden concept of disease. Alcohol dependence syndrome is based on the more specific formulation that an occurrence of a clinical phenomenon distinct from (but not mutually exclusive of) alcohol-related disabilities (and consequences or both) is recognizable and quantifiable. The alcohol dependence syndrome, as described by Edwards and Gross, is characterized by narrowing of the drinking repertoire, salience of drink-seeking behavior, increased tolerance, repeated withdrawal symptoms, relief and avoidance of withdrawal symptoms, subjective awareness of a compulsion to drink, and reinstatement (of drinking) after abstinence. Both the *DSM-III-R* and the proposed 10th revision of the *International Classification of Diseases* include, in addition to alcohol dependence syndrome, criteria referring to persistent drinking despite adverse consequences (or "problems," as in *DSM-III-R*).

Patterns of Use

Despite this diagnostic use of the term *alcohol dependence*, the term *alcoholism* continues to be widely used among professionals and the general public alike. Alcoholism is vaguely referred to under "patterns of use" in *DSM-III-R*. Yet it is not directly compared or contrasted with the terms *alcohol dependency* and *alcohol abuse*. Thus, it remains unclear whether these concepts are interchangeable or inconsistent with each other.

To establish a more precise use of the term *alcoholism*, the National Council on Alcoholism and Drug Dependence and the American Society of Addiction Medicine created a Joint Committee to Study the Definition and Criteria for the Diagnosis of Alcoholism. This 23-member multidisciplinary group (scientists, physicians, and lay leaders) formulated a revised definition of alcoholism that the group hoped would be (1) scientifically valid, (2) clinically useful, and (3) understandable by the general public. Clearly, this is a difficult task and one that is necessarily ongoing and incomplete. Well-intentioned scientists continue to debate basic concepts of alcoholism. Some argue that it is mainly a disorder of appetite, that is, a pathologic or abnormal appetite (not present in nonalcoholics) for a particular substance. Others, after the work of A. Wikler, emphasize the principles of classical conditioning. Physicians from the various specialties, such as psychiatry and internal medicine, tend to view alcoholism from slightly different perspectives, and some of the informed lay public disagree with the above concepts and focus instead on the cultural, legal, or moral aspects of alcoholism. That the joint committee could arrive at a consensus is a tribute to the persistence, open-mindedness, and goodwill of its members.

> *"The term alcoholism has been used over the years as a vague, poorly understood, and sometimes morally flavored term."*

Without undertaking an exhaustive scientific review of the subject, we at least hoped not to be at odds with currently known and accepted concepts in this rapidly evolving field.

The revised definition proposed by the committee recognizes alcoholism as a heterogeneous disease (that is, biopsychosocial factors are implicated in the causes, signs and symptoms, complications, and treatment of alcoholism). The definition acknowledges a genetic vulnerability in the evolution of alcoholism in many alcoholics: broadens the scope of the 1976 definition to include the basic behavioral changes that are symptomatic of the disease; and, for the first time, formally incorporates denial as a major concept. By giving greater consideration to these factors, the committee hopes that the revised definition will encourage earlier intervention in the course of alcoholism by professionals and the general population. The revised definition of alcoholism more closely approximates that of alcohol dependence as outlined in *DSM-III-R* and the proposed 10th revision of the *International Classification of Diseases*. Although the term *alcoholism* has been used over the years as a vague, poorly understood, and sometimes morally flavored term, we do not believe it necessary or desirable to discard it. Rather, we prefer to clarify its meaning with updated concepts and terminology so that its usage will be more meaningful.

Revised Definition of Alcoholism

Alcoholism is a primary, chronic disease with genetic, psychosocial, and environmental factors influencing its development and manifestations. The disease is often progressive and fatal. It is characterized by impaired control over drinking, preoccupation with the drug alcohol, use of alcohol despite adverse consequences, and distortions in thinking, most notably denial. Each of these symptoms may be continuous or periodic.

Alcoholism as a Disease

"Primary" refers to the nature of alcoholism as a disease entity in addition to and separate from other pathophysiologic states that may be associated with it. It suggests that as an addiction, alcoholism is not a symptom of an underlying disease state.

"Disease" means an involuntary disability. Use of the term *involuntary* in defining disease is descriptive of this state as a discrete entity that is not deliberately pursued. It does not suggest passivity in the recovery process. Similarly, use of this term does not imply the abrogation of responsibility in the legal sense. Disease represents the sum of the abnormal phenomena displayed by the group of individuals. These phenomena are associated with a specified common set of characteristics by which certain individuals differ from the norm and which places them at a disadvantage.

"Often progressive and fatal" means that the disease persists over time and that physical, emotional, and social changes are often cumulative and may progress as drinking continues. Alcoholism causes premature death through overdose; through organic complications involving the brain, liver, heart, and other organs; and by contributing to suicide, homicide, motor vehicle accidents, and other traumatic events.

"Impaired control" means the inability to consistently limit on drinking occasions the duration of the drinking episode, the quantity of alcohol consumed, and/or the behavioral consequences.

"Preoccupation" used in association with "alcohol use" indicates excessive, focused attention given to the drug alcohol and to its effects or its use (or both). The relative value the person assigns to alcohol often leads to energy being diverted from important life concerns.

"Adverse consequences" are alcohol-related problems, "disabilities," or impairments in such areas as physical health (eg, alcohol withdrawal syndromes, liver disease, gastritis, anemia, and neurologic disorders), psychologic functioning (eg, cognition and changes in mood and behavior), interpersonal functioning (eg, marital problems, child abuse, and troubled social relationships), occupational functioning (eg, scholastic or job problems), and legal, financial, or spiritual problems. Although the alcohol dependence syndrome may theoretically occur in the absence of adverse consequences, we believe that the latter are evident in

> *"Alcoholism is a primary, chronic disease with genetic, psychosocial, and environmental factors."*

virtually all clinical cases.

"Denial" is used in the definition not only in the psychoanalytic sense of a single psychologic defense mechanism disavowing the significance of events but more broadly to include a range of psychologic maneuvers that decrease awareness of the fact that alcohol use is the cause of a person's problems rather than a solution to those problems. Denial becomes an integral part of the disease and is nearly always a major obstacle to recovery. Denial in alcoholism is a complex phenomenon determined by multiple psychologic and physiologic mechanisms. These include the pharmacologic effects of alcohol on memory, the influence of euphoric recall on perception and insight, the role of suppression and repression as psychologic defense mechanisms, and the impact of social and cultural enabling behavior.

Our proposed definition should not be interpreted as a new set of criteria for making the diagnosis of alcoholism, even though certain criteria are implied in its terminology.

Alcoholism Is Not a Disease

by Jeffrey A. Schaler

About the author: *Jeffrey A. Schaler is a psychotherapist in Silver Spring, Maryland, and a lecturer on drugs, alcoholism, and society in the department of justice, law, and society at American University in Washington, D.C.*

"That was the disease talking . . . I was a victim." So declared Marion Barry, 54, mayor of the District of Columbia. Drug addiction is the disease. Fourteen charges were lodged against him by the U.S. attorney's office, including three counts of perjury, a felony offense for lying about drug use before a grand jury; ten counts of cocaine possession, a misdemeanor; and one count of conspiracy to possess cocaine.

Barry considered legal but settled for moral sanctuary in what has come to be known as the disease-model defense. He maintained that he "was addicted to alcohol and had a chemical dependency on Valium and Xanax." These are diseases, he asserted, "similar to cancer, heart disease and diabetes." The implication: It is as unfair to hold him responsible for drug-related criminal behavior as it is to hold a diabetic responsible for diabetes.

The suggestion was that his disease of addiction forced him to use drugs, which in turn eroded his volition and judgment. He did not voluntarily break the law. According to Barry, "the best defense to a lie is truth," and the truth, he contended, is that he was powerless in relation to drugs, his life unmanageable and "out of control." His behaviors or acts were purportedly the result, that is, symptomatic, of his disease. And jail, say those who agree with him, is not the answer to the "product of an illness."

Defendants of Addiction

This disease alibi has become a popular defense. Baseball's Pete Rose broke through his "denial" to admit he has a "gambling disease." Football's Dexter Manley claimed his drug use was caused by addiction disease. Addiction treatment professionals diagnosed televangelist Jimmy Swaggart as having "lost control" of his behavior and as being "addicted to the chemical released in his brain from orgasm." They assert that Barry, Rose, Manley and Swaggart all need "twelve-step treatment" for addiction, the putative disease that, claims the multimillion-dollar addiction treatment industry, is reaching epidemic proportions and requires medical treatment. To view addiction-related behaviors as a function of free will,

> *"The disease model is both paternalistic and mechanistic."*

they often say, is cruel, stigmatizing and moralistic, an indication that one does not really understand the disease.

Others are more reluctant to swallow the disease model. After testing positive for cocaine in 1987, Mets pitcher Dwight Gooden said he could moderate his use of the drug and was not addicted. This is heresy according to disease-model proponents, a sign of denial, the salient symptom of the disease of addiction and considered by some to be a disease itself. There is no such thing as responsible drug taking or controlled drinking for an addict or an alcoholic, they assert.

The tendency to view unusual or questionable behavior as part of a disease process is now being extended, along with the characteristic theory of "loss of control," to include all sorts of "addictive" behaviors. We are currently experiencing the "diseasing of America," as social-clinical psychologist Stanton Peele describes it in his book of the same name (1989). The disease model is being applied to any socially unacceptable behavior as a means of absolving people of responsibility for their actions, criminal or otherwise. The practice is justified on this basis: Drug use constitutes an addiction. Addiction is a disease. Acts stemming from the disease are called symptoms. Since the symptoms of a disease are involuntary, the symptoms of drug addiction disease are likewise involuntary. Addicts are thus not responsible for their actions.

Is this analogizing of drug addiction to real diseases like diabetes, heart disease and cancer scientifically valid? Or is the word "disease" simply a misused metaphor? Does drug use truly equal addiction? Are the symptoms of drug addiction really involuntary?

Loss of Control

At the heart of the idea that drug use equals addiction is a theory known as "loss of control." This theory may have originated among members of Alcoholics Anonymous "to denote," as described by researcher E.M. Jellinek in his book *The Disease Concept of Alcoholism* (1960), "that stage in the development of [alcoholics'] drinking history when the ingestion of one alcoholic drink sets up a chain reaction so that they are unable to adhere to their intention to 'have one or two drinks only' but continue to ingest more and more—often with quite some difficulty and disgust—contrary to their volition."

Loss of control also suggests that addictive drugs can start a biochemical chain reaction experienced by an addict as an uncontrollable physical demand for more drugs. Drug addicts are people who have allegedly lost their ability to control their ingestion of drugs.

In a speech in San Diego in 1989, National Drug Policy Director William Bennett explained that a drug "addict is a man or woman whose power to exercise . . . rational volition has . . . been seriously eroded by drugs, and whose life is instead organized largely—even exclusively—around the pursuit and satisfaction of his addiction."

Yet, there is a contradiction in Bennett's point of view. If an addict's power to exercise rational volition is seriously eroded, on what basis does the addict organize life "largely—even exclusively—around the pursuit and satisfaction of his addiction"? An act of organizing is clearly a volitional act, an act of will.

Three Models of Addiction

Etiological paradigms for understanding drug use can be distilled into three models. Aside from the disease model, there are two other ways of looking at drug addiction: the free-will model and the moralistic model. In the free-will model drug use is envisioned as a means of coping with environmental experience, a behavioral choice and a function of psychological and environmental factors combined. The nervous system of the body is conceived of as a lens, modulating experience as self and environment interact. The self is like the film in a camera, where experience is organized and meaning is created. The self is not the brain.

> *"There has been no confirmation of the notion that once drinking starts, it proceeds autonomously."*

Individual physiological differences affect the experience of self. They do not create it. The quality of a camera lens affects the image of the environment transposed to the film. When the image is unpleasant, drugs are used to modify the lens.

The self is the executor of experience in this model, not the nervous system. Drug use may or may not be an effective means of lens modification. The assessment of drug effectiveness and the price of drug use are viewed as moral, not medical, judgments.

The recommended therapy for the drug user is: 1) a matter of choice; 2) concerned with awareness and responsibility; 3) a process of values clarification; 4) a means of support to achieve specific behavior goals; and 5) an educational process that involves the learning of coping strategies.

The moralistic model harkens back to the days of the temperance movement and is often erroneously equated with the free-will model. Here, addiction is considered to be the result of low moral standards, bad character and weak will. Treatment consists of punishment for drug-using behavior. The punitive nature of America's current war on drugs with its call for "user accountability" is typical of the moralistic perspective.

Addicts are viewed as bad people who need to be rehabilitated in "boot camps." They are said to be lacking in values. President Bush gave a clear example of this during the televised debates of the 1988 presidential campaign. When asked how to solve the drug problem, he answered, "by instilling values."

The drug user's loss of values is often attributed to the presence of a disease. A "plague" and "epidemic" of drug use are said to be spreading across the land. Since users are sick and supposedly unaware of their disease, many people feel justified in coercing them into treatment, treatment that is primarily religious in nature. Thus, the moralistic model is paternalistic.

In the disease or medical model, addicts are considered to have physiological differences from normal people, differences based in a genetic source or created through the chemical effects of drugs. Instead of focusing on the interaction between the self and the environment, advocates of the disease model view the interaction between physiology and the chemicals in drugs as both the disease and the executor of behavior and experience. In this sense the model is mechanistic. The person is viewed as a machine, a highly complex machine, but a machine nevertheless. The disease of addiction is considered to be incurable. People in treatment can only reach a state of perpetual recovery. Treatment of symptoms involves admitting that one is ill by breaking through denial of the disease and turning over one's life to a "higher power" in a spiritual sense and psychological support to achieve sobriety. Addicts are not bad but sick people. Intervention is required because the machine has broken. Thus, the disease model is both paternalistic and mechanistic.

Addiction Redefined

Proponents of the will and the disease models disagree with the moralistic perspective, but for different reasons. The former believe addicts should not be punished for having unconventional values. They believe treatment should focus on changing the psychological and environmental conditions conducive to drug use. Coping skills should be taught along with the building of self-esteem and self-efficacy. The latter believe that addicts should not be punished for being sick and that treatment should focus on the biological factors that cause and reinforce drug use.

James R. Milam and Katherine Ketcham, authors of *Under the Influence* (1981), are popular spokespersons for the disease-model camp. They argue that alcoholics should not

> *"Alcoholics' drinking is correlated with their beliefs about alcohol and drinking."*

be held accountable for their actions because these are the "outpourings of a sick brain. . . . They are sick, unable to think rationally, and incapable of giving up alcohol by themselves."

Similarly, physician Mark S. Gold, an expert on cocaine use and treatment, says in his book *800-COCAINE* (1984) that cocaine should not be regarded as a benign recreational drug because it can cause addiction. As with alcoholism, says Gold, there is no cure for cocaine addiction except permanent and total abstention from its use. Cocaine produces "an irresistible compulsion to use the drug at increasing doses and frequency in the face of serious physical and/or psychological side effects and the extreme disruption of the user's personal relationships and system of values." According to Gold "if you feel addicted, you are addicted." Addiction, be it to alcohol or cocaine, is, as far as Milam, Ketcham and Gold are concerned, identical to loss of control. The drug itself and physiological changes in the addict's body are said to control further ingestion of drugs in what is viewed as an involuntary process.

> *"The ability of alcoholics to stop drinking alcohol is not determined by a physiological reaction to alcohol."*

It may be helpful to look at how the term "addiction" has developed. Its use in conjunction with drugs, disease, loss of control, withdrawal and tolerance developed out of the moralistic rhetoric of the temperance and anti-opium movements of the nineteenth century, not through scientific inquiry. Such a restrictive use of the word served multiple purposes according to psychologist Bruce Alexander of Simon Fraser University in British Columbia, lead author of an article on the subject. Linking addiction to drugs and illness suggested it was a medical problem. It also helped to scare people away from drug use, a tactic that became increasingly important with anti-opium reformers. Etymologically, the word "addiction" comes from the Latin "dicere" (infinitive form) and, combined with the preposition "ad," means "to say yes to," "consent." Consent implies voluntary acceptance.

The idea of choice, volition or voluntariness inherent in the meaning of the word "addiction" is significant to will-model proponents because the concept of addiction as a disease depends so much on the loss-of-control theory. Most people think of addiction with the element of volition decidedly absent. Studies of alcoholics and cocaine and heroin addicts conducted over the past twenty-six years appear to refute this claim, however.

The Myth of Loss of Control

In 1962 British physician and alcohol researcher D.L. Davies rocked the alcoholism field by publishing the results of a long-term follow-up study of patients treated for alcoholism at the Maudsley Hospital in London. Abstinence, long considered the only cure for alcoholism, was seriously questioned as the only form of treatment when seven out of ninety-three male alcoholics studied exhibited a pattern of normal drinking. Physiological differences purportedly present in alcoholics did not seem to affect their ability to control drinking.

Four years later, *The Lancet* published an important study by British psychiatrist Julius Merry that supported Davies's findings. Alcoholics who were unaware they were drinking alcohol did not develop an uncontrollable desire to drink more, undermining the assertion by supporters of the disease model that a small amount of alcohol triggers uncontrollable craving. If alcoholics truly experience loss of control, then the subjects of the study should have reported higher craving whether they believed their beverages contained alcohol or not.

According to the loss-of-control theory, those with the disease of alcoholism cannot plan their drinking especially when going through a period of excessive craving. Yet, psychologist Nancy Mello and physician Jack Mendelson, leading alcoholism researchers and editors of the *Journal of Studies on Alcohol*, reported in 1972 that they found alcoholics bought and stockpiled alcohol to be able to get as drunk as they wanted even while undergoing withdrawal from previous binges. In other words, they could control their drinking for psychological reasons; their drinking behavior was not determined by a physiologically uncontrollable force, sparked by use of alcohol.

As Mello and Mendelson wrote in summary of their study of twenty-three alcoholics published in *Psychosomatic Medicine:* "It is important to emphasize that even in the unrestricted alcohol-access situation, no subject drank all the alcohol available or tried to 'drink to oblivion.' These data are inconsistent with predictions from the craving hypothesis so often invoked to account for an alcoholic's perpetuation of drinking. No empirical support has been provided for the notion of craving by directly observing alcoholic subjects in a situation where they can choose to drink alcohol in any volume at any time by working at a simple task. There has been no confirmation of the notion that once drinking starts, it proceeds autonomously."

Beliefs Control Drinking Behavior

A significant experiment conducted by Alan Marlatt of the University of Washington in Seattle and his colleagues in 1973 supported these findings by showing that alcoholics' drinking is correlated with their beliefs about alcohol and drinking. Marlatt successfully disguised beverages containing and not containing alcohol among a randomly assigned group of sixty-four alcoholic and social drinkers (the control group) asked to participate in a "taste-rating task." One group of subjects was given a beverage with alcohol but was told that although it tasted like alcohol it actually contained none. Subjects in another group were given a beverage with no alcohol (tonic) but were told that it did contain alcohol.

> *"The Supreme Court upheld the right . . . to define alcoholism to be the result of willful misconduct."*

As Marlatt and co-authors reported in the *Journal of Abnormal Psychology,* they found "the consumption rates were higher in those conditions in which subjects were led to believe that they would consume alcohol, regardless of the ac-

39

tual beverage administered." The finding was obtained among both alcoholic and social drinker subjects. Marlatt's experiment suggests that according to their findings the ability of alcoholics to stop drinking alcohol is not determined by a physiological reaction to alcohol. A psychological fact—the belief that they were drinking alcohol—was operationally significant, not alcohol itself. . . .

These and similar studies support the idea that what goes on outside of a person's body is more significant in understanding drug use, including alcoholism, than what goes on inside the body. . . .

Addiction and the Law

The extent of an addict's responsibility for criminal behavior has been debated in the courts for more than twenty-five years. In *Traynor v. Turnage* (1988), the Supreme Court upheld the right of the Veterans Administration (VA) to define alcoholism to be the result of willful misconduct. The petitioner in this case asserted he was unable to claim VA education benefits because he was an alcoholic; he further claimed that he suffered from a disease called alcoholism and that the law prohibits discrimination on the basis of a disease. The VA called his alcoholism "willful misconduct." Soon thereafter, however, Congress passed a law for veterans that expressly forbids considering the disabling effects of chronic alcoholism to be the result of willful misconduct. However, this law does not define alcoholism as a disease, nor does it prohibit drug addiction from being regarded as "willful misconduct.". . .

> *"Smoking and drinking are behaviors. Cancer and cirrhosis are diseases."*

In *Powell v. Texas* the Court held against the use of status as an alcoholic as exculpatory. Powell, an alcoholic, was held to be responsible for his criminal actions. In *Traynor*, the Court upheld the decision made in *Powell*. Traynor and Powell were not absolved of responsibility for their actions because of their alcoholism disease. . . .

The critical point here is the inseparability of status and act. Certain acts are considered to be part of disease status. Disease is involuntary. Therefore, acts stemming from the disease are exculpable. Are the acts that stem from status really involuntary? This belief is the legal corollary to Jellinek's notion of loss of control.

According to professor of psychiatry Thomas Szasz at the State University of New York in Syracuse, a disease, as textbooks on pathology state, is a phenomenon limited to the body. It has no relationship to a behavior such as drug addiction, except as a metaphor. Szasz argues against the disease model of addiction on the basis of the following distinction between disease and behavior. In *Insanity: The Idea and Its Consequences* (1987) he writes:

> [B]y behavior we mean the person's 'mode of conducting himself' or his 'deportment'. . . the name we attach to a living being's conduct in the daily pursuit

40

of life . . . [B]odily movements that are the products of neurophysiological discharges or reflexes are not behavior. . . . The point is that behavior implies action, and action implies conduct pursued by an agent seeking to attain a goal.

The products of neurophysiological discharges or reflexes become behavior when they are organized through intent, a willful act. Drug-taking behavior is not like epilepsy. The former involves intentional, goal-seeking behavior. An epileptic convulsion is an unconscious, unorganized neurophysiological discharge or reflex, not a behavior.

> *"One leading alcoholism researcher asserts that alcoholism is a disease simply because people go to doctors for it."*

In another example, smoking cigarettes and drinking alcohol are behaviors that can lead to the diseases we call cancer of the lungs and cirrhosis of the liver. Smoking and drinking are behaviors. Cancer and cirrhosis are diseases. Smoking and drinking are not cancer and cirrhosis.

The alleged absence of voluntariness or willfulness forms the basis of legal rulings that extend beyond the minimalist interpretation of *Robinson v. California* (1962), exculpating criminal behavior on the basis of a person's supposed disease status. Yet because behavior such as drug use involves voluntariness it seems an individual who uses drugs should not be absolved of responsibility for criminal behavior on the grounds that his actions are involuntary symptoms of drug addiction disease.

Many advocates of the disease model cite as further evidence for their view the results of genetic studies involving the heritability of alcoholism. Recently, the dopamine D_2 receptor gene was found to be associated with alcoholism. A study by Kenneth Blum and co-authors, published in the *Journal of the American Medical Association*, suggests that this gene confers susceptibility to at least one form of alcoholism. The goal of this and similar studies is to identify the at-risk population in order to prevent people from becoming alcoholics and drug addicts.

Effect of Other Factors

What such studies do not tell us is why people who are not predisposed become alcoholics and why those who are predisposed do not. It seems more than reasonable to attribute this variance to psychological factors such as will, volition and choice, as well as to environmental variables such as economic opportunity, racism and family settings, to name just a few. Experimental controls accounting for genetic versus environmental influences on alcoholic behavior are sorely lacking in these studies.

The basis upon which people with alleged alcoholism disease are distinguished from mere heavy drinkers is arbitrary. No reliable explanation has yet been put forth of how the biological mechanisms theoretically associated with alcoholism and other forms of drug addiction translate into drug-taking behavior. Moreover, Annabel M. Bolos and co-authors, in a rigorous attempt to replicate the Blum findings, reported higher frequencies of the D_2 receptor gene found in their control population than in the alcoholic population in the same journal seven months later.

Treatment

Finally, the contribution of treatment to exposing the myth of addiction disease warrants mention. Since his arrest at the Vista Hotel in Washington, D.C., Marion Barry has undergone treatment for alcohol addiction and chemical dependency at the Hanley-Hazelden clinic in West Palm Beach, Florida, and at the Fenwick Hall facility near Charleston, South Carolina. Barry said he needs treatment because he has "not been spiritual enough." His plan is to turn his "entire will and life over to the care of God . . . using the twelve-step method and consulting with treatment specialists." He said he will then "become more balanced and a better person."

The twelve-step program Barry is attempting to follow is the one developed by Alcoholics Anonymous (AA), a spiritual self-help fellowship. AA is the major method dealing with alcoholism today. All good addiction treatment facilities and treatment programs aim at getting the patient into AA and similar programs such as Narcotics Anonymous. Yet several courts throughout the United States have determined that AA is a religion and not a form of medicine, in cases involving First Amendment violations, most recently in *Maryland v. Norfolk* (1989). Anthropologist Paul Antze at York University in Ontario has written extensively on AA and describes the "point-by-point homology between AA's dramatic model of the alcoholic's predicament and the venerable Protestant drama of sin and salvation."

Successful treatment from this perspective is dependent upon a religious conversion experience. In addition, patients are required to adopt a disease identity. If they do not, they are said to be in denial. But such an approach is a psychologically coercive remedy for a moral problem, not a medical one. And here—in their concepts of treatment—is where the disease model and moralistic model of addiction seem to merge.

> *"Addicts and alcoholics do not 'get better' because they do not want to."*

With so much evidence to refute it, why is the view of drug addiction as a disease so prevalent? Incredible as it may seem, because doctors say so. One leading alcoholism researcher asserts that alcoholism is a disease simply because people go to doctors for it. Undoubtedly, addicts seek help from doctors for two reasons. Addicts have a significant psychological investment in maintaining this view, having learned that their sobriety depends on believing they have a disease. And treatment professionals have a significant economic investment at stake. The more behaviors are diagnosed as diseases, the more they will be paid by health insurance companies for treating these diseases.

Most people say we need more treatment for drug addiction. But few people realize how ineffective treatment programs really are. Treatment professionals know this all too well. In fact, the best predictor of treatment success, says Charles Schuster, director of the National Institute on Drug Abuse, is whether the addict has a job or not.

George Vaillant, professor of psychiatry at Dartmouth Medical School, describes his first experience, using the disease model and its effectiveness in diagnosing alcoholism, in *The Natural History of Alcoholism* (1983):

> . . . I learned for the first time how to diagnose alcoholism as an illness. . . . Instead of pondering the sociological and psychodynamic complexities of alcoholism . . . [A]lcoholism became a fascinating disease . . . [B]y inexorably moving patients into the treatment system of AA, I was working for the most exciting alcohol program in the world. . . . After initial discharge, only five patients in the Clinic sample never relapsed to alcoholic drinking, and there is compelling evidence that the results of our treatment were no better than the natural history of the disease.

"Research suggests that drug addiction is far from a real disease."

This is important information because the definition of who an alcoholic or drug addict is and what constitutes treatment as well as treatment success can affect the lives of people who choose not to use drugs as well as those who choose to. For example, Stanton Peele has written extensively on how studies show that most people arrested for drinking and driving are directed into treatment for alcoholism disease, yet the majority are not alcoholics. Those receiving treatment demonstrate higher recidivism rates, including accidents, driving violations and arrests, than those who are prosecuted and receive ordinary legal sanctions.

Furthermore, in a careful review of studies on treatment success and follow-up studies of heroin addicts at the United States Public Health Service hospital for narcotics addicts at Lexington, Kentucky, where "tens of thousands of addicts have been treated," the late Edward M. Brecher concluded in *Licit & Illicit Drugs* (1972) that "[a]lmost all [addicts] became readdicted and reimprisoned . . . for most the process is repeated over and over again . . . [and] no cure for narcotics addiction, and no effective deterrent, was found there—or anywhere else."

The Role of "Resistance"

Brecher explained the failure of treatment in terms of the addictive property of heroin. Vaillant suggested that tuberculosis be considered as an analogy. Treatment, he said, rests entirely on recognition of the factors contributing to the "resistance" of the patient. And here is the "catch-22" of the disease model.

Addiction is a disease beyond volitional control except when it comes to treatment failure, wherein "resistance" comes into play.

Neither Brecher nor Vaillant recognized that treatment does not work because there is nothing to treat. There is no medicine and there is no disease. The notions that heroin as an addictive drug causes addicts not to be treated successfully, or that "resistance" causes alcoholics to be incurable, are mythical notions that only serve to reinforce an avoidance of the facts: Addicts and alcoholics do not "get better" because they do not want to. Their self-destructive behaviors are not disturbed. They are disturbing. . . .

The legal arguments set forth to exculpate criminals because of addiction disease do not seem to be supported by scientific findings. Quite to the contrary, research suggests that drug addiction is far from a real disease. And as long as drug addiction can be blamed on a mythical disease, the real reasons why people use drugs—those related to socioeconomic, existential and psychological conditions including low self-esteem, self-worth and self-efficacy—can be ignored.

Alcoholism Is Not Genetically Inherited

by Alfie Kohn

About the author: *Alfie Kohn is the author of several books on human behavior including* The Brighter Side of Human Nature: Altruism and Empathy in Everyday Life.

What does it mean when someone drinks too much? Is hitting the bottle every day best viewed as a private decision, a reflection of hard times, a response to peer pressure, a sin, or an inherited disease? Any of these accounts might help to make sense of alcohol abuse, but only one—the last—is currently fashionable. Echoing the position of much of the mental health establishment and Alcoholics Anonymous, nearly nine of every 10 Americans think alcoholism is a disease, according to a Gallup poll.

Steven Paul, who directs all in-house research for the National Institute of Mental Health, says: "There is very good evidence that genetic factors play an important role. Certain forms of alcoholism seem to be highly inherited."

But a growing number of recent studies are challenging the assumption that excessive drinking can best be explained as an illness that simply happens to people. "AA wants it to be a genetic disease, and people seem overly willing to accept the hypothesis of genetic influence," says Robert Plomin, one of the country's leading behavioral geneticists. But "the evidence isn't all that convincing."

The traditional wisdom has been that the best way to predict who will abuse alcohol is to look for a family history of such abuse—are children of alcoholics especially likely to drink heavily themselves? But several new studies raise doubts. In 1989, for example, a group of researchers in Philadelphia surveyed 83 male college students and found no differences in the amount or frequency of drinking between the sons of alcoholics and the sons of non-alcoholics.

Children Do Not Repeat Their Fathers' Addiction

Even more remarkable were the results of a study at the University of Michigan published in 1990. An examination of hundreds of offspring of men with drinking problems found that nearly two-thirds drank very little or not at all. The implication is not only that many such sons and daughters had an aversion to their fathers' destructive habit but that they were able to choose moderation. "There is a strong, predictable generational pattern among the adult offspring 'of heavy drinkers' of . . . drinking less than their parents," Dr. Ernest Harburg and his colleagues wrote in the *Journal of Studies on Alcohol.*

But even in cases where parent and child do share a tendency to drink to excess, it cannot be taken for granted that the problem is inherited. Junior's similarity to dad may be due to sharing his home rather than his genes. This is why some researchers have conducted twin studies: to try to tease apart nature and nurture. If identical (monozygotic or MZ) twins are more likely than fraternal (dizygotic or DZ) twins to share the tendency to abuse liquor—which some studies have found—this is taken to mean the problem has a genetic component. The reason: MZs are genetically the same while DZs (like other siblings) share only about half their genes.

> *"A growing number of recent studies are challenging the assumption that excessive drinking can best be explained as an illness."*

But not all studies have discovered such a gap. University of Minnesota research psychologist Matt McGue and his colleagues found little difference between the likelihood that two MZs, on the one hand, and two DZs, on the other, would share a diagnosis of alcohol abuse or dependence. There was no evidence at all, moreover, to support a genetic explanation for the drinking habits of women or older men.

Regardless of their findings, though, twin studies have a problem: MZ twins share more of their environment than DZs, not just more of their genes. They're raised more similarly, they spend more time with each other, and, as a 1988 study confirmed, the frequency of their contact is directly related to the similarity of their personalities.

According to research conducted in London, the greater similarity in drinking patterns between two MZs is substantially reduced once the tendency for identical twins to live together is factored in. In fact, fraternal twins who lived together were more likely to share a drinking problem than identical twins who lived apart. Once again, this is unsettling news for those who think that genes explain who abuses alcohol.

Environmental Pressures

Another paper adds further doubt. Taking a careful second look at the Swedish study that is most often cited to support the idea that alcoholism is inherited, psychologist John Searles of the University of Pennsylvania found that a peculiar criterion had been used to decide who qualified as a heavy abuser. When he analyzed the data again, he found that "environmental pressures . . . are substantially more important in determining alcohol abuse than are genetic factors."

More recently, Kenneth Blum at the University of Texas, Ernest Noble at UCLA, and their colleagues announced that they had demonstrated a genetic contribution to alcoholism without doing a twin study. Following a path taken by other researchers, they conducted a "linkage" study in the laboratory to try to locate a particular gene that corresponds to the appearance of the disorder.

Controversy Over Gene's Link to Alcoholism

In April, 1990, they announced they had found it. After looking at the brain tissue of 70 deceased subjects (half of whom had been alcoholics), Blum and Noble said a particular gene appeared in 24 of the alcoholics but in only seven of the non-alcoholics. Newspapers across the country trumpeted the news—even though previous claims to have found a gene linked to schizophrenia and manic-depressive illness, respectively, had to be retracted.

Sure enough, a team of researchers at the National Institute on Alcohol Abuse and Alcoholism (NIAAA) reported later that year that they were unable to replicate those results. Pointing out that Blum and Noble's alcoholic brains had suspiciously low rates of the gene in question, they went on to show no difference in their own study. Blum and Noble struck back, claiming to have replicated their original findings and faulting the NIAAA group for excluding subjects with severe alcoholism. That controversy will likely continue for some time.

But despite their disagreement with Blum and Noble, the NIAAA researchers share the commonly accepted view and have written that "studies of twins, families and adopted children have indicated that genetic predisposition is significant in determining the risk for alcoholism."

On the other hand, even researchers who insist that genes do play a role generally add that drinking is profoundly affected by one's social and family environment, and the choices one makes—which means that the popular belief that some individuals are powerless over alcohol finds very little scientific support. Even Robert Cloninger of Washington University in St. Louis, a leading champion of the genetic position, has written that "major changes in social attitudes about drinking styles can change dramatically the prevalence of alcohol abuse regardless of genetic predisposition."

The nature of that genetic predisposition—if it does exist—is also widely misunderstood. Students of the subject, including UCLA's Noble, point out that there is almost cer-

"There is almost certainly no gene just for alcohol abuse."

tainly no gene just for alcohol abuse. "No geneticist claims that you inherit an inability to control your drinking—that doesn't make sense genetically," says Stanton Peele, a psychologist whose books on the subject include "Diseasing of America." If genetics plays any role, it probably has to do with a person's general inclination to act impulsively in seeking pleasure.

Nor have scientists found any proof that some people inherit an inability to metabolize alcohol efficiently and therefore become alcoholics. Two University of Colorado researchers reported in 1987 that people with a close relative who was an alcoholic were no different from other people "on alcohol metabolism, on sensitivity and acute tolerance to alcohol across several behavioral measures, or on perceived intoxication."

Peele cites evidence to debunk still other myths on the subject. Most problem drinkers outgrow their tendency to abuse alcohol, or stop drinking on their own—meaning that alcoholism isn't always a progressive disorder or one that requires a particular kind of treatment. And some former abusers manage to cut down their intake to an occasional drink—suggesting that quitting cold turkey isn't necessary for everyone.

The current climate in our culture is "dominated by the view that alcoholism is a biologically determined medical disease," McGue and his colleagues have written. That may be part of the reason that NIAAA will be spending about $25 million during the first half of the 1990s to look specifically for a genetic basis rather than to investigate the social and economic forces that might lead to excessive drinking.

But the fact is, McGue and his colleagues continued, that "serious questions remain concerning the consistency of the empirical support for the existence of a genetic influence on alcoholism." While McGue thinks genes will turn out to be related somehow to a risk for alcoholism, he adds that as far as the idea that alcohol abuse is simply a genetic disease is concerned, "The public has been sold a bill of goods."

Alcoholics Anonymous Created the Myth That Alcoholism Is a Disease

by Jack Trimpey

About the author: *Jack Trimpey founded the Rational Recovery Systems for overcoming alcohol and drug dependence in 1986. RRS emphasizes the importance of thinking and self-reliance in conquering addiction. In his book* The Small Book, *excerpted in the following viewpoint, Trimpey details the concepts behind Rational Recovery.*

Is Alcoholism a Disease? There is bitter debate over this question, as if the answer would have great importance to those who drink too much. Alas, it doesn't matter, because the solution is the same. If alcoholism is a disease and you have a drinking problem, you will become progressively more sick unless you stop drinking. But if alcoholism isn't a disease, and you are having persistent problems related to drinking, you had also better learn to abstain. Abstinence is simply the final stage in one's effort to moderate, when it becomes easier to quit *for good* than to moderate. Abstinence is also a commonplace thing that human beings have been achieving for millennia without the assistance of Alcoholics Anonymous or any other recovery program. In RR, we know that either way, disease or not, we are not powerless.

The Motivation for Making Alcoholism a Disease

But many people *do* care if alcoholism is a disease. Many people's jobs depend on alcoholism being a disease. Others make "I am an alcoholic" their personal identity and this admission the password to their recovery clubs. Still others can forgive themselves for their drunken behavior only if they believe the disease was responsible. Many accept the disease idea as an article of faith and in normal conversation feel compelled to join the word "alcoholism" with "the disease of . . ." Some others use the disease idea as a gun to their heads, imagining catastrophic results if they have just a sip of alcohol, ever. Still others seek leniency in court by focusing on the powerlessness that is said to accompany the disease of alcoholism.

Historically, alcoholism referred simply to the excessive drinking of alcohol. With the advent of AA in the 1930s, alcoholism became a term describing a specific physical disease, although there was no medical evidence to that effect. AA merely assumed that peo-

> **"Many people's jobs depend on alcoholism being a disease."**

ple with extreme dependence on alcohol were physically different, either inherently or as a result of exposure to the substance alcohol. AA not only created this disease called alcoholism but also devised a treatment. None of this occurred in a laboratory, clinical, or academic setting. It happened in church basements.

Prior to AA, problem drinkers were seen as morally defective and weak of character. AA gained strength on the idea that if problem drinkers are sick with a disease called alcoholism, then who can really *blame* them? This relieved some of the social stigma and guilt that problem drinkers encounter, and also had the beneficial effect of attracting many guilt-ridden addicts to AA meetings.

The data are now catching up with AA, and it seems they may be partly right in their claim that problem drinkers are physically different. There are differences between alcoholics and nonalcoholics in their blood chemistry and in measures of their tolerance patterns. Sons of alcoholics tolerate alcohol without motor impairment better than sons of nonalcoholics. It also appears there are different types of alcoholics whose patterns of onset and patterns of abuse differ markedly. Degrees of dependency are also recognized.

All of which points to the conclusion of the American Psychiatric Association. The medical diagnosis "alcoholism" has been dropped from the Diagnostic and Statistical Manual (DSM-3R) in favor of two others: "alcohol dependence" and "alcohol abuse." These two terms now describe the vast majority of persons who experience serious problems associated with the use of alcohol.

The Word Game

"Alcoholism" and "alcoholic" are *folk expressions*. Neither word is a medical term; when doctors sign insurance claims for treating someone who drinks too much, they write "alcohol dependence." The doctor who wrote the word "alcoholism" in the space for the diagnosis would not be paid.

I use the term "alcoholic" to refer to people who believe they are powerless over their addictions and act accordingly, and to those who call themselves "alcoholics." They are practicing the *philosophy* of "alcohol-*ism*," just as Catholics practice the philosophy of Catholicism.

I prefer the correct term "alcohol dependence" to describe the problem of persistent, heavy drinking. (The reader may substitute "drug dependence" for "alcohol dependence"; recovery is the same game for boozers and junkies.) If you think about this, you will probably see that alcohol dependence is a much clearer expression. It actually *describes* the problem, i.e., "I am *dependent* on alcohol," and it also even suggests what you may *do* about it, i.e., "I had better become *independent* from alcohol."

Some other "-isms" come to mind that are not diseases but only patterns of discomfort. Rheumatism is really arthritis. Another is priapism, not a disease but a symptom of one. Most other "-isms" are doctrines or *philosophies*, such as capitalism, communism, Methodism, Catholicism, and catechism. Alcoholism, like other "-isms," is not a disease but rather a *philosophy* that has affixed itself to a particular human problem—that of habitual, self-destructive drinking of alcohol. The same philosophy has attached itself to other medical and psychiatric diagnoses, under the various names of "———Anonymous," especially when the symptoms of those conditions are morally tinged, social vices.

By recognizing that alcoholism is a *personal philosophy*, a mode of thinking that allows one to slowly self-destruct while under the influence, you should also recognize that you can change your thinking about drinking, and recover. By so doing, you can recover from "alcohol-ism" as well as alcohol dependence.

Chapter 2

Is Alcoholics Anonymous the Most Effective Treatment for Alcoholism?

Chapter Preface

Alcoholics Anonymous is America's most well known and popular treatment for alcoholism. Established in 1935 by two recovering alcoholics, AA's unique twelve-step program has attracted millions and helped many recover from their addiction.

AA's philosophy requires alcoholics to admit that they are powerless over alcohol, to turn to a higher power to help them control their addiction, to evaluate their lives and acknowledge the harm their alcoholism has caused them and others, and to help other alcoholics achieve and maintain sobriety. Membership in AA is free and anonymous. The organization encourages members to attend as many meetings as they need to and to support one another in maintaining sobriety.

Many Americans trust that AA is the best treatment for alcoholism. Physicians and therapists often refer their alcoholic patients to AA, and increasingly courts are requiring those convicted of alcohol-related crimes to attend AA as part of their sentence. This confidence in AA is expressed by Ronald L. Rogers, Chandler Scott McMillin, and Morris A. Hill, authors of *The Twelve Steps Revisited:*

> AA found that what alcoholics could not do by themselves, could be done when they worked together. A disease which resisted all efforts of individual will, could in fact be controlled within the structure of a fellowship and its simple program for recovery. It worked. It grew into what we know as the Twelve Steps. And that, more than anything else, is AA's gift to humanity.

In recent years, however, this unquestioning faith in AA has begun to erode. Many critics oppose AA's emphasis on spirituality and on the alcoholic's need to rely on a higher power to conquer the addiction. As Jack Trimpey, a former alcoholic and one of AA's foremost critics, argues:

> Because of the organizational success of Alcoholics Anonymous and its twelve-step spiritual healing program, it has become a universal component in addiction care. Unfortunately, millions of alcoholics are not good candidates for spiritual healing, and can best regain control of their lives through a program that does not require their moral betterment or belief in a Higher Power, a Supreme Being, or other articles of faith.

Other critics maintain that by emphasizing the alcoholic's powerlessness over alcohol, AA only convinces alcoholics that they are weak victims of alcohol rather than strong, responsible people able to conquer their addiction. These critics also point out that, although AA may have helped thousands, most alcoholics do not join AA, and most of those who do join fail to remain abstinent.

The debate over AA's effectiveness is an emotional one. AA has rescued many from lives of abuse and addiction, and these people often have an unshakeable faith in the twelve steps. Those who have found AA wanting are eager to offer alternative solutions. The authors in the following chapter debate whether AA's widespread popularity is justified.

Alcoholics Anonymous Is the Most Effective Treatment for Alcoholism

by Terence T. Gorski

About the author: *Terence T. Gorski is the president of the CENAPS Corporation, a training, consultation, and research firm specializing in chemical dependency treatment and relapse prevention therapy. He is the author of* Passages Through Recovery: An Action Guide for Preventing Relapse; Staying Sober: A Guide for Relapse Prevention; The Staying Sober Workbook; *and* Understanding the Twelve Steps, *from which this viewpoint is excerpted.*

The single, most effective program for the treatment of alcoholism . . . is Alcoholics Anonymous, best known as A.A. Alcoholics Anonymous is a worldwide fellowship of men and women who share their experience, strength, and hope with each other in an effort to recover from alcoholism. It is a voluntary fellowship. No one is forced to belong, but millions of voluntary members benefit greatly from their involvement. . . .

Many people find the miracle of sobriety by working the Twelve Steps. Since nothing else has worked for them, many believe that the Steps are mystical and magical, and, as a result, these same persons fail to search for and identify the underlying principles that make them work. Working the Steps can create the miracle of sobriety, but the miracle isn't magic. The miracle occurs because working the Twelve Steps allows people to use powerful principles of recovery. Those who are willing to dig beneath the surface and truly understand the principles upon which the Steps are based are better able to use the principles in their lives.

The Twelve Steps and Twelve Traditions

The primary purpose of A.A. is to help alcoholics stop drinking. It was never intended to be all things to all people; however, A.A. recognizes that the

Twelve Steps can help people with other problems. Thus, it allows organizations such as Narcotics Anonymous, Cocaine Anonymous, Marijuana Anonymous, Overeaters Anonymous, and others to use its Steps and principles. These related fellowships are developing as separate organizations so that A.A. can keep its primary focus on helping alcoholics to stop drinking.

> *"The single, most effective program for the treatment of alcoholism . . . is Alcoholics Anonymous."*

A.A. is based upon a program of Twelve Steps to recovery that act as a personal guide to sobriety, and Twelve Traditions that act as guiding principles or bylaws for A.A. as a whole. Knowledge of the Twelve Steps is of critical importance to all recovering people for two reasons: (1) The Steps work if you work them, and (2) Twelve Step programs are inexpensive and readily available in most communities. As a result, they are the most widely used lifeline for people recovering from chemical dependence, codependence, and other compulsive or addictive disorders. . . .

Levels of Twelve Step Involvement

Nobody is forced to do anything in A.A. It is one of the few organizations I know that supports the inherent constitutional right to do what we want. There is no coercion to participate on any level. If you want to belong, that's fine. You are welcome to attend meetings and work the Steps. If you don't want to belong, that's also fine.

For most members, however, their involvement progresses through a number of levels. At the first level, they attend meetings. At the second, they read Twelve Step literature and discuss it with other members of the program. At the third level, they get a sponsor who can show them how the program works. At the fourth level, they start working the Twelve Steps. As members start to grow and change—a result of attending meetings and working the Steps—they are ready to move to a fifth level of involvement and begin sponsoring others. After they gain experience as sponsors, they are then ready for the sixth level of involvement, general service work, guided by A.A.'s Twelve Traditions, the set of principles that act as bylaws. General service work is designed to benefit A.A. as a whole. Notice the progression: Individuals help themselves first, then they help other people in the program, then they help the program as a whole. In summary, the levels of involvement are as follows:

1. Attending meetings
2. Reading and discussing A.A. literature
3. Getting a sponsor
4. Working the Twelve Steps
5. Sponsoring others
6. Service guided by the Traditions

Attending Meetings. You start working a Twelve Step program by regularly attending meetings. In A.A. it is said, "If you bring the body, the mind will follow," because the Twelve Step program rubs off on people if they hang around long enough. Attending meetings isn't a passive process. Working a program means you need to get actively involved, participating at the meetings you attend. The easiest way to take part is to say, "I pass"—a perfectly acceptable remark. No one in a Twelve Step program is obligated to say more. Most people, however, want to say more because they find it both enjoyable and beneficial. The more open and honest your comments, the faster you get well.

"Ninety in Ninety"

There is a joke that asks, "What is the difference between a drunk and an alcoholic?" Answer: "A drunk doesn't have to go to meetings; an alcoholic does!" A.A. stresses the importance of attending meetings, especially during the first three months of sobriety. Many members suggest attending ninety meetings in ninety days. By doing "ninety in ninety," beginners receive an intense exposure to the Twelve Step program and the people who use it. The principle that underlies doing "ninety in ninety" is a simple one—the more meetings you attend early on, the greater your chances of long-term recovery. There is no rule, of course, that you have to attend exactly ninety meetings in the first ninety days; go as often as your lifestyle allows. But keep in mind that the more meetings you attend, the faster you will get well.

> *"Many people find the miracle of sobriety by working the Twelve Steps."*

Many members complain about having to attend meetings, but those who recover keep going even when they don't feel like it. You don't have to like going to meetings, you just have to keep going. Meetings are the lifeline to sobriety. When you attend meetings, you take a needed time-out from an alcohol- and drug-centered world and remind yourself that you are an alcoholic, cannot safely use alcohol and other drugs, and that you need the fellowship of other sober alcoholics to stay sober.

Reading Twelve Step Literature. The second level of involvement is to read Twelve Step literature and discuss your reactions, both positive and negative, with other members. The early members of A.A. identified the basic principles needed to get sober and stay that way. They compiled that information in two books—*Alcoholics Anonymous* (often called the Big Book) and *Twelve Steps and Twelve Traditions*. Both books are available from the central office of Alcoholics Anonymous in New York City. These books provide the basic principles needed to begin living the sober life.

Getting a Sponsor. After you feel comfortable going to meetings, making comments, and reading the basic literature, the third level of involvement is to get a sponsor. A sponsor is another member of the Twelve Step program who has more experience at recovery than you do. In order to get a sponsor, you must have participated in the program long enough to get to know people. Listen to the comments of others. Try to find someone you respect and admire, someone who knows more than you do about the program and can show you the ropes. In the business world, a sponsor is called a mentor.

When you find such a person and ask him or her to be your sponsor, you are in essence asking, "Would you be willing to spend time with me and teach me how you work the program?" There's a slogan in the Twelve Step program: "If you want what we have, you do what we did." And it's primarily in the sponsorship relationship that this principle comes alive. You find a sponsor who has the type of recovery you would like to have, ask him to teach you what steps he took, and then try to do those things in your recovery.

Therapists and A.A.

A therapist does not take the place of a sponsor. You need a Twelve Step sponsor even if you have the best therapist in the world. A good therapist will encourage recovering people to become involved in Twelve Step programs and to get a sponsor. As a therapist, I don't mandate Twelve Step attendance, but I do strongly encourage it. If someone refuses to attend even one meeting to see what the organization is all about, I may say, "If you're not willing to go to Twelve Step meetings, I'm not willing to treat you. Why? Because if you're not willing to go and find out what Twelve Step programs involve, I don't think you really want to do what's necessary to recover." I base this attitude on an A.A. slogan: "We must be willing to go to any lengths to get sober." If you are not willing to clear a few evenings and attend some meetings, I question your willingness to do what is necessary to recover.

Work the Steps. Once you have a solid relationship with a good sponsor, you move to the fourth level: working the Twelve Steps. Step work under the guidance of a sponsor is literally the heart and soul of most Twelve Step programs. . . . Members who go to meetings but refuse to work the Steps are not really working the program. To quote the Big Book, "Rarely have we seen a person fail who has thoroughly followed our path." People who genuinely want to recover do more than just go to meetings: They work the Steps under the guidance of their sponsor. Those who are not serious about recovery don't work the steps. It's just that simple.

Sponsoring Others. By attending meetings, reading Twelve Step literature, talking frequently with sponsors, and working the Steps, you begin to grow and change. The program will start to transform you. As you learn and grow, you need to reach out and start giving back to others what has been given to you so freely. In short, it is time to move onto the fifth level and begin sponsoring others.

> *"[A.A.] meetings are the lifeline to sobriety."*

Sponsorship has two purposes: to help yourself and to help the person you sponsor. It is important to remember that you sponsor others in order to help yourself. You are in no way responsible for the recovery or relapse of the people you sponsor. The primary goal is to share freely your own experience, strength, and hope, and by doing so, you help yourself and may help the person you are sponsoring. But there are no guarantees. A.A. is a selfish program: Recovering people help others in order to help themselves. This attitude is clearly summed up in an A.A. slogan: "In order to keep it, you have to give it away."

By pairing with someone who is less experienced with the Twelve Steps than you are, and by trying to help him or her, you gain new insights into your own recovery. When I first started teaching courses on counseling, I realized how much I didn't know. I became motivated to learn more. The same is true in sponsorship. When you try to answer the questions of a newcomer, you become aware of your own ignorance. You gain the courage to stretch and to grow. When someone you are sponsoring asks you a question and you don't know the answer, it is time to go to your own sponsor. By helping others, we have been forced to learn. The formula is simple: Attend meetings, work the Steps, have a sponsor, and sponsor others.

Service Guided by the Traditions. The sixth level of involvement is service guided by the Traditions. Every organization needs bylaws, and Twelve Step programs are no exception. The twelve fundamental bylaws

> *"A good therapist will encourage recovering people to become involved in Twelve Step programs."*

that govern the operation of Twelve Step programs are called the Traditions. There is a need to maintain the organization of a Twelve Step program in order to make sure that the program continues to be available to help others. It is important to keep first things first. Service work is secondary to working the Steps and learning how to stay comfortable in recovery. But once A.A. members have a firm handle on their own recovery, service work is important to ensure the survival of the organization as a whole.

To Keep It, You Have to Give It Away

Father Joseph Martin, the creator of the film *Chalk Talk* and cofounder of the Ashley treatment center in Havre de Grace, Maryland, told me this story of A.A.'s cofounder Bill Wilson. Bill tried to stay sober all by himself for a long period of time, but he could never manage more than a few weeks of sobriety. Then he had this crazy notion that maybe he could help himself stay sober by helping other people to stay sober. The first approach Bill tried was what I call the "scrape them off the bar stool" approach. He talked to all of his friends with drinking problems and tried to convince them to stop. Basically, he went on a crusade to sober up drunks. Six months later, he told his wife, Lois, "I've failed. I've been trying to help alcoholics now for six months, and I haven't helped one person to get sober." Lois looked at him and said, "Bill, you're wrong. You have helped someone. *You* haven't had a drink in six months." Thus, one of the first principles of A.A. was born. It is summarized in the slogan, "In order to keep it, you have to give it away." The benefit of A.A. is that its members, recovering people in Twelve Step programs, get well by helping others to get well.

> *"The program will start to transform you."*

By trying to help others, people in recovery transcend their own selfishness; they interrupt the self-centeredness that is central to most addictions and compulsions. By trying to help others, addicts no longer remain the central part of their own personal addictive network. They begin to expand their world beyond the tip of their nose. In doing so, they find new values to govern their lives.

A.A. provides a number of crystal-clear guidelines: Don't drink, go to meetings, get a sponsor, work the Steps. Beyond these basics, there is a lot of ambiguity. After reading A.A. literature or attending a meeting, it is common for a member to scratch his or her head and ask, "What does that mean?" Part of the power of A.A. lies in this ambiguity, which forces people to provide their own meaning when working the program. Recovering people must make up their own minds and decide what the A.A. principles mean for them. One of the hallmarks of A.A. is that it's a "selfish" program. Members decide for themselves what they take out of the meetings. Nobody tells them what their experience is. They take what fits them and they leave the rest. . . .

The Trend Toward Self-Care

Twelve Step groups are everywhere—or so it seems. Alcoholics Anonymous, starting with its quiet beginnings in 1935, has emerged as a major influence that is shaping the future of America. John Naisbitt, a man who earns his living by analyzing future trends, confirms that A.A. and other self-help groups are part of a major national trend from professional care to self-care.

In the past, most Americans turned to professionals for help and support when things went wrong. But all that is changing as people take control of and responsibility for their own lives. Growing numbers of people are turning to self-help support groups as their primary source of assistance when trouble hits. Many of these groups are based upon the Twelve Steps of A.A.

There is a "statement of responsibility" in A.A. that says, "Anytime, anyone, anywhere reaches out for help, the hand of A.A. will be there, for this I am responsible." The incredible thing about this is that most A.A. members mean it! Any alcoholic who calls A.A. is referred to another member who gets that person to a meeting and orients him or her to the program. There is no charge for this highly personalized service. It happens because one alcoholic who feels that A.A. has saved his or her life is returning the favor to another alcoholic. The same is true in most other Twelve Step fellowships. Why? Because it is part of the program. Remember: "In order to keep it, you have to give it away!"

The popularity of A.A. and the Twelve Steps is not a fad. The Twelve Step philosophy is emerging as a powerful social trend. The Twelve Step movement is slowly creating a new way of thinking—one person at a time, one day at a time, in a very "easy does it" manner. The number of A.A spin-off groups that use the Twelve Steps is growing every day. Al-Anon was the first such group designed to help people who were affected by the alcoholism of another. Adult Children of Alcoholics (ACoA) is another major spin-off of A.A. As America moved into the age of "better living through chemistry," a number of other drug-addiction recovery groups, such as Narcotics Anonymous, Marijuana Anonymous, Cocaine Anonymous, and Pills Anonymous, were begun for people whose primary drug of choice is one other than alcohol. There are also Overeaters Anonymous, Gamblers Anonymous, Families Anonymous, Emotions Anonymous, and more than 200 other Twelve Step recovery groups. We are seeing a very powerful self-care movement that is readily available in most communities throughout the world.

A Source of Hope

In order to recover, chemically dependent people need to understand how to access the power of this movement to recover. Twelve Step groups provide a powerful source of information, courage, strength, and hope. And even though they will never totally replace professional care, these Twelve Step programs can be an effective, low-cost, and readily available adjunct to professional treatment.

Because A.A. is the single, most effective way to recover from chemical dependence, I strongly recommend it to all recovering people. If someone were to say to me, "I am only willing to do one thing for recovery. What should I do?" my answer as a professional counselor would be: "Go to A.A." Why? Because A.A. as a single, stand-alone source of help, is the most effective means of getting sober. There are more people sober as a result of attending A.A. and nothing else, than there are people who participate in all other forms of counseling and therapy combined. A.A. is by far the most powerful and most readily available recovery resource.

> *"A.A. is by far the most powerful and most readily available recovery resource."*

Treatment Centers Effectively Use Twelve-Step Programs to Help Alcoholics

by Norman S. Miller and John C. Mahler

About the authors: *Norman S. Miller and John C. Mahler are physicians affiliated with the New York Hospital/Cornell Medical Center in White Plains, New York.*

The principles and philosophy of the abstinence-based Twelve Step Program of Alcoholics Anonymous can be incorporated into the treatment process for alcohol and drug addiction. Current inpatient and outpatient psychiatric treatment may utilize the first five steps as an approach to alcohol and drug addiction. Furthermore, the program of Alcoholics Anonymous is recommended as a mainstay of continued treatment in the long term follow-up. However, AA limits its affiliation with rehabilitation centers as suggested in the Sixth Tradition: "An AA group ought never endorse, finance, or lend the AA name to any related facility or outside enterprise, lest problems of money, property, and prestige divert us from our primary purpose." Adherence to this principle ensures that AA remains focused on helping alcoholics recover from alcoholism and drug addiction.

Treatment for Alcoholism: The Disease Concept

Alcoholism and drug addiction are diseases for which treatment is essential and relatively sophisticated. One of the important reasons why Alcoholics Anonymous enjoys the popularity and success that it does today is because of advances in the effective treatment for alcoholism. Conversely, treatment for alcoholism has been enhanced by the inclusion of the principles of Alcoholics Anonymous. The two have benefited each other reciprocally. A basic tenet of the treatment approach as in AA is that alcohol and drug addiction are physical, mental and spiritual diseases. Treatment centers employ physicians, psycholo-

Norman S. Miller and John C. Mahler, "Alcoholics Anonymous and the 'AA' Model for Treatment," *Alcoholism Treatment Quarterly* 8 (no. 1, 1991): 39-49 (footnotes omitted). Copyright 1991 by The Haworth Press, Inc., 10 Alice St., Binghamton, NY 13904. Reprinted with permission.

gists, counselors and social workers who treat the diseases of alcoholism and drug addiction. The fundamental treatment focus is on the alcoholic; however, alcoholism (alcohol addiction) is considered a family illness so that the family is also intimately involved in the treatment process. Alcoholism and drug addiction will, and often do, affect each family member as severely and insidiously as they do the alcoholic.

Step One. Denial in both the alcoholic and the family members is an essential feature of addiction. Without denial, alcohol addiction could not exist in the proportions we know today. There is a significant amount of denial in virtually every alcoholic entering treatment.

Much of the treatment process occurs in both large and small groups. These groups are usually directed by a psychiatrist, psychologist or counselor. Patient interaction is encouraged and treatment begins when group members reach out to each other. In addiction, identification of one alcoholic with another is a critical step in the alcoholic's ability to accept treatment.

Confronting Denial

A substantial amount of the treatment process centers around the First Step where the denial of alcoholism and its consequences is gradually confronted. This confrontation of the alcoholic by the group is frequently accomplished by presenting the alcoholic with the evidence of the drinking and drug use that includes the consequences affecting him and others.

As a part of the treatment programs, the First Five Steps of Alcoholics Anonymous may be addressed and completed.

The First Step. "We admitted we were powerless over alcohol—that our lives had become unmanageable." The requirement for this step is complete abstinence from alcohol and other drugs to which the alcoholic may be addicted. The alcoholic admits that he has a loss of control over alcohol use and accepts the requirement of complete abstinence from alcohol. The alcoholic at some point has lost his ability to control the amount of alcohol drunk and the resolve to abstain from alcohol. The word "unmanageable" refers to the effects of alcoholism on the alcoholic and others around him. The admission and acceptance of "powerlessness" over alcohol are essential for continued abstinence and change in attitude and mood that occurs as a result of applying the remaining Eleven Steps to the alcoholic's daily life.

> *"The program of Alcoholics Anonymous is recommended as a mainstay of continued treatment in the long term follow-up."*

The disease concept of alcoholism purports a physical, mental and spiritual triad. Dr. William Silkworth referred to alcoholism as an "allergy" in Doctor's Opinion in the book *Alcoholics Anonymous*. Dr. Silkworth instilled the disease concept of alcoholism to the co-founders of Alcoholics Anonymous,

Bill Wilson and Dr. Robert Smith, who incorporated it into the program of recovery of AA.

Well-known toxic consequences of alcohol on the brain and body have been described in detail in a variety of medical sources. These physical and neuropsychological consequences of alcohol use include widespread involvement of many organ systems in the body. Cognitive, mood and memory disturbances emanate from direct toxic perturbations of the brain cells in a diffuse distribution in both higher cerebral and lower limbic centers. A multitude of medical sequelae ensue from disruption of function, and at times pathological injury, in the gastrointestinal-intestinal, cardiovascular, pulmonary, endocrine and integumentary systems as well as others.

The Alcoholic Personality

The mental consequences are dramatically illustrated in the psychological state of the alcoholic that contains many paradoxical characterizations. The outer phenomenology provides a portrait of a defiant, overconfident, exuberant and independent personality behind which is a victim who feels inferior, depressed, dependent, hopeless, helpless and worthless. The disease of alcoholism (and drug addiction) has rendered the individual powerless over alcohol and self. An added mental agony is that the alcoholic (addict) is at least partially aware of the hopelessness of this predicament, but is unable by resolve and will to deter his apparent self-inflicted demise.

> *"Treatment for alcoholism has been enhanced by the inclusion of the principles of Alcoholics Anonymous."*

The spiritual consequences are devastating. Usually, the alcoholic has been acting and thinking contrary to his moral standard or values, i.e., sense of right and wrong, which has produced a significant sense of guilt and isolation from himself and others. The price of denying his conscience its proper and sufficient expression is enormous and uncompromising. The existential state of the alcoholic is to not believe in any power that is greater than himself to maintain the illusion of self-reliance and the pattern of addiction which is loss of self-control. The chaos produced by the alcoholic's exercising his self-will in the face of an overpowering addiction is evident in all aspects of these attitudes, moods and perceptions. The complexity of the addictive state is greater than the simple inebriation from alcohol and drugs; the sense of "being" is corrupted. The sense of well being is replaced by a profound loss of meaning. Self-centered purpose and direction masquerade as a contemporary justification of Machiavellian thinking and action.

A profound lowered mood and a change in self-attitude of worthlessness, hopelessness, helplessness and self-blame constitute a syndrome of depression, sometimes very severe. Disturbances in vegetative functions such as altered sleep and eating patterns may occur. A blunted affect and psychomotor retardation may accompany the depressive state induced by alcoholism and drug addiction. The specific treatment of the alcohol and drug addiction with abstinence and the addict's application of the Steps will often relieve and resolve the severe depressive syndrome. Action taken in these Steps will often result in an elevation of mood and an establishment of an improved self-attitude. Spontaneous and expressive affect and behaviors replace the earlier dour and downtrodden appearance. The Twelve Step Program frequently is not only necessary, but sufficient for the reversal of "endogenous" or "biological depressions." The Dexamethasone Suppression Tests and Thyroid Releasing Stimulation test are frequently abnormal in active alcoholics and drug addicts and normal during abstinence to suggest an alcohol- and drug-induced biological substrate for the major depression seen in this population.

Threat of Suicide

A common conclusion and an almost natural sequelae to the cumulative effects of the physical, mental and spiritual deterioration and degradation induced by alcohol and drugs is suicidal thought and sometimes actions. Next to advancing age, alcoholism and drug addiction are the most serious risk factor for suicide, at least equal and probably above idiopathic depression that occupies a lower position among risk factors.

The adverse consequences are evident in the disruption of family harmony and cohesiveness; impaired performance at work; an array of legal entanglements and social infringements; and a wide variety of personal indiscretions and violations. These add to the already substantial guilt and isolation of the alcoholic.

The alcoholic now experiences a severe impairment in the perception of his "reality" and in the ability to discern and judge accurately. If honesty or self-insight uncovers this state of powerlessness and irrationality then the need for a power greater than the alcohol and drugs is required to relieve the insanity of continued addictive use.

Step Two. "Came to believe that a power greater than ourselves could restore us to sanity." The alcoholic on willpower, wits and character is unable to keep from drinking and in reality, drinks addictively against his will. The insanity of the second step is that the alcoholic takes the first drink in the first place. The assumption is that same person would not drink at all, knowing the consequences of another bout of drinking and the loss of control if when one drink is taken to set into motion an unyielding, compulsive consumption of alcohol. The alcoholic has lost the willpower to refuse a drink or a drug. The dilemma of the alcoholic is a lack of power of choice to avoid drinking and drug use that is the basis of an addiction. Furthermore, the misconcep-

> *"The Twelve Step Program frequently is not only necessary, but sufficient for the reversal of . . . 'biological depressions.'"*

tion that the alcoholic enjoys drinking at the point of addictive use perpetuates the moral condemnation of the alcoholic. The euphoria or enjoyment has usually long waned from the drinking experience of the alcoholic. The mystery is that the alcoholic continues to drink without pleasure; despite the anhedonia produced by addictive drinking.

An addiction has three components; a preoccupation with alcohol and other drugs, compulsive use, and relapse to alcohol and other drugs. In order for the alcoholic to successfully resist the addiction, outside help must be accepted. The insanity is that the alcoholic drinks even though to drink may mean significant adverse consequences and perhaps death, slow or fast; however, the alcoholic will often drink because of the addiction. Paradoxically, the power utilized by the alcoholic can only be other than or outside the alcoholic. The power, while under treatment, is often the physician or counselor, or the group of alcoholics in the treatment program at the time.

The Concept of Choice

Step Two is incorporated into this treatment program by introducing the concept of choice to the alcoholic. The alcoholic can learn to exercise his choice not to drink if he accepts his/her "powerlessness" or loss of control over alcoholism. The sanity is restored when the alcoholic is able to grasp the consequences of alcoholic drinking before taking a drink. The choice is maintained as long as abstinence and a commitment to recovery remain in effect.

Step Three. "Made a decision to turn our will and our lives over to the care of God as we understood Him." No attendance in a church nor adherence to theological dogma is required to accomplish this step, only a decision. The important factor in initiating this step is for the alcoholic to make a decision to turn his "will and life" over to the care of God. This step is spiritual and not religious in nature. The alcoholic volunteers some confidence and faith that accepting therapy for the alcoholism will work. The requirement is to "make a decision" to accept help from a power greater than himself.

A critical issue of this step is control. Repeatedly the alcoholic has failed at efforts to control his drinking patterns and alcoholism and has made persistent, although unsuccessful attempts to control time, quantity and places of alcohol and drug consumption. More importantly, the emotional loss of control and "instincts" that have gone awry have produced a state of fury and confusion in the alcoholic. The need for sex, food, love and security has been often exaggerated, distorted and misdirected by the alcohol and drugs sometimes into forms of other illnesses such as sexual and eating disorders. The basis of these distortions in sex, food and emotions is complex, derived from disturbances in the limbic system by the toxic effects of alco-

> *"The alcoholic can choose to believe in any power that is greater than himself to avoid . . . loss of control with alcohol."*

hol and drugs. The limbic system contains the neurosubstrate for emotions (such as anger, placidity, fear), sexual drive and expression, hunger and memory. The drive states and emotions may have been entrained by, and associated with alcohol and drugs. An increase in the tension of the drive states may signal the pursuit and use of alcohol and drugs. A reduction in the drive state may be satisfied by the reinforcement produced by alcohol and drugs.

Giving Up Control to Gain Control

A caricature develops of a self-centered, immature, self-seeking, self-willed, fearful and resentful personality. A defiance of the superego and its punitive exhortations is costly in the degree of guilt that is inflicted on the victim. The addictive process forces the individual to defy important moral values and ethical directives. The cumulative effect is destructive and overwhelming to the individual that is attempting to "control" all the diverse impulses and conflicts.

The alcoholic must paradoxically relinquish these attempts at control to regain mastery over self, emotions and instincts. The belief that a power both spiritual and human will return the control to the alcoholic is an essential step in recovery. A self-trust begins with a trust in others, both visible and invisible.

> *"Step Four ... is a necessary step for the alcoholic to achieve full awareness ... of the alcoholism."*

The key phrase in this step is God "as we understand Him," where the alcoholic can choose to believe in any power that is greater than himself to avoid the return to ruinous reliance and patterns of addiction and loss of control with alcohol. The alcoholic chooses to apply his will to a source of strength and help rather than the addictive mode directed by the drives in the limbic system that has been occupying his attitude, mood and perceptions.

Step Four. "Made a searching and fearless moral inventory of ourselves." This step requires recounting and detailing the consequences of the alcoholism and drug addiction admitted in the First Step. The alcoholic takes an inventory of the way in which alcohol had adversely affected him and others. The expression of conscious and unconscious material to the self is of paramount importance for the alcoholic to achieve a psychodynamic equilibrium. The inventory pertains to conscious and unconscious conflicts that represent the obstacles, that may or may not include moral judgments, within the alcoholic to future recovery. These obstacles frequently include defects in emotions (mood) and attitudes such as resentments, anger and fears, immaturity and sources of guilt. Some mastery over emotions, change in attitudes and resolution must occur for the alcoholic to achieve and maintain recovery, enjoy satisfactory sobriety and to avoid the syndrome of "depression" that is the total expression of these derangements in emotions, attitudes and guilt. A self-mastering over the limbic system by higher brain function is promoted by the use of the intellectual and spiritual exercise of self-inventory.

Step Five. "Admitted to God, to ourselves, and to another human being the exact nature of our wrongs." This is a Step of confession or in psychodynamic terms, a release of conscious and unconscious conflict to achieve an intrapsy-chic equilibrium between ego, id and superego. The alcoholic confides in and confesses to someone else the obstacles in the form of distorted atti-tudes and deranged morals uncovered in Step Four. This is a necessary step for the alcoholic to achieve full awareness regarding his intrapsychic

> *"Alcoholics Anonymous' . . . principles and practices may be incorporated into forms of acute intervention and treatment programs."*

state and effect of the consequences of the alcoholism. Confidentiality is a criti-cal requirement for this step. A skilled and compassionate listener, knowledge-able to the purpose of the alcoholic, is essential. The other person frequently is a sponsor in AA or a clergyman, although it can be a psychiatrist or counselor. The confession is therapeutic by itself, relieving depressive moods and dis-torted attitudes and frequently leads to a solid foundation for recovery if done with a measure of honesty and sincerity.

Alcoholism as a Family Illness

The family undergoes a similar clinical evaluation, self-scrutiny and treat-ment. The family members must examine their state of denial and how the dis-eases of alcoholism and drug addiction have affected them over the years. Those non-alcoholics affected by alcoholism are said to be as "ill" as the alco-holic. The recognition of their illness is often difficult because the identification of the alcoholic as the primary problem tends to distract attention from the non-alcoholic and to disguise the severe personality disturbances which can occur in those affected by the alcoholic. Often resentments that are directed towards the alcoholic are key offenders present within the family.

It is critically important for the entire family to be included in the treatment process at the same time as the alcoholic. Not doing so can delay not only the alcoholic's progress, but can also delay the treatment of the family. Alcoholics who are more likely to recover are those who have the support and involvement of their family and significant others. The alcoholic who is alone without fam-ily, social and community support is statistically less apt to recover. The more the family knows and the healthier it becomes through treatment, the better able the alcoholic and the family are to recover together.

Follow-Up

Follow-up and continued treatment after discharge from an inpatient program for alcoholism and drug addiction can contain a variety of ingredients. It may be only an entrance into Alcoholics Anonymous in the community as a continuation by the alcoholic who began attending AA meetings while in treatment. The family members and significant others who are not alcoholic are encouraged to attend Al-Anon on a regular basis. Some alcoholics need placement in residential treatment facilities which are called "half-way houses." This is a misnomer since these facilities are actually extended treatment care facilities where the alcoholic continues to receive group therapy and individual counseling, has employment, and attends meetings of Alcoholics Anonymous.

Day or partial hospital treatment programs are currently available in some centers. These programs provide the full range of group and individual therapies that are available to the inpatients and outpatients. The patients may have completed inpatient programs and have progressed to a stable state not requiring the therapeutic structure of a full-time stay in the hospital. Patients may also attend partial or day hospital programs de novo without a prior inpatient program if their clinical state and social supports are sufficiently stable to promote abstinence from alcohol and regular attendance in the program.

For many alcoholics, aftercare treatment on a follow-up basis after discharge from a hospital program is important and often involves the family. The treatment program may include discussions, education and group therapies which address current problems shared by the alcoholics and their families. These are more than support groups. They are actual therapy groups that meet on a regular basis between one to five times a week with a duration of one or more hours a day or evening. The total duration of treatment may be weeks, months or years.

In addition, alcoholics have other psychiatric problems more frequently than other populations that include eating, sexual, mood, and personality disorders that can also be addressed in the hospital programs and in the follow-up treatment plans. Special types of treatments and therapies from psychiatrists and psychologists are available for these recovering alcoholics and drug addicts. There are also support groups in the community for bulimia and anorexia patients and for individuals with particular sexual problems.

> *"Application of the AA model into treatment programs has resulted in effective ... treatments for alcohol and drug addiction."*

Although Alcoholics Anonymous remains a mainstay for "long term" treatment of the alcoholic, its principles and practices may be incorporated into forms of acute intervention and treatment programs. Considerable refinement and application of the AA model into treatment programs has resulted in effective inpatient and outpatient treatments for alcohol and drug addiction.

The forms of treatment that are effective for other disorders are employed in the treatment of addiction: these include group and individual therapies. The Steps of Alcoholics Anonymous can be effectively incorporated into the modalities of group and individual therapies. The concepts and application of these Steps are readily applied in formal treatment settings for alcoholism and drug addiction.

The Spirituality of AA Helps Alcoholics

by Monty Roberts

About the author: *Monty Roberts is a senior associate at Zoetics, Inc., a New York City marketing think tank.*

I found God in an Exodus community called Alcoholics Anonymous. My primary conversion text is the healing of the Gerasene demoniac, which concludes, "The man from whom the demons had gone begged that he might be with him; but Jesus sent him away, saying, 'Return to your home, and declare how much God has done for you'" (Luke 8:22-39).

Jesus made a conscious decision to cross the lake from his own town, Capernaum, to Gerasa before encountering the demoniac. It was not a whim. Just as the evil spirits invariably recognize Jesus as the Christ before we do, so Jesus invariably goes to confront evil before we recognize it as such. The basic story epitomizes my experience of recovering from a demon named alcoholism—how God's power will heal the addict who is willing to put down his ego and ask for help, who will name his disease and admit his powerlessness before it.

Alcoholism is a three-faced disease: physical, psychological, and spiritual. It is chronic, progressive, and fatal. There is no cure.

The process of recovery from alcoholism is not a matter of medical science curing the disease. Recovery is grace—a process of being healed by God's love.

Shared Suffering

The fact that sharing our suffering can bring the redemption of God's love is something which is lost in society at large and in most mainstream churches. But it is not lost in Alcoholics Anonymous. It may explain why AA membership is growing at a high rate while mainstream church rolls are declining. The *New York Times* once noted that "religious leaders have begun suspecting that more lives are being transformed in church basements than in the pews."

The church's problem is contextual. It is upstairs talking about abstract theol-

Monty Roberts, "Home at Last," *Sojourners*, August/September 1992. Reprinted with permission from *Sojourners*, PO Box 29272, Washington, DC 20017.

ogy while Jesus is downstairs, drinking coffee with the recovering drunks and drug addicts. The church caters to Wall Street when the hungry are homeless on Main Street.

In AA, to keep your sobriety you must give it away; and the process for doing this is to share your experience, strength, and hope with the community. An AA slogan states: "I get drunk, we get sober." The 12 Steps of AA provide a framework for moving through the phases of suffering outlined by theologian Dorothee Soelle, from mute isolation to lamentation to repentance in solidarity with the community.

> *"AA teaches rigorous honesty, obedience to God's will, and humility."*

Suffering is what holds the community together in common union. Shared suffering is what brings redemption to others. Just as Jesus shared his suffering with us and for us, so the recovering addict/alcoholic shares her or his suffering with others and for others in the AA community.

AA teaches rigorous honesty, obedience to God's will, and humility. The slogan is HOW (Honest, Open, and Willing). The model for turning our will and our life over to the care of God is Jesus, who "emptied himself, taking the form of a slave, being born in human likeness. And being found in human form, he humbled himself and became obedient to the point of death—even death on a cross" (Philippians 2:7-8).

For Those Who Have Been to Hell

The foundation of recovery is not willpower but surrender of one's will to God. Although AA is not a religion, since its founding 57 years ago, many have pointed out how much the church needs to learn or reclaim from AA. In AA, like the early church, there are no "good Christians," only sinners. It is said: "Religion is for those afraid of going to hell, and AA spirituality is for those who have already been there."

Theologian Richard Rohr notes a parallel between AA spirituality and the call of liberation theology that we make a preferential option for the poor. Rohr points out that the practice of the 12 Steps "calls us to embrace and love the poor part of ourselves—to find Christ in the wounded, needy depths of our own souls."

And theologian Leonardo Boff says, "Only a society of sisters and brothers whose social fabric is woven out of participation and communion of all in everything can justifiably claim to be an image and likeness (albeit pale) of the Trinity, the foundation and final resting place of the universe."

God and Chaos

AA is such a society. It is open to the chaos; it allows anxiety to be freely, honestly expressed and finds joy in dancing with human diversity. AA's old-timers say all you need to know to believe in God is to know you are not God.

The AA group is a community where it is OK to make mistakes and where we are home at last. We know we are in the presence of God when our experience is supported, shared, challenged, or refined by those called by God to journey with us.

Studies Show Alcoholics Anonymous Is Ineffective

by Charles Bufe

About the author: *Charles Bufe is the author of* Alcoholics Anonymous: Cult or Cure? *from which this viewpoint is excerpted.*

Is A.A. an effective treatment for alcoholism? That seemingly simple question is far more difficult to answer than one would expect. A major problem is the difficulty of defining the terms "alcoholism" and "alcoholic." Since the terms were invented over 100 years ago, a great variety of definitions have been offered, and there is still no uniformity of opinion among the "experts" about what constitutes alcoholism nor about what constitutes an alcoholic. The safest thing that can be said is that definitions are largely arbitrary and can (and do) change over time. For example, in the first edition of the "Big Book," Bill Wilson mentions "a certain type of hard drinker. He may have the habit badly enough to gradually impair him physically and mentally. It may cause him to die a few years before his time." Wilson goes on to say that this person is not a real alcoholic because he can learn to "stop or moderate." Needless to say, virtually all A.A. members, as well a very large majority of alcoholism professionals, would now label such a person "alcoholic."

How Many Alcoholics?

Another indication of the difficulties involved in defining the word "alcoholic" can be seen in the wildly varying estimates of the number of alcoholics in the United States. In the 1986 best-seller, *The Courage to Change*, Dennis Wholely estimates that there are 20 million American alcoholics. This figure is twice as high as the figure of 10 million which is found in many professional journal articles and alcoholism reference texts published in the 1970s and early 1980s, and which is still occasionally cited. A facts sheet circulated by the NCA [National Council on Alcoholism and Other Drug Addictions] estimates that there are 12.1 million heavy drinkers exhibiting one or more of the signs of alcoholism. And if you accept the commonly cited figure that 10 percent of American adults are alcoholics, you arrive at a figure of roughly 18 million.

The primary reason why these estimates vary so greatly is that "alcoholism" is an elusive concept with several defining factors, the limits of which are seemingly arbitrary, with the exceptions of physical dependency and tolerance (the need to drink larger amounts than the average person in order to reach a similar state of intoxication). In addition to physical dependency and tolerance, commonly cited defin-

> *"At least some disturbed persons . . . are attracted to A.A. because it's an easy way to meet their social needs."*

ing factors include level of alcohol consumption, legal problems (e.g., DWIs [driving while intoxicated]), psychological dependency, and family, social, psychological, and economic problems. Obviously, any definition based upon such factors must be imprecise and at least somewhat arbitrary. For example, what is the precise amount of alcohol consumption which separates the alcoholic from the social drinker? And what relation does alcohol consumption have to the other defining variables? Would someone who drank 7 ounces of alcohol per day but who had relatively minor problems in other areas be defined as an alcoholic? Would someone who drank only half that amount but had severe problems in other areas be defined as an alcoholic? It's difficult to view answers to such questions as anything other than arbitrary.

One thing that is certain is that the typical A.A. member today is different than the typical A.A. member in 1940. In the early days of A.A., members were primarily "low-bottom" alcoholics who had been hospitalized for their drinking problems, and whose drinking had had devastating effects on their lives. At present, at least a large minority, perhaps a majority, of A.A. members are "high-bottom" problem drinkers who were never physically dependent upon nor tolerant of alcohol and who still functioned reasonably well socially and economically when they quit drinking. Thus, a well-designed study of the effectiveness of A.A. today would very probably yield a different result than a similar study conducted 50 years ago would have, simply because of the differences in the makeup of both A.A.'s membership and the much-expanded pool of drinkers from which it is now drawn.

The Changing Composition of AA

With the trend toward inclusion of those with shorter and shorter and ever-less-serious drinking problems in A.A., the composition of A.A.'s membership will very likely continue to change for some time to come. (According to A.A.'s 1989 membership survey, 3 percent of A.A.'s members are *teenagers*. In the 1930s, A.A.'s early members would have considered the idea of teenage "alcoholics" ludicrous.) One question which arises from this is what percentage of A.A.'s members are now "real alcoholics"? A complicating factor is the fact that at least some disturbed persons whose primary problems are almost certainly not alcohol related are attracted to A.A. because it's an easy way to meet their social needs.

The changing makeup of A.A.'s membership is, however, a minor problem compared with several others. The most important problem is that in attempting to gauge the effectiveness of A.A. it's very difficult to tell if you're gauging results due to the A.A. program or results due to the characteristics of A.A.'s membership. There are several factors predictive of a positive outcome to alcoholism treatment—motivation, middle-class status, marital stability, employment, relatively mild and short-term problems with alcohol, and absence of serious mental illness being probably the most important—with most being found in higher-than-average percentages (for problem drinkers) in A.A.'s membership; and it should be noted that these factors are *pre*determining factors which were operative in a great many A.A. members *before* they joined A.A. An indication of the importance of these predictive factors is found in an evaluation by Frederick Baekeland of different varieties of alcoholism treatment. Baekeland compared studies of four group therapy programs serving high socioeconomic status (SES—an important prognosticator of treatment outcome) patients with studies of four group therapy programs serving skid row alcoholics and other low SES patients. The improvement rates of the programs serving the skid row alcoholics were only 18 percent, 7.9 percent, 2 percent, and 0 percent, while the improvement rates of the programs serving high SES patients were 32.4 percent, 46.4 percent, 55.8 percent, and 68 percent.

> *"Certain aspects of A.A. are so unpleasant . . . that continued attendance in itself implies a high degree of motivation."*

As is almost universally recognized in treatment literature, the most important favorable prognosticator is "motivation." Like most cliches, the truism that "once you admit you have a problem, it's half-licked" seems to have a basis in fact. Simply showing up at an A.A. meeting implies that an individual recognizes that s/he has a problem, and in itself this self-selection seems predictive of a successful outcome. Further, certain aspects of A.A. are so unpleasant—especially the religiosity, anti-intellectuality, and the gas chamber-like, tobacco smoke-filled atmosphere at many meetings—that continued attendance in itself implies a high degree of motivation, at least for non-religious and critically minded (not to mention nonsmoking) members.

Few Alcoholics Join AA

Biasing factors, such as "motivation," are a serious problem, but it does seem possible to draw at least tentative conclusions about the effectiveness of Alcoholics Anonymous. A good starting point is A.A.'s most recent triennial membership survey. At the present time A.A. claims only 900,000 members in the

U.S. and Canada, while there are an estimated 10 to 20 million alcoholics in the U.S. alone. The population of the U.S. is about ten times that of Canada, and for the purposes of this analysis we can assume that the ratio of A.A. members to general population is about the same in the United States and Canada. Thus, there should be approximately 820,000 A.A. members in the U.S., so in all probability only 4.1 percent to 8.2 percent of the nation's alcoholics are members of A.A. And the percentage of those who reach the A.A. goal of lifelong sobriety is much lower than that.

A noticeable feature of A.A. is that a large number of its members have been in the organization for a relatively short time. Based on my attendance at A.A. meetings in San Francisco, I would estimate that over 50 percent of those attending meetings in this city have been A.A. members for less than one year and, in fact, that a majority have been members for only a few months.

This estimate is more or less in line with the figures given by Bill C. in a 1965 article in the *Quarterly Journal of Studies on Alcohol*. In it, he reports that of 393 A.A. members surveyed, 31 percent had been sober for more than one year; 12 percent had been sober for more than one year but had had at least one relapse after joining A.A.; 9 percent had achieved a year's sobriety; 6 percent had died; 3 percent had gone to prison; 1 percent had gone to mental institutions; and 38 percent had stopped attending A.A. What makes these numbers even more dismal than they appear is the fact that Bill C. defined a member as someone who attended 10 or more A.A. meetings in a year's time. When you take into account the "revolving door effect," it becomes apparent that far more persons attended A.A. meetings than the 393 "members" Bill C. lists. It seems quite probable that he picked the figure of 10 meetings in a year as a membership criterion because A.A.'s success rate would have been revealed as microscopic if he had used a smaller number of attendances as his membership-defining device. (It should also be mentioned that attendance at 10 meetings in itself seems to imply a fairly high degree of motivation.)

Poor Success Rates

The success rate calculated through analysis of the 1989 A.A. membership survey is hardly more impressive. The summary of the membership survey indicates that only 29 percent of members have at least five-years' sobriety. Using the figure of five-years' sobriety as the criterion of success, one arrives at an A.A. success rate of approximately 1.2 percent to 2.4 percent (in comparison with the total number of alcoholics in the U.S.). If success is defined as one or more years of sobriety, A.A.'s success rate improves considerably, to 2.7 percent to 5.4 percent, as, according to A.A.'s survey, 65 percent of A.A. members have been sober at least one year.

> *"Only 29 percent of members have at least five-years' sobriety."*

It could be argued that this is an unfair way of evaluating the effectiveness of A.A., and that only alcoholics who have investigated sobering up via A.A. should be considered. That's a reasonable argument, but it's virtually impossible to know the exact percentage of American alcoholics who have participated in A.A. Anyone who has attended many A.A. meetings can testify that droves of newcomers show up, attend one, or a few, meeting(s), and then are never seen again—the "revolving door effect." Based on the

> *"Only 5 percent of those who investigate A.A. are still attending meetings one year after they first walked through the door."*

sheer numbers of such persons, it seems probable that well over 50 percent, perhaps as many as 90 percent, of the nation's problem drinkers investigate A.A. at some time during their drinking careers. In fact, A.A.'s 1989 membership survey lends support to this estimate. According to the survey, only 5 percent of those who investigate A.A. are still attending meetings one year after they first walked through the door.

Low Success Rates

If success is defined as one-year's sobriety, on the face of it this 95 percent dropout rate gives A.A. a *maximum* success rate of only 5 percent; and a great many new members do not remain continuously sober during their first year in A.A., which causes the apparent A.A. success rate to fall even lower. Of course, many of the 95 percent who drop out within the first year are probably "repeaters" who have previously investigated A.A., and this would increase the apparent A.A. success rate; but at least for the present there is no way to know what percentage of the dropouts are repeaters. Additionally, at least some of the 95 percent who drop out of A.A. during their first year do manage to sober up; but to date there's no way to know what their numbers are. As well, it seems quite probable that most of those who drop out early in the program do so because they dislike and disagree with A.A., so it could be argued that most of them who attain sobriety do so in spite of, not because of, A.A.

One thing, however, is certain: An extremely high percentage of American drinkers who have been hospitalized for alcoholism or who have participated in other institutional alcoholism programs have participated in Alcoholics Anonymous. The number of patients treated for alcoholism is now close to two million annually, which (because A.A. is a part of treatment in virtually all institutional programs) is a good indication that the proportion of alcoholics who have been exposed to A.A. is very high. It should also be kept in mind that convicted drunk drivers are routinely forced to attend A.A. as a condition of probation—which pushes the percentage of alcoholics exposed to A.A. even higher. Further, in most areas A.A. is the only widely available—and widely media-promoted—alcoholism treatment program, so A.A. has a very high volume of "walk in" traffic.

But let's give A.A. the benefit of the doubt and estimate that only 50 percent of U.S. alcoholics have tried A.A. That would double the success rate calculated earlier (based on the total number of U.S. alcoholics), and it would increase to 2.4 percent to 4.8 percent of alcoholics who have investigated A.A. if the criterion of success is defined as five-years' sobriety, and 5.4 percent to 10.8 percent if the criterion is set at one-year's sobriety. (The variation is due to the widely differing estimates of the number of American alcoholics.)

In a worst case scenario, where 90 percent of the nation's alcoholics have looked into A.A., where success is defined as five or more years of sobriety, where 29 percent of A.A. members have been sober for five or more years (as A.A. indicates), and where there are 20 million alcoholics in the country, the A.A. success rate would be about 1.3 percent (and even lower than that if the criterion of success is lifelong sobriety rather than five-years' sobriety). The true success rate of A.A. is very probably somewhere between these two extremes, depending, of course, on how one defines "success"; that is, A.A.'s success rate is probably somewhere between 1.3 percent and 10.8 percent (of those who have attended A.A.).

> *"Contrary to popular belief, alcoholism is not a progressive and incurable 'disease.'"*

This is far from impressive, especially when compared with the rate of "spontaneous remission." Contrary to popular belief, alcoholism is *not* a progressive and incurable "disease." Several studies have been conducted on so-called spontaneous recovery by alcoholics (that is, recovery without treatment, which can refer to achievement of either sobriety or controlled drinking), and the consensus of these studies is that "spontaneous" recovery occurs in a significant percentage of alcoholics, though the calculated rates of recovery vary considerably. Other consistently supported conclusions are that the rate of alcoholism among individuals past the age of 40 declines far faster than can be explained by mortality, and that "spontaneous" recovery normally occurs for identifiable reasons. In many cases remission comes suddenly after a particularly dangerous or humiliating incident shocks the drinker into realization of the seriousness of his or her drinking problem. In other, probably fewer, cases, recovery occurs as the result of an "existential" decision to quit based on a gradually increasing realization of the seriousness of the problem. Whatever its causes, spontaneous recovery occurs at a significant rate. One review of available literature estimated the rate of spontaneous recovery at 3.7 percent to 7.4 percent per *year*. Compared with this, the above-calculated rate of recovery via A.A. is not impressive. In fact, it appears to be no better than the rate of spontaneous recovery.

Scientific Investigations of AA

But haven't there been scientific investigations of the effectiveness of A.A.? There have been, but there haven't been many. One reason for this could well be that, [as Helen Annis states,] "A.A. does not like to have researchers around," that it is highly reluctant to "open its doors to researchers," [according to Baekeland]. Whatever the truth of these charges, there have only been two well-designed studies of the effectiveness of A.A.—that is, studies which have included control groups and the random assignment of subjects. Both studies indicated that A.A. is *not* an effective across-the-board treatment for alcoholism. The subjects in both studies were, however, court-referred alcoholic offenders and hence different from the general alcoholic population in certain respects. Thus one important distinguishing feature is the fact that they did not voluntarily seek treatment; they were forced to attend A.A. and the other treatments studied.

Are Factors Biased?

On the surface, these factors—the employment of coercion and the special-population status of alcoholic offenders—seem to lessen the credibility of the two controlled studies of A.A.'s effectiveness. But it could be argued that one factor is irrelevant and the other actually enhances the studies' credibility. If, as is commonly asserted, A.A. is a universally applicable treatment for *all* alcoholics, the makeup of the study populations shouldn't have mattered a wit as long as assignment of subjects to A.A. and control groups was truly random. And the fact that the studies' subjects were coerced into participating could well *increase* the validity of the studies' findings because a very important biasing factor, subject motivation, was eliminated, and the remaining biasing factors were spread out fairly evenly among the groups studied because of the random assignment procedure. Further, since a large number of present-day A.A. participants are coerced into attendance either by alcoholism treatment programs or the courts, through programs for DWI offenders, the populations of these studies were perhaps not as different from the general A.A. population as one might suspect.

The first of these controlled studies of A.A.'s effectiveness was conducted in San Diego in the mid-1960s. In the study 301 public drunkenness offenders were randomly divided into three groups. One group was assigned to attend A.A., another to attend an alcoholism treatment clinic, and a third group, the control, was not assigned to any treatment program. All of the study's subjects were followed for at least one full year following conviction. Results were calculated by counting the number and frequency of rearrests for drunkenness. Surprisingly, the control group was the most successful of the three, with 44 percent of its members having no rearrests; 32 percent of the subjects in the clinic group had no rearrests; and 31 percent of those assigned to A.A. had no rearrests. As well, 37 percent of the members of the no-

> *"A.A. is not an effective across-the-board treatment for alcoholism."*

treatment control group had two or more rearrests, while 40 percent of the alco-holism clinic attendees were rearrested at least two times, and 47 percent of the A.A. attendees were arrested at least twice. While far from a definitive debunk-ing of A.A.'s alleged effectiveness, these results are certainly suggestive.

The other controlled study of A.A.'s effectiveness was very carefully designed and conducted and was carried out in Kentucky in the mid-1970s [by Jeffrey Brandsma, Maxie Maultsby, and Richard J. Welsh]. A large majority of its subjects were obtained via the court system, and seemed to be "rep-

> *"A significant percentage of alcohol abusers can become moderate drinkers."*

resentative of the 'revolving door' alcoholic court cases in our cities." The study's conductors divided 197 subjects into five randomly selected groups: a control group given no treatment; a group assigned to traditional insight therapy adminis-tered by professionals; a group assigned to nonprofessionally led Rational Behav-ior Therapy (lay-RBT); a group assigned to professionally led Rational Behavior Therapy; and a group assigned to A.A. Length of treatment varied from 202 to 246 days, and subjects were evaluated at the end of treatment and also at three months and 12 months following its termination.

Professional Treatment

In general, the groups given professional treatment did better than the non-professionally treated groups and the control group. A significant finding, how-ever, was that treatment of any kind was preferable to no treatment at all.

Since professional treatment is not an option for many, perhaps most, alco-holics, it's particularly important to compare the results of the A.A., lay-RBT, and control groups. Lay-RBT was clearly superior to A.A. in terms of dropout rate. During the study 68.4 percent of those assigned to A.A. stopped attending it, while only 40 percent of those attending lay-RBT sessions stopped attending them. Further, at the termination of treatment all of the lay-RBT participants who had persisted in treatment reported that they were drinking less than they were before treatment, while only two-thirds of those who had continued to at-tend A.A. reported decreased drinking. As well, during the final three months of treatment, the mean number of arrests was 1.24 for the lay-RBT group, 1.67 for the A.A. group, and 1.79 for the control group. Perhaps most interestingly, the number of reported binges at three months after termination of treatment was far higher for the A.A. group than for the lay-RBT or control groups. The mean number of reported binges by the A.A. attendees was 2.37 over the previ-ous three months, while the mean number reported by the controls was 0.56, and the mean for the lay-RBT group was only 0.26. This finding strongly sug-gests that the A.A. attendees had been affected by A.A.'s "one drink, one drunk" dogma, had accepted it, and had then proceeded to "prove" it. It should be pointed out, however, that at 12 months following the termination of treatment there were no significant differences between the A.A., lay-RBT, and control groups.

A particularly interesting aspect of this study is that the relatively successful (compared with A.A. and the no-treatment controls) lay-RBT group utilized a treatment based on Rational Emotive Therapy (RET). The reason this is so interesting is that the program of Rational Recovery (R.R.), a new self-help secular alternative to A.A., is based entirely upon RET, and RET is utilized at least to some extent within Secular Organizations for Sobriety (S.O.S.), another of the new alternatives to A.A. To date, no scientific evaluations of the effectiveness of R.R. or S.O.S. have been published, but in light of the study just discussed it seems reasonable to suspect that both of them, though particularly R.R., might be more effective than A.A.

Other Forms of Treatment

Such speculation is, however, just that—speculation. What is certain is that certain types of alcoholism treatment work better than others, and some have shown very high success rates in controlled studies. For example, the Community Reinforcement Approach (CRA)—a treatment method utilizing behavioral family therapy, job-finding training (for unemployed clients), problem-solving training and social skills training—has shown extremely high success rates in two carefully controlled studies, with CRA-treated clients in one of the studies drinking on only 2 percent of days versus 55 percent of days for control-group clients; and the gains made by CRA-treated clients persisted throughout a 24-month follow-up period.

It appears that even that bugaboo of abstinence advocates, controlled drinking, is an effective alternative to uncontrolled drinking or abstinence for many problem drinkers. A number of studies have indicated that a significant percentage of alcohol abusers *can* become moderate drinkers. It's important to point out, though, that "one highly consistent finding is that individuals with less severe problems are more likely to succeed in achieving controlled drinking, whereas more severe alcoholics show better prognosis with abstinence," [according to William R. Miller and Nick Heather]. That is, the chances of a problem drinker's achieving controlled drinking are inversely related to the seriousness and length of his or her drinking problem. Thus, it seems quite probable that abstinence is a preferable goal for those with long-term and serious drinking problems, especially if those problems involve (or involved) physical dependency and/or physical damage. . . .

"There is virtually no overlap between alcoholism treatments known to be effective and those which are widely employed."

It's very interesting to note that two prominent alcoholism treatment researchers, William R. Miller and Nick Heather, state that there is virtually no overlap between alcoholism treatments known to be effective and those which are widely employed. Treatments which they list as "currently supported by controlled outcome research" are aversion therapies, behavioral self-control training (controlled drinking and drink refusal), community reinforcement approach, marital and family therapy, social skills training, and stress management. The treatment methods which they list as "currently employed as standard practice in alcoholism programs," but which are not supported by controlled research, are Alcoholics Anonymous, alcoholism education, confrontation, disulfiram (antabuse), group therapy, and individual counseling.

AA Works Sometimes

Is A.A. totally useless as a treatment for alcoholism? Perhaps not. One of the current trends in alcoholism treatment is "client matching," that is, the matching of clients to particular treatments based upon the clients' needs, personalities, and social characteristics. Since A.A. inspires fanatical loyalty in certain members, it would be surprising if A.A. wasn't an appropriate treatment method for certain alcoholics; and it seems logical that the characteristics of those for whom A.A. is appropriate would in general match the characteristics of those already succeeding in the program.

Many studies of the characteristics of A.A. members have been conducted, and based on them Baekeland comments that the typical A.A. member is "likely to be a single, religiously oriented [middle class] individual . . . He is not highly symptomatic, and is a socially dependent guilt-prone person with obsessive-compulsive and authoritarian personality features, prone to use rationalization and reaction formation. Finally, he is a verbal person who can share his reactions with others and is not threatened by groups of people."

Alan C. Ogborne and Frederick B. Glaser list the characteristics of successful A.A. members as "male, over forty years of age, white, middle or upper class, socially stable, . . ." binge/heavy drinker, physical dependency and loss of control when drinking, "authoritarian personality, high affiliative needs, high group dependency needs, prone to guilt, external locus of control . . . cognitive simplicity, low conceptual level . . . religious orientation . . . conformity orientation, deindividuation potential."

What is striking about both of these lists is that they describe the original members of A.A. almost perfectly. This, as well as A.A.'s previously discussed overall lack of efficacy, strongly suggests that A.A. would do well to stop presenting itself as a universally effective treatment program for alcoholism and instead return to its original mission of recruiting and treating "low-bottom" "up and outers"—severely dependent, middle-aged, middle- and upper-middle-class, religious, politically conservative white males. For clearly A.A. is neither a suitable nor an effective form of treatment for the vast majority of alcohol abusers.

AA's Focus on Spirituality Is Harmful and Unnecessary

by Jack Trimpey

About the author: *Jack Trimpey founded Rational Recovery Systems, an organization that helps people overcome alcohol and drug dependence, in 1986. RRS emphasizes the importance of self-reliance in conquering addiction. Trimpey is the author of* The Small Book, *which details the concepts behind Rational Recovery and from which this viewpoint is excerpted.*

This viewpoint will do two things. First, it will summarize the common objections that many people have to the 12-step program. These are not necessarily my objections, but a summary of the objections of the thousands of frustrated people who have contacted RRS [Rational Recovery Systems] and told us their stories. Second, this chapter will bring to the public eye what is happening in our national addiction care system. It is not my intention here to persuade AA members or devout theists that their views are wrong, or to discredit any successes of the AA treatment approach. Instead we will simply examine each of the steps from the perspective of an inquiring mind, asking the questions that come naturally to *anyone* who is not already convinced of the overall correctness of the 12-step creed.

Nonbelievers

The idea that an author must be angry in order to criticize or express dissent is an *ad hominem* response that seeks to sidestep the author's argument. It is also typical for proponents of faith-based systems of thought to believe that there must be something wrong with someone who disagrees. There is an AA pamphlet titled *AA: An Interpretation for the Nonbeliever* (Jon Weinberg, Ph.D., Hazelden Foundation) that is worth getting and reviewing first hand. On the front cover of this fourteen-page booklet, a "nonbeliever" is depicted in caricature, and one must see it to believe it. This is an ugly person—his mouth is twisted into a scowl, his eyeglasses are slipping down his nose, his double chin protrudes over his collar, and his entire face is furrowed with deep, angry wrinkles. He is pitiful. He is a stereotype that is central to AA tradition, and we may find the image of this troubled soul described throughout "The Big Book." He is "the angry one," a pathetic dumbbell who denies God, then sees the error of his ways, surrenders to his Higher Power, has a spiritual awakening, and then lives happily ever after.

One of the barriers to progress in addiction care is what we might call "blasphobia," or the morbid fear of being associated with anything that could be construed by anyone as being blasphemous, anti-God, anti-Christ, antireligion, satanic, demonic, etc. As it stands, AA represents America's "traditional values"—the good, the true, and the beautiful. What could be more publicly appealing than a secret society of altruists who themselves were redeemed from iniquity through faith in God? But I must ask, "What is the state's interest in protecting the 12-step ideology from meticulous scrutiny?"

As strange as it may sound, I feel *AA is not responsible for the deplorable condition in which it is participating*. The responsibility for AA's inappropriate dominance of the American addiction care system lies within the leadership of our public health care institutions and within the helping professions. AA is blameless for behaving exactly like other faith-based, expansionist organizations, and no one should be surprised that, once inside the door, and with decades of progressive momentum and administrative passivity, it has become a socio-medical behemoth. The task before us is to help our health care system backpedal on its excessive commitment to the venerable 12 steps and achieve a two-party system —the spiritual and the rational—in publicly supported agencies.

The Beatification of Bill Wilson

When Bill Wilson came to national consciousness a few decades ago, the orderly progression of national health care was diverted into the arena of spiritual healing. Referred to in those times as "the religious solution," AA was viewed as an inspirational example of people helping others to overcome the behavioral problem "dipsomania." AA fulfilled the nation's desire for anything that would help problem drinkers just at the time Prohibition was being repealed. A social movement—a religious movement—had been born, and its charismatic leader was "Bill W.," who was intensely admired as a very good man. He symbolized the triumph of the human spirit over adversity, and his humble, down-home charm made him a role model for others struggling with their own addictions. As time passed, his humility inspired fierce loyalty among his followers.

> *"AA ... has become a socio-medical behemoth."*

When Bill Wilson died in 1971, there began a beatification process that by 1980 led to his elevation to folk saint. So powerful are the symbols of Bill Wilson's charismatic leadership that his simple message and 12-step spiritual healing program have penetrated the barrier separating church and state. It is of no importance whether or not Bill Wilson knew what he was doing when he founded "the religion that is not a religion," but it is clear that in doing so, he created *an ambiguous organism* that defies definition. "We are *not* a religion" is commonly heard from the employees and officials of public institutions throughout the land, "we are only a *spiritual* organization."

> *"Under the charismatic leadership of the founders of AA and their successors, addiction care has run amok."*

American health care, of which addiction care is an important part, is science-based. Under the charismatic leadership of the founders of AA and their successors, addiction care has run amok. It has evaded public accountability by using strong symbols, by borrowing protections normally reserved for religions, and through the use of charismatic authority. Until the public is awakened to the religious fundamentalism contained in our addiction care system, many people will continue to receive unwanted religious indoctrinations during their times of special vulnerability.

A Critique of the 12 Steps

As you read this short critique of the 12 steps, you will notice that taken together they implement a philosophy in which one is powerless, submissive to authority, unequipped to function independently, and in endless need of external support and guidance. This should not be surprising to anyone, and to take offense that this is pointed out would seem to be a *denial* of reality. The 12 steps are derived from an ancient philosophy with which we are all familiar. Like it or not, the twelve numbered ideas below reflect just one of the major philosophical traditions of American society, even though they have often been held up as a universal ideal.

Step 1: *"We admitted we were powerless over alcohol—that our lives had become unmanageable."*

Step 1 actually teaches addicts that they are not responsible for what they put in their mouths, that they have no capacity to refrain from ingesting alcohol. Could it be that alcoholism is largely a *result* of this idea? That is, isn't the alcoholic already acting out the idea that his desire for alcohol is an *absolute* need, that a craving is *irresistible* or *intolerable*, and that, when the desire to drink occurs, it *must* be gratified *immediately* and *completely*? To the extent that this is so, the message in this first step could be counterproductive to those who are concerned enough to attend a few meetings but not really inclined to adopt the social or theological elements of AA spiritualism.

Learned helplessness from Step 1 often can be a self-fulfilling prophecy in which the addict retains this central spiritual principle of surrender even after quitting AA. For example, after attending a few meetings you may decide that AA isn't for you, that you can get sober on your own. So you stop attending meetings, resolved to quit drinking. However, something lingers in your thinking and it won't go away. When you feel like having a drink, you think back to what was said at the AA meetings, and you remember the sincere people and their stern warnings:

> You are powerless over alcohol and you have no control; only a Higher Power can restore you to sanity. We all tried it on our own and none of us could remain sober until we found our Higher Power. You can't resist the overpowering urge to drink, and if you leave this group you will drink again; then it's all downhill. This group is a lifeboat; leave us and you'll sink. There's no escape except through our loving God, Who gives us the strength to stay sober, one day at a time.

This kind of indoctrination does *nothing* to help your resolve to not drink; it is probably *the worst thing* to tell someone who is having problems with impulse control and who does not believe in a rescuing deity. If you are seriously tempted to have a drink and all those experienced people say you're powerless over alcohol, who are you to argue the point? "Down the hatch—cheers." Your decline is highly predictable.

Self-Sobriety

The chief problem with the idea of powerlessness, even greater than the negative psychological impact it has on certain addicts, is its utter falsity. There are simply too many examples of alcoholic persons, including this writer, who "wise up and sober up" when the consequences of chemical dependency become too costly, too risky, or too painful. Self-initiated sobriety is far more common than generally supposed, and I have encountered many such persons in both my personal and professional life. It is doubtful that any of us could have helped ourselves if we were really convinced of the truth of Step 1. Some people find within themselves the ability to stop drinking independently, while the large majority of us achieve our goal of sobriety and abstinence by getting professional help or attending AA. The charge that when an alcoholic seeks help for his problem he is admitting powerlessness is simply not true; reaching out for help is in itself a powerful act of self-determination.

Step 2: *"We came to believe that a Power greater than ourselves could restore us to sanity."*

"Step 1 actually teaches addicts that they are not responsible for what they put in their mouths."

"The Big Book" of Alcoholics Anonymous, about three inches thick, is the central document of the AA movement, and its influence on thinking about alcoholism is pervasive and profound. It was written by the founders of AA fifty years ago, two men who attained sobriety following the Christian plan of salvation. Several of their contemporaries, members of "the Oxford Group," attempted earlier to found a sect of recovering alcoholics based on a more orthodox interpretation of Christian theology. They failed, partly because of the explicit religious dogma they sought to incorporate, leaving the "Akron Group," with its ambiguous "Higher Power," to evolve into the dominant theistic organization it is today.

> *"The 12-step program is a* **direct attack** *on the nonreligious."*

It is important to address the aspersions of "The Big Book" upon atheists, agnostics—about whom an entire, derisive chapter is devoted— skeptics, "disbelievers," and those whose religious views do not include a rescuing deity. "AA bashing" (a euphemism for "blasphemy!") is not our purpose in challenging "The Big Book"; our concern is for the desperate persons who are harmed by its dogmatic stance. The 12-step program is a *direct attack* on the nonreligious groups listed above. With our constitutional guarantees, all's fair in the discourse between religionists and humanists, but little attention is paid to the intellectual violence done to troubled people who do not endorse God, Jesus, the Bible, Christianity, or religion in general. . . .

No Proof That God Exists

Major problems develop when a particular branch of medicine is given over to a treatment approach that includes divine intervention, or what is commonly called "faith healing." Simply put, there is not a shred of objective evidence for the existence of a sentient, supernatural being in the universe. If such evidence existed, there would be no need for religions to endlessly indoctrinate people into such an idea. People would have no trouble in comprehending the obvious, proven truth. Deities, gods, and the like are imaginary, and people must *make* themselves *believe* in them because there is no evidence that they exist. For many people, making believe this way comes easily, while others find it virtually impossible to believe in improbabilities such as supernatural beings. It is such a being, a benevolent, rescuing deity called "God," upon which AA rests.

"But," the AA elders insist, "there is room for all degrees of disbelief in AA. *Anything* can be your Higher Power! Your HP can be a wrench, a tree, music, the AA group, even Wisdom, but you absolutely *must* place your faith in something greater than, and outside of, yourself."

This tactic is, in a word, unethical. Very often, it is also harmful. It is practiced everywhere in the AA spiritual network, and obviously has the sanction of key AA leaders. This is a cult tactic that, in the view of many, detracts from the dignity and credibility of the 12-step program. It's a bait-and-switch head game in which the real intention is to convert a neophyte to hard-core belief in God Almighty. Suppose a doubting newcomer accepts a bedpan as his Higher Power on the advice of well-intended members. Granted, he may get through detox while meditating on the finer dimensions of the bedpan, but what about the next hurdle, Step 3?

Step 3: *"We made a decision to turn our will and our lives over to the care of God, as we understand Him."*

Ah, now—it isn't the bedpan, is it? Would you turn your will and your life over to a bedpan? Now our newcomer is faced with the task of reconciling his newfound sobriety with a new, poorly understood "God." Bye-bye, bedpan.

Deceptive Indoctrination

The Higher Power of AA is a flexible "training deity" devised to (1) help neophytes complete early detox and withdrawal, (2) avoid disclosing the inflexible theism behind AA, and (3) provide a progressive relaxation of critical judgment so that neophytes can be further indoctrinated in AA theology. Notice that there is still equivocation with ". . . as we understand Him." Even though "He" rates a capital letter, you are led to believe that you are still at liberty to make "Him" what you believe "Him" to be. Sure you are.

Robert Helmfelt, co-editor of *The Serenity Bible*, explains how the 12-step program works:

> We may start as agnostics. We may then come to view the group or the recovery process as our Higher Power, looking to other people for strength. Gradually, we accept a vague notion of God, which grows to a more specific monotheistic God. Eventually we come to know the one true God. Unless we are growing spiritually in recovery, we are going backwards.

In other words, AA presents God to sick people, using a bait-and-switch technique. That's all RRS is saying here.

Step 4: *"We made a searching and fearless moral inventory of ourselves."*

Here we find that recovering alcoholics are expected to become better people. Is adult life really a struggle to "be good"? Come on, now. If someone defines adult life that way, then that's fine for that person, but it would seem that there are far better reasons for seeking sobriety than to "be a good person." We find here also the pernicious idea that good people are less likely to suffer a relapse than less "moral" people. Why should an alcoholic be required to search introspectively for "moral defects" in himself? Is this really relevant to alcohol dependence? Do we want alcoholics to become "good people" or just sober people? Are alcoholics bad, in need of moral betterment? (Good people, of course, never get hooked on alcohol.) Are diabetics similarly obliged to make searching and fearless moral inventories? If not, why not? If an alcoholic stops drinking through a chemical dependency program but still robs banks, was the treatment successful? Of course it was!

> *"Little attention is paid to the intellectual violence done to troubled people who do not endorse God."*

The Christian roots of AA are most conspicuous here, where the neophyte is required to debase himself, to grasp downward at "humility" as an avenue to spiritual redemption through faith. "We are all sinners" supposedly gives way to moral ascendancy.

Step 4 presents difficulties for many disturbed persons whose defenses against self-condemnation are poor. There is speculation that persons are most prone to suicide or self-destructive relapses during this phase of AA indoctrination, when the inductee is flooded with conditioned guilt and remorse and is unable to stem the tide of his self-condemnation. Unfortunately, data regarding this problem are scarce. "The Big Book" does give a vivid example of an individual who did commit suicide while trying unsuccessfully to "get his Higher Power together," and the writer describes this incident almost cavalierly as *something to be expected when one fails the test of faith*. The wages of sin is death. This all gets very, very Christian, which is fine for Christians. But can we really expect most substance abusers to accept Christian theology? Wouldn't a fearless inventory of irrational ideas that perpetuate the intoxication cycle be more appropriate?

Step 5: *"We admitted to God, to ourselves, and to another human being the exact nature of our wrongs."*

The idea here is that by confessing our sins, the listener will forgive us in spite of our having committed the misdeed. Forgiving is the opposite of blaming someone for committing an antisocial or other unacceptable act. Forgiveness by God is a temporary antidote for guilt because its message

> *"AA presents God to sick people, using a bait-and-switch technique."*

is, "God says you are still a good person even though you acted badly, and who are you to question the opinion of God?"

Borrowing Egos

At this point we come to the AA sponsor system. Briefly, it is a "buddy system" of interpersonal dependency, where the neophyte "borrows the ego" of a program veteran, and attempts to identify with one who has "been through it." There are many inspiring stories about how a faltering neophyte called his sponsor in the wee hours and found strength and encouragement to resist the temptation to drink. I have also spoken with alcoholics who believe that their dependency on a sponsor was unwarranted considering that sponsors have no special training or skills, and alcoholics whose emotional entanglement with a sponsor led to serious problems. One case involved a member whose sponsor resumed drinking and died, leaving the member disillusioned and demoralized. Another account is of a sponsor who took on the role of spiritual therapist, financial adviser, and vocational counselor with a susceptible member. While there will probably be occasional abuses in any kind of human relationship, it is worth pointing out here that emotional dependency among normal adults is categorically self-defeating, even when one party is deemed the helper. The sponsor system seems to encourage the irrational idea that one needs someone other or greater than oneself upon whom to rely.

Sponsors hear confession from neophytes with the understanding that confession is intrinsically beneficial and healing. This assumption is contradicted by the fact that confession programs are interminable, open-ended affairs in which the confessor never attains liberation from guilt *or from the confession ritual.* In AA, God listens to and forgives confessions eternally.

Step 6: *"We were entirely ready to have God remove all these defects of character."*

It is probably difficult for religious persons to imagine why this idea is so offensive to some people who are not religious, but I will attempt to explain anyway. What is being asked for in Step 6 is a miracle. Members

> *"AA sobriety is a supernatural miracle, not really the product of our own self-determination."*

must believe that miracles are possible and theirs for the asking. Accepting the miracles of sobriety, survival, and serenity from a Higher Power while other group members fail to qualify for miracles is thought to be character-building. In Step 5, there is some connection between what the neophyte is being asked to do and a potential benefit. If you confess, you may be forgiven, and that may help somewhat. But now the neophyte is being asked to get ready for a miracle—entirely ready. Well, suppose he's only *partly* ready? Or *almost* ready? Would this rescuing deity hold out on a sincere person who is not *entirely* ready? Is "entirely" inserted to cover for when the rescuing deity, in His infinite wisdom, *doesn't* come through with the desired character repairs? Why did this rescuing deity endow us with "alcoholic" genes in the first place—just to stir up a little trouble? So He could show off later with character repairs? To test our mettle? To lead us to AA? As you can see, the situation becomes absurd.

Character Defects

The "wrongs," or mistakes, or misdeeds, that one confessed to in Step 5 (after the "fearless moral inventory" of Step 4) have now been converted to "defects of character," which are to be removed through divine intervention after some additional qualifying steps. The passive-dependent theme in this step is apparent.

Step 7: *"We humbly asked Him to remove these shortcomings."*

Any priest or minister will immediately recognize here the setting of "a proper worshipful attitude" that is a requisite for prayer and ritual. We do not firmly or politely request favors from the deity, nor do we expect a decent response to a request we think would be just and fair unless *we* humbly *submit ourselves to the Lord, unworthy as we are, in the hope our pleas for mercy will not be dismissed or ignored.* It is to escape precisely this kind of groveling and self-abasement that many people flee from churches. It is in this step that we learn that AA sobriety is a supernatural miracle, not really the product of our own self-determination. Is it really character-building to believe that our well-being is subject to the whims of a rescuing deity?

A curious thing about the 12 steps is that not even a single word is said about how a substance abuser might arrive at a decision to not drink or use drugs. The idea of personal choice is absent. The program simply assumes that by becoming morally good, people will stay sober. Conversely, alcoholism is viewed very clearly as a moral failure, as separation from God, as a spiritual deficit to be remedied by a religious conversion.

Step 8: *"We made a list of all the persons we had harmed, and became willing to make amends to them all."*

A list? Became willing? Something's brewing here.

Step 9: *"We made direct amends to such people wherever possible, except when to do so would injure them or others."*

Freud and others have written about the common defense mechanism "undoing," where guilt-flooded persons seek to compensate for earlier misdeeds by symbolically or actually acting out scenarios that absolve the offense. To the extent that Steps 8 and 9 are to absolve persistent guilt about past alcoholic "sins," wouldn't making amends to *oneself* be more appropriate than dwelling on past mistakes and possibly opening old wounds? Aren't most people happy just to be rid of those who were once obnoxious drunks? Is it really constructive to exhume the past in this way? Do recipients of amends often appreciate surprises like this? Isn't the greatest gift of a substance abuser to society the mere fact of his or her sobriety? Aren't Steps 8 and 9 melodramatic and cloying? Are they really relevant to recovery from chemical dependency? Are Steps 8 and 9 intended to help others or are they part of a ritual for conditional self-esteem?

> *"The program simply assumes that by becoming morally good, people will stay sober."*

Step 10: *"We continued to take personal inventory and when we were wrong promptly admitted it."*

Here we find out that AA is forever. The program is interminable; members continue—and continue and continue and continue year after year, decade after decade, to take searching and fearless moral inventory and promptly admit when they are wrong. The idea of leaving the fold, leaving Mother Group, is anathema to AA. Members dwell on stories of those who "tried it on their own" only to drink again, and then, if they were fortunate enough, by the grace of God, to survive their inevitable alcoholic downfall, came crawling back to old Mother Group. Occasionally mention is made of so-and-so, who left ten years ago, and who was sober until last heard from but "he's still a dry drunk; he *can't* really be happy, we *know* he's really miserable . . ." The message of personal powerlessness is so strong that it becomes a self-fulfilling prophecy. Those who quit AA are likely to remember the grim pronouncements that those who leave the group are surely doomed. Then, in a moment of indecision, they succumb to the "inevitable," and take a drink of alcohol.

Good and Evil

Doesn't almost everyone, except possibly some sociopathic or mentally ill persons, try to "be good"? Aren't people who try to recover from alcohol dependence *already* trying to "be good"? Are chemically dependent people so morally defective as to need constant indoctrination, constant and repeated FMI's (fearless moral inventories)? Does Step 10, with its insistence that life is a constant struggle to remain moral and sober, contribute to self-doubt rather than to a healthy sense of personal competence and "goodness"? Doesn't Step 10 really reflect the idea that life is only a stage for acting out the pervasive forces of good and evil?

Step 11: *"We sought through prayer and meditation to improve our conscious contact with God as we understand Him, praying only for knowledge of His will and the power to carry that out."*

When AA finally loses its secular identity in court, as it seems likely to in time, this is the step that will probably be Exhibit A. As it stands, each member is expected to become an agent of God, praying for instructions from on high, and for the strength to carry out those instructions. AA adherents achieve a state of bliss, or inner peace, through meditation and prayer, a state they call "serenity," which is actually salvation through faith; this serenity is a major goal in the earthly lives of recovering substance abusers. Serenity, the peace which passeth all understanding, is regarded as a powerful hedge against alcoholic relapse. The phrase "as we understand Him" is repeated, but by now it is clear that the deity in question is highly *specific:* One Who is interested in substance abusers and listens to them, One Who sends messages and advice to the faithful, and One Who expects worship, prayer, meditation, obedience, and frequent meeting attendance as conditions to be met before special favors are granted and before character repairs are made. Wouldn't "as AA understands Him" be more accurate? Isn't this intensely religious? Could any program short of a monastery be *more* religious than this?

Step 12: *"Having had a spiritual awakening as a result of these Steps, we tried to carry this message to others, and to practice these principles in all our affairs."*

> *"Those who attend 'We Agnostics' groups are, in effect, 'riding in the back of the bus.'"*

Is a "spiritual awakening' different from religious conversion? If so, in what ways? If not, and the awakening occurred "as a result of these Steps," is not the 12-step program a religious doctrine of redemption and salvation? If 12-steppers try to "practice these principles in all our affairs," are they not practicing the religious life? Are many substance abusers really good candidates for this? If 12-steppers try to "carry this message

91

to other alcoholics," aren't they proselytizing, or witnessing, for an evangelical faith? There is no mention here of trying to dissuade other alcoholic people from drinking alcohol, or to help alcoholics get whatever help they might choose, but only to "carry *this* message" (the profoundly religious 12-step program of Alcoholics Anonymous) to others so that they might increase their faith in a Higher Power outside of themselves. After that, as part of their orientation, they are beseeched to refrain from alcohol.

If one completes the first eleven steps and then balks at this one, will he or she risk relapse? How does this step fit in with state-certified substance abuse counseling programs? Are states now participating in this step? Does this step ever create professional conflict of interest?

No Attempt to Help Agnostics

The above discussion of the AA spiritual healing program should identify some of the issues that affect each American who seeks help with an addictive disorder. None of the above is really new. These questions have been asked for years, ever since success spoiled a good thing, ever since the helping professions gradually sold out to AA.

A recurring question is, "Wouldn't it be good if AA were to change, to 'lighten up on the God part,' to make concessions to the 'agnostics,' to recognize that everyone, regardless of religious faith or the lack thereof, deserves a chance to get better?"

There have been some attempts to accommodate agnostics by segregating them into informal groups that meet independently, but no program designed for them is provided by AA national offices. There is no alternative literature and no plan for recovery except what interested persons might try to derive from the 12 steps. Some white out "God" and inject other abstracts, like "self" or "wisdom," but the result is always incoherent. Those who attend "We Agnostics" groups are, in effect, "riding in the back of the bus," and one will likely feel "marginal" as an agnostic in AA after reading Chapter 4, "We Agnostics," of "The Big Book."

Robert M., a recovered alcoholic from California, had attended AA for many years, but being a devout atheist, never came to believe in a rescuing deity. He achieved a durable sobriety his own way, using the AA group as a support and social outlet. He finally wrote *The Grapevine*, the internal newsletter of AA, stating that he believed that all the praying and religion during meetings were discouraging newcomers. He asked that his letter be published in the opinions column. Over the next three years, an escalating series of thirteen letters between Robert and various levels of the AA hierarchy were exchanged, hotly contesting whether or not the controversial 200-word letter should be published. It finally was, in an edited form. Robert was told that any change regarding the use of the Lord's Prayer in AA meetings would have to be voted on *by the entire membership*. So much for AA's capacity to change with regard to its theology.

AA's Coercive Tactics Are Harmful

by Archie Brodsky and Stanton Peele

About the authors: *Archie Brodsky is a senior research associate at the Harvard Medical School's Program in Psychiatry and the Law in Cambridge, Massachusetts. Stanton Peele, a psychologist and health care researcher, is the author of several well-known books on addiction. Brodsky and Peele are the authors, with Mary Arnold, of* The Truth About Addiction and Recovery: The Life Process Program for Outgrowing Destructive Habits.

A high-level delegation from the Soviet Union visited Quincy, Massachusetts, to learn how District Court Judge Albert L. Kramer handles drunk drivers. Kramer routinely sentences first-time driving-while-intoxicated (DWI) offenders to Right Turn, a private treatment program for alcoholism that requires participants to attend Alcoholics Anonymous meetings. The Soviet visitors enthusiastically embraced Kramer's program, which is also a favorite of the American media.

One would think that the Soviets were ahead of us in therapeutic coercion, given their history of incarcerating political dissenters under bogus psychiatric labels. But from their perspective Kramer's approach is innovative: A.A. treatment is a process of spiritual conversion that requires submission to a "higher power" (a.k.a. God). By adopting compulsory A.A. treatment, the Soviets would be shifting from a policy of enforced atheism to one of enforced religion.

Alcoholism treatment is today the standard sanction for DWI offenses in the United States, according to Constance Weisner of the Alcohol Research Group in Berkeley. "In fact, many states have transferred much of the handling of DWI offenses to alcohol treatment programs," she writes. In 1984, 2,551 public and private treatment programs in the United States reported providing DWI services for 864,000 individuals. In 1987, the 50 states devoted an average of 39 percent of their treatment units to DWI services. Some states continue to accelerate such treatment: From 1986 to 1988, Connecticut reported a 400-percent increase in the number of DWIs referred to treatment programs.

The response to drunk driving is part of the widespread American practice of forcing or pressuring people into A.A.-style treatment. The courts (through sentencing, probation, and parole), government licensing and social-service agencies, and mainstream institutions such as schools and employers are pushing more than a million people into treatment each year. The use of coercion and pressure to fill the rolls of treatment programs has distorted the U.S. approach to substance abuse: The A.A. model, which uses a spiritual approach to treat the "disease" of alcoholism, would not have as pervasive an influence under conditions of free choice.

> *"Alcoholics Anonymous was not always tied to coercion."*

Treatment or Sanctions?

Furthermore, prescribing treatment as a substitute for normal criminal, social, or workplace sanctions represents a national revision of traditional notions of individual responsibility. When called to account for misbehavior, the criminal, the delinquent teenager, the malingering employee, or the abusive supervisor has an out: Alcohol (or drugs) made me do it. But in exchange for the seductive explanation that substance abuse causes antisocial behavior, we allow state intrusion in people's private lives. When we surrender responsibility, we lose our freedom as well.

Consider some of the ways in which people end up in treatment:

• A major airline ordered a pilot into treatment after a fellow employee reported that he had twice been arrested for drunk driving a decade earlier. To keep his job and his FAA license, the pilot has to continue treatment indefinitely, despite an impeccable work record, no work-related drinking incidents, no drinking problems or DWI arrests for years, and a clean diagnosis by an independent clinician.

• Helen Terry, a city employee in Vancouver, Washington, was ostracized on the job after she testified in support of a colleague's sexual-harassment suit. Terry never drank more than a glass of wine in the evening. Nonetheless, based on an unconfirmed report that she had drunk too much at a social event, her superiors ordered her to admit she was an alcoholic and enter a treatment center, under threat of dismissal. A court awarded her more than $200,000 in damages after she sued the city for wrongful discharge and denial of due process.

• A man seeking to adopt a child admitted he had used drugs heavily almost a decade earlier. Required to submit to diagnosis, he was labeled "chemically dependent" even though he had not used drugs for years. He now worries that he will be followed for the rest of his life by the stigma of "chemical dependence."

• States routinely require "impaired" physicians and attorneys to enter treatment to avoid having their licenses revoked. A certified addiction counselor for the American Bar Association's Commission on Impaired Attorneys reports: "I do an assessment and tell that person what they have to do to get well. Part of that component is A.A. They must attend A.A."

The Roots of AA

Alcoholics Anonymous was not always tied to coercion. It began in 1935 as a voluntary association among a handful of chronic alcoholics. Its roots were in the 19th-century temperance movement, as reflected in its confessional style and sin-and-salvation spirit. A.A., and the alcoholism-as-disease movement it inspired, translated American evangelism into a medical world view.

Originally antimedical, A.A. members often emphasized the failure of physicians to recognize alcoholism. Marty Mann, a publicist and early A.A. member, correctly saw this as a self-limiting strategy. In 1944, she organized the National Committee for Education on Alcoholism (now the National Council on Alcoholism and Drug Dependence) as the public-relations arm of the movement, enlisting well-placed scientists and physicians to promote the disease model of alcoholism. Without this medical collaboration, A.A. could not have enjoyed the enduring success that distinguishes it from earlier temperance groups.

A.A. has now been incorporated into the cultural and economic mainstream. Indeed, many view A.A.'s 12-step philosophy as a cure not only for alcoholism but for a host of other problems. Twelve-step programs have been developed for drug addicts (Narcotics Anonymous), spouses of alcoholics (Al-Anon), children of alcoholics (Alateen), and people with literally hundreds of other problems (Gamblers Anonymous, Sexaholics Anonymous, Shopaholics Anonymous). Many of these groups and "diseases," in turn, are linked to counseling programs, some conducted in hospitals.

The medical establishment has come to recognize the financial and other advantages of piggybacking on the A.A. folk movement, as have many recovering alcoholics. A.A. members frequently make counseling careers out of their recoveries. They and the treatment centers they staff can then benefit from third-party reimbursement. In a recent survey of 15 treatment centers across the country, researcher Marie Bourbine-Twohig found that all of the centers (90 percent of which were residential) practiced the 12-step philosophy, and two-thirds of all counselors in the facilities were recovering alcoholics and addicts.

> *"Many people identified as alcoholics don't see themselves as sick and don't want to be treated."*

Early A.A. literature emphasized that members could succeed only if "motivated by a sincere desire." As their institutional base widened, A.A. and the disease approach became increasingly aggressive. This proselytizing tendency, originating in the religious roots of the movement, was legitimized by the association with medicine. If alcoholism is a disease, then it must be treated—like pneumonia. Unlike people with pneumonia, however, many peo-ple identified as alcoholics don't see themselves as sick and don't want to be treated. According to the treatment industry, a person with a drinking or drug problem who does not recognize its nature as a disease is practicing "denial."

In fact, denial of a drinking problem—or other disease diagnosis and A.A. rem-edy—has come to be a defining characteristic of the disease. But indiscriminate use of the denial label obscures important distinctions among drinkers. While people sometimes do fail to recognize and acknowledge the severity of their problems, a drinking problem does not automatically prove a person is a lifelong alcoholic. Indeed, most people "mature out" of excessive, irresponsible drinking.

The disease approach uses the concept of denial not only to force people into treatment, but to justify emotional abuse within treatment. Drug and alcohol programs typically rely on confrontational therapy in which counselors and groups deride the inmates for their failings and their reluctance to accept the program's prescriptions. Most of the celebrities who graduate from such pro-grams, out of either genuine belief or judicious discretion, report tough but pos-itive experiences.

But the remarks of a critical minor-ity are revealing. Actor Chevy Chase, for example, criticized the Betty Ford Center in *Playboy* and on TV talk shows after his 1986 stay there. "We called the therapy 'God squadding,'"

> *"The disease approach uses the concept of denial . . . to justify emotional abuse within treatment."*

he said. "They get you to believe that you're at death's door . . . that you've ru-ined it for everybody, that you're nothing and that you've got to start building yourself back up through your trust in the Lord. . . . I didn't care for the scare tactics being used there. I didn't think they were right."

In a 1987 *New York Times* article, New York Mets pitcher Dwight Gooden de-scribed the group indoctrination at the Smithers Center in New York, where he was sent for cocaine abuse. Gooden, who had used cocaine at off-season par-ties, was browbeaten by fellow residents: "My stories weren't as good [as theirs]. . . . They said, 'C'mon, man, you're lying.' They didn't believe me. . . . I cried a lot before I went to bed at night."

A Draining Ordeal

For every Dwight Gooden or Chevy Chase, there are thousands of less-famous people who have bitter experiences after being roped into treatment. Marie R., for example, is a stable, married woman in her 50s. One evening she drove after drinking beyond the legal limit and was apprehended in a police spot check. Like most drunk drivers, Marie did not meet the criteria for alco-holism, which include routine loss of control. (Research by Kaye Fillmore and Dennis Kelso of the University of California has found that most people ar-rested for drunk driving are able to moderate their drinking.)

Marie admitted that she deserved to be penalized. Nonetheless, she was shocked when she learned that she faced a one-year license suspension. Although irresponsible, her carelessness was not as serious as the recklessness of a DWI whose driving clearly endangers others. Such disproportionate sentences push all but the most stubborn DWIs to accept "treatment" instead; indeed, this may be their purpose. Like most offenders, Marie thought treatment was preferable, even though she had to pay $500 for it.

> *"Not every employee who screws up at work is screwing up because of drugs or alcohol."*

Marie's treatment consisted of weekly counseling sessions, plus weekly A.A. meetings, for more than four months. Contrary to her initial expectations, she found the experience "the most physically and emotionally draining ordeal of my life." At A.A. meetings, Marie listened to ceaseless stories of suffering and degradation, stories replete with phrases like "descent into hell" and "I got down on my knees and prayed to a higher power." For Marie, A.A. was akin to a fundamentalist revival meeting.

In the counseling program provided by a private licensee to the state, Marie received the same A.A. indoctrination and met with counselors whose only qualification was membership in A.A. These true believers told all the DWIs that they had the permanent "disease" of alcoholism, the only cure for which was lifetime abstinence and A.A. membership—all this based on one drunk-driving arrest!

In keeping with the self-righteous, evangelistic spirit of the program, any objection to its requirements was treated as "denial." The program's dictates extended into Marie's private life: She was told to abstain from all alcohol during "treatment," a proscription enforced by the threat of urinalysis. As Marie found her entire life controlled by the program, she concluded that "the power these people attempt to wield is to compensate for the lack of power within themselves."

No Help for Emotional Problems

Money was a regular topic at the sessions, and counselors constantly reminded group members to keep up their payments. But the state picked up the tab for those who claimed they could not afford the $500 fee. Meanwhile, members of the group who had serious emotional problems searched vainly for competent professional counseling. One night, a woman said she felt suicidal. The group counselor instructed her, "Pray to a higher power." The woman dragged on through the meetings with no apparent improvement.

In lieu of real counseling, Marie and the others were forced to participate in a religious ritual. Marie became preoccupied by "the moral, ethical, and legal issue of coercing citizens into accepting dogma which they find offensive." Having had only a vague idea of the A.A. program, she was astounded to discover that "God" and a "higher power" are mentioned in half of A.A.'s 12 steps. For Marie, the third step said it all: "Made a decision to turn our will and our lives over to the care of God." Like many, Marie was not consoled that it was God "as we understood him."

She wrote in her diary: "I keep reminding myself that this is America. I find it unconscionable that the criminal justice system has the power to coerce American citizens to accept ideas that are anathema to them. It is as if I were a citizen of a totalitarian regime being punished for political dissent."

Client Pools for AA

As Marie's story shows, court-mandated DWI referrals generate income for treatment entrepreneurs from insurance companies and state treasuries. The director of one treatment center says: "Approximately 80 percent of my clients come via the courts and deferred prosecution agreements. Many are simply taking advantage of the opportunity to avoid jail, increased insurance premiums, blemished driving record, etc., and have no intention of changing their behavior."

Although DWIs constitute the largest number of referrals from the criminal-justice system, defendants are required to enter substance-abuse treatment for other crimes as well. In 1988, a quarter of Connecticut's probationers were under court order to enter alcohol or drug treatment. Penal systems are opting to treat the large number of drug offenders they face, both as an alternative to sentencing and as a condition of parole. The potential flow of treatment clients is huge: New York prison authorities estimate that three-quarters of all inmates in the state have abused drugs.

Adolescents are another rich source of treatment clients. High schools and universities regularly direct students into A.A., sometimes based on isolated incidents of drunkenness. In fact, people in their teens and 20s represent the fastest-growing segment of the A.A. membership. The incarceration of adolescents in private mental institutions—primarily for substance abuse—grew by 450 percent during the 1980s. Teenagers almost always enter treatment involuntarily, whether under court order or under pressure (on them or their parents) from schools and other public agencies. In treatment, they undergo "tough love" programs, which strip children of their pretreatment identities through techniques that often border on physical abuse.

"Teaching life-management skills, rather than lecturing about the disease of addiction, is the most productive form of treatment."

In *The Great Drug War*, Arnold Trebach documents the shocking case of 19-year-old Fred Collins, who was pressured into residential treatment in 1982 at Straight Inc. near St. Petersburg, Florida, by his parents and the organization's staff. Collins's and other inmates' parents collaborated with Straight in forcibly confining him for 135 days. Isolated from the outside world, he was subjected to 24-hour surveillance, sleep and food deprivation (he lost 25 pounds), and constant intimidation and harassment.

Collins eventually escaped through a window and, after months of hiding from his own parents, sought legal redress. In court, Straight did not contest Collins's account but instead claimed the treatment was justified because he was chemically dependent. Collins, an above-average student, presented psychiatric testimony that he had merely smoked marijuana and drunk beer occasionally. A jury found for Collins and awarded him $220,000, mostly in punitive damages. Nonetheless, Straight has never admitted its treatment program was flawed, and Nancy Reagan has continued to be a staunch advocate for the organization. Meanwhile, ABC's "Primetime Live" and "20/20" have documented similar abuses in other private treatment programs.

Employee Interventions

Another major group of treatment clients are those referred by employee-assistance programs (EAPs). While some employees seek counseling for a variety of problems, the main focus of EAPs has been substance abuse. Typically the initiative for treatment comes from the EAP rather than the employee, who must undergo treatment to keep his or her job. There are now more than 10,000 EAPs in the United States, and the number continues to grow. The majority of companies with at least 750 employees had EAPs by the mid-1980s.

> *"We have undermined the right of people to change their behavior on their own."*

EAPs often use "interventions," a technique that is popular throughout the treatment industry. An intervention involves surprising the targeted individual with a phalanx of family members, friends, and co-workers who, under the supervision of treatment personnel, browbeat the person into accepting that he or she is chemically dependent and requires treatment. Interventions are often spearheaded by counselors who are themselves recovering alcoholics. And usually the agency that assists with the intervention ends up treating the accused substance abuser.

"Interventions are the greatest advance in alcoholism treatment since Alcoholics Anonymous was founded," says the director of a California treatment center that depends on such clients. In a 1990 article in *Special Report on Health* entitled "Drunk Until Proven Sober," journalist John Davidson offered a different assessment: "The philosophical premise behind the technique appears to be that anyone—especially a recovering alcoholic—has the right to invade another's privacy, as long as he's trying to help."

Although employees who are subjected to such interventions are not coerced, they are usually threatened with dismissal, and their experiences often parallel those of criminal defendants who are forced to undergo treatment. Companies confronting employees suspected of drug or alcohol abuse make the same mistakes as courts do in handling drunk drivers. Most important, they fail to distinguish among different groups of employees suspected of substance abuse.

As the stories of Dwight Gooden and Helen Terry indicate, employees may be identified by an EAP even though their job performance is satisfactory. Random urinalysis may find drug traces, a record search may turn up an old drunk-driving arrest, or an enemy may submit a false report. Furthermore, not every employee who screws up at work is screwing up because of drugs or alcohol. Even when an employee's performance is suffering because of drug or alcohol use, this does not mean he or she is an addict or alcoholic. Finally, those employees who do have serious substance-abuse problems may not benefit from the 12-step approach.

> *"The courts have ruled that A.A. is equivalent to a religion."*

An Ineffective Treatment

For all its strong-arm tactics, mainstream drug and alcohol treatment does not seem to work very well. The few studies that have used random assignment and appropriate control groups suggest that A.A. works no better, and perhaps worse, than no treatment at all. The value of A.A., like that of any spiritual fellowship, is in the perceptions of those who choose to participate in it.

A study in *The New England Journal of Medicine* reported, for the first time, that employee substance abusers sent to private hospital programs had fewer subsequent drinking problems than employees who selected their own treatment (which generally meant either a hospital or A.A.). A third group sent to A.A. fared the worst of all.

Even in the hospital group, only 36 percent abstained throughout the two years following treatment (the figure was 16 percent for the A.A. group). Finally, although hospital treatment produced more abstinence, no differences in productivity, absenteeism, and other work-related measures were found among the groups. In other words, the employer who was footing the bill for treatment realized no greater benefit from the more expensive option.

Moreover, this study looked at private treatment centers, which cater to the sort of clients—well-to-do, educated, employed, with intact families—who most often straighten out on their own. The results for public treatment facilities are even less encouraging. A national study of public treatment facilities by the Research Triangle Institute in North Carolina found evidence of improvement for methadone maintenance and therapeutic communities for drug addicts, but no positive changes for people entering treatment for marijuana abuse or for alcoholism. A 1985 study published in *The New England Journal of Medicine* reported that just 7 percent of a group of patients treated in an inner-city alcoholism ward had survived and were in remission when followed up several years later.

All of these studies suffer from the flaw of not including a nontreatment comparison group. Such comparisons have most often been carried out with DWI populations. A series of such studies has shown that treatment of drunk drivers is less effective than judicial sanctions. For example, a major study in California compared four counties where drunk drivers were referred to alcohol-rehabilitation programs with four similar counties where drivers' licenses were suspended or revoked. After four years, DWIs in the counties imposing traditional legal sanctions had better driving records than those in the counties relying on treatment programs.

Lessons on Life

For nonalcoholic DWIs, programs teaching drivers the skills with which to manage or avoid risky situations have proven superior to conventional A.A. education programs. Indeed, research has shown that, even for highly alcoholic drinkers, teaching life-management skills, rather than lecturing about the disease of addiction, is the most productive form of treatment. The training covers communication (particularly with family members), job skills, and the ability to "cool out" under stressful conditions that often lead to excessive drinking.

Such training is the standard for treatment in most of the world. Given the spotty record of disease-model treatment, one would think that U.S. programs would be interested in exploring alternative therapies. Instead, these remain anathema to treatment

"Treatment should reflect individual needs and values."

facilities, which see no possibilities beyond the disease model. In 1990, the Institute of Medicine of the prestigious National Academy of Sciences issued a report calling for a much wider range of treatments to respond to the variety of individual preferences and drinking problems.

By accepting the notion that people who having drinking or drug problems (or are merely identified by others as having such problems) suffer from a disease that forever negates their personal judgment, we have undermined the right of people to change their behavior on their own, to reject labels they find inaccurate and demeaning, and to choose a form of treatment they can be comfortable with and believe will work for them. At the same time, we have given government support to group indoctrination, coerced confessions, and massive invasions of privacy.

Fortunately, the courts have supported those seeking protection from coercive treatment. In every court challenge to mandated A.A. attendance to date—in Wisconsin, Colorado, Alaska, and Maryland—the courts have ruled that A.A. is equivalent to a religion for First Amendment purposes. The state's power is limited to regulating people's behavior, not controlling their thoughts.

In the words of Ellen Luff, the ACLU [American Civil Liberties Union] attorney who successfully argued the Maryland case before a state appeals court, the state may not "intrude further into the probationer's mind by forcing sustained attendance in programs designed to alter . . . their belief in God or their self identity." Whether or not any established religion is involved, she concludes, "if the state becomes a party to attempt-ing to precipitate a conversion experi-ence, the First Amendment has been violated."

> *"Coercive treatment on a religious model is notably ineffective."*

Decisions like the one in Maryland, issued in 1989, have not deterred the director of the court-sanctioned Right Turn program in Massachusetts, who de-clares: "The basic principle about entering A.A. voluntarily is debatable, be-cause most non-Right Turn members of A.A. were forced into the program by other pressures; for instance, a spouse or an employer delivered a last ultima-tum." Leaving aside the assumption that the typical drunk driver resembles the alcoholic who voluntarily goes to A.A., the equation of judicial coercion with social or economic pressure would leave us with no Bill of Rights.

Punishment for Alcohol Abusers

In place of today's confused, corrupt tangle of treatment, law enforcement and personnel management, we propose the following guidelines:

Punish misbehavior straightforwardly. Society should hold people account-able for their conduct and penalize irresponsible, destructive behavior appropri-ately. For example, drunk drivers should be sentenced, irrespective of any pre-sumed "disease state," in a manner commensurate with the frequency and severity of their reckless driving. At the lower end of DWI offenses (borderline intoxication), the penalties are probably too severe; at the upper end (repeat of-fenders, reckless drunk driving that endangers others, vehicular homicide), they are too lenient. Penalties should be uniform and realistic—for example, a one-month license suspension for a first-time drunk driver who did not otherwise drive recklessly—since they will actually be carried out.

Similarly, employers should insist that workers do their jobs properly. When performance is not satisfactory, for whatever reason, it may make sense to warn, suspend, demote, or fire the employee, depending upon how far short of accepted standards he or she falls. Treatment is a separate issue; in many cases—for example, when the only indication of substance abuse is a Monday-morning hangover—it's inappropriate.

Offer treatment to those who seek help, but not as an alternative to account-ability. Coercive treatment has such poor results in part because offenders typi-cally accept treatment as a way to avoid punishment. Courts and employers should provide treatment referrals for those who want help in extricating them-selves from destructive habits, but not as a way of avoiding penalties.

Offer a range of therapeutic alternatives. Treatment should reflect individual needs and values. For treatment to have its greatest impact, people must believe in it and take responsibility for its success because they have chosen it. Americans should have access to the range of treatments used in other countries and proven effective in clinical research.

Emphasize specific behaviors, not global identities. "Denial" is often a response to the mindless insistence that people admit they are addicts or alcoholics. This resistance can be circumvented by focusing on the specific behavior that the state has a legitimate interest in modifying—for instance, driving while intoxicated. A practical, goal-oriented approach, implemented through situational and skills training, has the best chance of changing behavior.

There is no better motivation for change than the experience of real-world punishments for misbehavior. By comparison, coercive treatment on a religious model is notably ineffective. And it is one of the most blatant and pervasive violations of constitutional rights in the United States today. After all, even murderers on death row are not forced to pray.

Forcing Alcoholic Prisoners to Join AA Is Ineffective

by Corey Weinstein

About the author: *Corey Weinstein is a physician and medical consultant to the Prisoners Rights Union, a civil rights group for prisoners. He also chairs the Jail and Prison Health Committee of the American Public Health Association.*

Alcoholics Anonymous has dominated the addiction recovery field for many years. AA and its offshoots for narcotics (NA), cocaine (CA), and [adult] children of alcoholics (ACA) are available in most communities. While these programs have helped many drug addicts, their effectiveness within the California prison system has been curbed by CDC's [California Department of Corrections] over-reliance on AA and NA as the principal means to recovery.

The courts, parole boards and Board of Prison Terms (BPT) frequently require AA and NA for prisoners being considered for release from custody or parole. Thus, AA and NA mandated by judges, in effect become part of a prisoner's or parolee's sentence and thus achieve the force of law in our courts and prisons.

The law is used to make people participate despite the fact that 50% of AA's new members in the community quit within three months and 75% quit by one year. Prisoners are forced to attend regular AA/NA meetings that are known to be generally unsuccessful.

No Belief in God

While there are many reasons why these programs fail, one important cause of failure is that many addicts do not believe in God or a higher power. Such a belief in God is a central idea in the AA Twelve Step recovery program.

AA members must admit that they are powerless over their drug use and accept that only by turning their lives over to the care of God can they overcome their addiction. Staying sober becomes a test of a person's faith and ability to

Corey Weinstein, "Is Alcoholics Anonymous Illegal?" *The California Prisoner*, Spring 1992. Reprinted with permission of the author and the Prisoners' Rights Union, Sacramento, California.

submit to a supreme being. Drug use is seen as a moral failure which needs to be confessed to God and other people.

For those addicts with Christian beliefs and training, these ideas and techniques can be very useful. There are many addicts, however, who do not find such Christian spiritualism or any religion important. Still others have religious views that are not based in guilt and confession.

There are two problems with court- and BPT-ordered participation in AA. First, the value of any drug program is in the voluntary participation of the attenders. The choice to seek help is the first step in breaking the cycle of drug abuse.

Legally mandated participation removes choice and undermines the drug program by forcing addicts to attend who do not want to be there. The sincerity and honesty that is necessary for growth and change is not important to those coerced by law into attendance. These reluctant chair warmers are there only for show, making it more difficult for those genuinely seeking self-improvement. Thus, it is likely that NA and AA programs involving coerced members in prison are even less successful than their community counterparts.

The second problem is the fact that forced participation in AA and NA violates a prisoner's right to freedom of choice of religion. The Twelve Step program demands a belief in God, not just any god, but a God who is interested in a prisoner's submission and who will care for the supplicant. For buddhists, atheists and agnostics, such a God is not necessarily a part of their belief system.

> *"AA programs involving coerced members in prison are even less successful than their community counterparts."*

Thus, not only are AA and NA irrelevant to people who do not share the proper belief system, it is likely illegal to force a nonbeliever to attend such religious indoctrination. North American Indians in Canada have demanded and received more culturally relevant addiction services on these grounds alone.

Many Programs Are Needed

A variety of addiction services that draw prisoners based on sincere interest are needed in prisons today. AA will only help some.

Therapeutic communities, which provide a positive social environment, are proven to be the most effective and meaningful path to recovery. Such a community has been developed in the Washington, D.C., prison system where a whole wing has been turned into a community for drug recovery.

Acupuncture has been used with excellent results in Minnesota prisons following pioneering work in acupuncture, detox and drug rehabilitation at the Lincoln Hospital drug clinic in New York City.

A new program developed by Jack Trimpey entitled Rational Recovery is based on non-religious, humanist ideas that could be of great use in prison as part of a variety of addiction services.

Rational Recovery is a program for recovery from addiction that teaches the addict to develop and use the mental tools necessary to stop abusing drugs. RR views drug overuse and dependence as a behavior disorder, not a spiritual failure.

The approach of RR is that you need to change the way you think in order to stop using drugs. Support groups, individual study books and professional counselors are available for assistance through the RR program.

> *"A variety of addiction services that draw prisoners based on sincere interest are needed in prisons today. AA will only help some."*

I have long observed the fact that addicts are very determined people. A drug is used daily and in excess despite the warnings of the body: the cough and shortness of breath of the smoker, the hangover of the drinker, or the infections (including HIV) and debility of the IV drug user.

Rather than being powerless, the addict rigidly chooses drugs against many health, social and legal warnings. Every addict knows that the pain, ill-health, confusion and risk of serious disease would disappear once sobriety is achieved, yet he overrides all of these concerns and picks up the bottle or syringe.

A common belief among addicts is that in order to feel like a worthwhile person, one must stop using. RR points out that it is more accurate to say it is because a person is worthwhile that he will stop using drugs and build a more decent life. A part of this sense of being a worthwhile person is the understanding that some discomfort is an inevitable and common part of life and of being drug free.

RR teaches a way of coping with troublesome feelings called the ABCs. Using this method, the addict is first encouraged to accept responsibility for his feelings and not persist in the idea that feelings are forced on us by outside people and events.

The Activating events might be conflicts with another, disappointments, or just inner feelings. Certain Beliefs follow these events and feelings which bring about the Consequence of troublesome emotions that call to mind the "solution" of drug use. RR teaches to Dispute in the mind the Beliefs that follow the Activating stimulus. Such inner arguments will begin to create a different Effect and lead to solutions to inner sufferings that do not include drugs.

By using Rational Recovery's ABCs, the addict develops useful control over feelings and inner distress.

A Need for Acceptance

A central issue of Rational Recovery is the idea of our need for love and approval. Humans have a deep need for acceptance from others. We are a very social species. Yet is it not true that if we love ourselves first, we then will be more able to find support and approval from others? The adage to "love your neighbor as yourself" supports how important self-love is. In loving ourselves, we recognize that we all have flaws and weaknesses.

We should seek not to harshly blame ourselves for our failures, but to take responsibility for our actions with appropriate regret for our errors. RR teaches ways to think about our troubles and problems that produce effective action. This includes the development of emotional coping skills.

RR recognizes that complete abstinence is a goal for those who habitually overuse drugs. A single drink during recovery, however, is not considered a downfall and, in fact, is quite common. Again, the tools of rational thought are used to cope with relapse.

Chapter 3

Do Alcohol Advertisements Encourage Alcohol Abuse?

Chapter Preface

Most attempts to reduce alcoholism focus on getting addicts to stop consuming alcohol. Today, however, some critics are directing their focus not on the consumer—the alcoholic—but on the producer—brewers, distillers, and others who manufacture alcoholic beverages.

These critics' main target is alcohol advertisements. Such ads may show young people drinking beer at a party or after playing sports. They may portray a romantic scene in which a couple shares a bottle of wine. Or they may show a successful executive enjoying a drink at the end of a long day. The ads suggest that alcohol can be entertaining and relaxing.

On the surface, these ads may seem benign. Critics, however, contend that such ads imply that alcohol helps you have a good time, and perhaps even that alcohol is a *necessity* for a good time. "These ads deny the consequences of alcohol use," states Patricia Taylor, co-chair of the Center for Science in the Public Interest. Much of the nation's alcoholism, alcohol abuse, drunken driving, and accidents related to alcohol use are tied to alcohol ads, Taylor maintains.

She and others believe alcohol producers have a social responsibility to understand how their products and ads affect Americans. "Corporations have a moral and ethical responsibility to lower pain and misery—not increase it. It is individually our responsibility to use our collective power to minimize the impact alcohol has on our families and communities," contends Jesse W. Brown Jr., co-chair of the Philadelphia-based National Association of African-Americans for Positive Imagery.

Brown and other minority leaders are especially concerned about ads that target specific minority groups, such as blacks or Hispanics. Studies have shown that 60 to 70 percent of the billboards in black neighborhoods advertise alcohol or tobacco. Because alcohol is often a factor in a high rate of accidents, murders, and crimes among blacks, Brown believes these billboards and other alcohol ads must be regulated. "Because African-Americans share a disproportionate burden of the pain and suffering associated with alcohol, elimination of the advertising and promotion of alcoholic products in the African-American community has become a moral and ethical quest," Brown concludes. "We can no longer sit idly by and allow the alcohol industry to disrespect African-Americans and abuse the privilege of marketing to African-American communities with such a lethal and misery-inducing product."

But the alcohol industry and even some black leaders argue that such attitudes are patronizing. Benjamin Hooks, former executive director of the NAACP (National Association for the Advancement of Colored People), believes that behind the movement to regulate ads targeted at blacks "is the rationale that blacks are not capable of making their own free choices and need some guardian angels to protect their best interests." Joseph P. Castellano, vice president of consumer awareness and education at the Anheuser-Busch brewery, echoes Hooks, stating that those who oppose alcohol ads directed at specific minorities are actually saying "that members of certain groups should not be entrusted to make their own decisions, including which ads they should see and what they should buy."

Finally, the alcohol industry maintains that no proof exists that connects alcohol ads with alcohol abuse. Consequently, there is no rationale for regulating such ads. "The U.S. is not awash in alcohol," asserts Janet Flynn of the Distilled Spirits Council. "According to the United States' own statistics, underage drinking is at its lowest level since 1974, fatal accidents involving teen-age drunk drivers are down 39 percent since 1982." Flynn and others also believe that even if such a connection existed, advertisements are protected by the First Amendment right to freedom of speech, and therefore cannot be regulated. "We're a legitimate industry and a legal product and have every right to First Amendment rights," she concludes.

Because the debate concerning alcohol advertisements involves such disparate and sensitive issues as freedom of speech, corporate responsibility, and the needs and rights of minorities, it is not an easy debate to resolve. The authors in the following chapter present their arguments concerning the effect of alcohol advertisements on Americans and whether regulating such ads is justified.

Alcohol Advertisements Encourage Alcohol Abuse

by Patricia Taylor

About the author: *Patricia Taylor is the director of the Alcohol Policies Project of the Center for Science in the Public Interest, a nonprofit organization dedicated to promoting public health.*

Together, [tobacco and alcohol] are responsible for far more harm, both in loss of life and societal cost, than all other drugs combined. And when alcohol and tobacco are used together, their impact can be even more devastating. There are, however, some important differences between these two products.

Advertising and Addiction

One is the rate at which individuals using the products become addicted to them. For alcohol, 10-15 percent of drinkers become dependent on alcohol. Alcohol is used by more Americans than any other drug, including cigarette tobacco. According to the U.S. Department of Health and Human Services' 7th Report to Congress on Alcohol and Health, 18 million Americans suffer from alcohol problems, with a projected increase of almost one million more Americans who will exhibit symptoms of alcohol dependence by 1995.

Another critical difference between these two products is *when* the negative impacts occur. Alcohol-related problems can result immediately, even after short-term use, unlike tobacco, which causes long-term adverse effects. For example, I know of no cases of acute nicotine poisoning resulting in death, whereas acute alcohol poisoning is a far too common occurrence. Drinking, unlike smoking, is also linked with violent crime, suicide, spousal and child abuse, and drinking and driving crashes—the leading cause of death for young Americans.

And, contrary to what the alcoholic beverage companies would have members of Congress and the public believe, the majority of alcohol-related problems are *not* caused by heavy drinkers—but by light to moderate drinkers, ac-

From Patricia Taylor's testimony before the U.S. House of Representatives Subcommittee on Transportation and Hazardous Materials, March 1, 1990.

cording to a report issued by the Institute of Medicine in January 1990.

A third important distinction between these products is the fact that alcoholic beverage producers spent over $1 billion in 1989 advertising their products on radio and TV, compared to no broadcast expenditures for cigarettes. According to New York University professor Neil Postman and his colleagues in "Myths, Men, and Beer," a report funded by the AAA Foundation for Traffic Safety, young people

> *"The average 8- to 12-year-old child could name 5.2 alcoholic beverages, but only 4.8 presidents."*

see tens of thousands of television commercials for beer alone before they reach the legal drinking age of 21. . . .

Alcohol Advertisers and Youth

Even though youths cannot legally purchase alcoholic beverages, alcohol advertisers target under-age drinkers. Who do they think will see, and purchase, products like beer-can candies or race cars adorned with alcohol company logos? I never imagined there would actually be an alcohol equivalent to candy cigarettes.

At the Center for Science in the Public Interest, we have conducted two surveys of young people, to learn more about the influence of alcohol advertising on youth. In one survey of 4th and 5th graders in metropolitan Washington, D.C., we found that the average 8- to 12-year-old child could name 5.2 alcoholic beverages, but only 4.8 presidents. And they didn't just know the brand names, they could spell them remarkably well also. One 11-year-old boy who spelled Matilda Bay, King Cobra, and Bud Light correctly, couldn't do any better than presidents "Nickson" and "Rosselvet." We suspect that much of this brand awareness is due to billboards, TV and radio commercials, and other forms of advertising.

In 1989, we conducted another survey, this time of teenagers, asking them to name their favorite TV ads. Once again, we found that kids are attracted to these clever, well-produced ads. Boys cited beer ads more often than any other type of ad as their favorite. The 40 percent of the boys who named one or more beer ads as their favorite, put beer ahead of ads for fast foods, cars, running shoes, and even soft drinks.

Beer companies know what they're doing. That's why many of the ads favored by these young men featured music and depicted athletes and sporting activities. In 1988, breweries paid for about 10 percent of all sponsorships of athletic, music, cultural, and other special events. But it's not just the ads on TV that influence young people, young men in particular, who are the largest consumers of beer.

America's largest brewer, Anheuser-Busch, helps finance all U.S. Major League baseball teams, 20 of the 28 NFL teams, more than 300 college teams, and about 1,000 other sporting events. The alcoholic beverage industry may give lip service to their concerns about under-age drinking, but high school coaches, who work with young athletes, are worried. They view alcohol as the main threat to high school athletes. In a *USA Today* survey of 798 high school coaches conducted October 25-31, 1989, 88% of coaches identified alcohol as the greatest threat to their athletes. Only 6% identified crack-cocaine, and even fewer, 3%, identified marijuana.

But the alcoholic beverage industry's sponsorship of athletic events belies these problems and promotes a dangerously misleading myth among youth—that drinking is linked to athletic success. They certainly don't let under-age drinkers know that alcohol is a drug, that it may be addictive, or that drinking can in fact lead to serious health problems that undermine athletic prowess.

In 1989, concern about the power and pervasiveness of pro-drinking messages that target and influence youth prompted then Surgeon General C. Everett Koop to issue recommendations for restricting these marketing practices. Based on advice from a panel of experts, Dr. Koop's recommendations included the elimination of alcohol advertising and promotions on college campuses; restrictions on alcohol advertising, promotions, and sponsorships of public events; and the elimination of official sponsorship of athletic events by the alcoholic beverage industry. Later, Dr. Koop went even further, calling for a complete ban on all broadcast advertising of alcoholic beverages.

Targeting Minorities

Some Americans are changing their drinking habits, partly in response to the health information that has been provided by Dr. Koop and other prominent health officials. But, to maintain sales, the $90 billion a year alcoholic beverage industry spent over $2 billion on advertising and promotions in 1989. That money lines the pockets of ad agencies and media that are only too willing to testify on behalf of the First Amendment rights of some of their best customers.

This $90 billion a year industry is also investing in Congress—in two election cycles, the alcoholic beverage industry stuffed over $4 million in PAC, honoraria, and individual contributions into Congressional pockets. The broadcasters and their allies also gave generously, as did the outdoor advertisers who are responsible for the billboards littering our inner cities with messages promoting drinking and smoking. I'm sure that these facts are all too familiar to critics of smoking, because the methods and strategies of alcohol producers are similar to those of tobacco producers.

> *"High school coaches . . . view alcohol as the main threat to high school athletes."*

Both industries selectively target certain segments of our population with various products. Malt liquors are clearly targeted at minorities. Blacks account for only about 10 percent of sales of regular beer, but about 30 percent of sales of malt liquor, according to *Impact*, an alcohol trade publication. And, while regular beer contains about 4.6 percent alcohol, malt liquors range in alcohol content from 5.6 percent to a whopping 10.9 percent. Four cans of malt liquor have as much alcohol as five to eight cans of regular beer.

Despite the beer industry's written, voluntary policy of not touting the potency of their products, producers have named or advertised these brews specifically to imply high potency. Names like Schlitz Malt Liquor, with its bull crashing through a wall; Elephant; Midnight Dragon; and Turbo 1000 convey the impression that these beers are higher octane than regular beer.

Seductive Selling

But there's more to the story than the high alcohol content and the advertisements that connote strength and power. Ads for these products are explicitly targeted to Blacks and Latinos. I have here promotional materials, available in English and Spanish, for Pabst's Olde English 800. Provocatively dressed Black and Latina models, posing as "Lady and the Tiger," are accompanied by the slogan, "It's the Power." Most telling is the back page of a sales brochure that states, ". . . brewed for relatively high alcohol content (important to the Ethnic market!)." In another ad, this one for something called Midnight Dragon malt liquor, a seductively dressed woman sits backward on a chair, saying, "I could suck on this all night."

"Malt liquors are clearly targeted at minorities."

A coalition of 22 Black, Latino, and health organizations joined together to protest this marketing formula. They stressed that these aggressive marketing campaigns undermine the nation's anti-drug programs.

According to Dr. Walter Fagget, representing the National Medical Association, "The War on Drugs is doomed to failure when slick ads for Colt 45 and other malt liquors tell young men that drinking is the key to fun and sexual success. Not only are malt liquor products harmful themselves, but they're 'gateway' drugs that could pave the way to crack-cocaine and other illegal drugs." The groups called unsuccessfully on Secretary of HHS [Health and Human Services] Dr. Louis Sullivan and Treasury Secretary Nicholas Brady to demand that the companies stop targeting Blacks and Latinos and that they limit the alcohol content of malt liquor to 5 percent. . . .

In addition to particular products, alcohol and tobacco producers also utilize selected advertising techniques to reach minority markets. One advertising medium, billboards, has been under growing attack by citizen activists and elected officials across the country. Billboards target inner-city neighborhoods with 24-hour-a-day messages to smoke and drink. Scenic America and the Center for Science in the Public Interest released a report, "Citizens' Action Handbook on Alcohol and Tobacco Billboard Advertising."

The impetus for our report was the growing grass-roots activism of neighborhood residents who were fed up with the proliferation of pro-drinking and smoking messages in their neighborhoods—many of which tower over playgrounds and residential neighborhoods. One such activist, who calls himself Mandrake, has been painting over offensive alcohol and tobacco billboards in his neighborhood on the South Side of Chicago.

> *"Producers have named or advertised these brews specifically to imply high potency."*

These billboards are found predominantly in Black and Latino neighborhoods. The Call to Action in our handbook was written by Alberta Tinsley-Williams, a Wayne County, Michigan, Commissioner and the inspiration for some of the grass-roots activity around this issue. Her experiences have included debates with Billy Dee Williams, star of Colt 45 malt liquor ads; winning the removal of a Wild Irish Rose billboard that featured a seductively posed woman and was situated between a runaway shelter and a church; and a campaign to remove all alcohol and tobacco billboards from the city of Detroit.

She was peripherally involved in a very telling experience that demonstrates the ability of alcoholic beverage companies to influence policy debates by using their financial largesse.

In the summer of 1988, a conference to address alcohol advertising and marketing practices aimed at Blacks was to be held at Wayne State University. The day-long program was to be co-sponsored by the State of Michigan, Wayne State, and the Detroit Urban League. Alberta Tinsley-Williams, Representative John Conyers, who has been involved in efforts to publicize the problem of targeting of minority communities by alcohol and tobacco companies, and other speakers were invited to participate.

The Detroit Urban League's Board of Directors includes a Stroh Brewery Co. executive. The Stroh's board representative phoned the local league president. Shortly thereafter, the Detroit Urban League withdrew its sponsorship of the event.

Although the Detroit Urban League disassociated itself from the conference and the National Urban League has yet to criticize alcohol advertising targeted to minorities, one good thing did come out of that display of corporate muscle—Alberta Tinsley-Williams decided that she needed to become a national spokeswoman for eliminating 24-hour-a-day drug-promoting billboards from communities.

Alcohol and Tobacco Use Among Hispanics

Alcohol and tobacco companies haven't restricted their targeting practices to billboards or to Black communities. In a report we issued in October 1990, "Marketing Disease to Hispanics," Representative Matthew Martinez underscored the growing concern about the escalating cancer rates among Hispanics: more Hispanics are smoking, and smoking more cigarettes than in the past. Meanwhile alcohol-related problems, which had been limited almost exclusively to men, are now spreading to Latina women, who traditionally drank little.

According to Representative Martinez, "Many factors obviously play a role, but one clear contributor is the slick advertising campaigns that alcohol and tobacco companies have aimed at Hispanics for years. The glamorous images in the ads, which are particularly enticing to young people, saturate Hispanic neighborhoods across the country." "Marketing Disease to Hispanics" examines the pervasive influence of the alcohol and tobacco industries in the Hispanic community and the impact this influence is having on health.

> *"The War on Drugs is doomed to failure when slick ads for Colt 45 and other malt liquors tell young men that drinking is the key to fun and sexual success."*

I would like to cite one example of the differences in how alcoholic beverages are marketed to the majority population compared to Hispanics. There has been a long-standing voluntary restraint on the part of liquor producers from advertising on television, as you know. In 1988, we were informed by a Spanish-language TV viewer that similar restraint was not being exercised on Spanish-language TV. As a matter of fact, not only were ads being aired, but ads for one particular product even had a man drinking on a boat from a gallon-sized bottle and then jumping in the water, while a gaggle of admiring, bikini-clad women, also drinking, admired his exploits from a nearby boat. We, along with a number of Hispanic and public health organizations, were eventually successful in persuading Telemundo and Univision to halt the airing of ads for hard liquor.

In their afterword to the report, Rodolfo Acuna and Juana Mora call on the Latino community "to end the domination by the beer and tobacco companies that . . . have written our history through the production of their calendars, radio and TV commercials, magazine ads, donations to civic groups, and other forms of influence." According to Acuna and Mora, "Solutions have to go beyond just saying no and having the pushers of alcohol and tobacco pay for an occasional public service message about the disease that they profit from.". . .

Need for Alcohol Advertising Reforms

Which gets us back to the heart of the problem—how is it that alcohol and tobacco aren't part of the nation's anti-drug effort? Part of the problem clearly lies in the powerful pro-drinking messages that fill our airwaves. In response to public criticism about these messages, the alcoholic beverage industry has appointed itself the purveyor of so-called moderation messages, which are oftentimes nothing more than an extension of their advertising, creating a "Good Guy" image and geared to undermine demands for governmental action.

Have you thought about what Spuds McKenzie telling your 10 year old to "Know When To Say When" really means? First, your child is getting a pro-drinking message. "Know When To Say When" assumes that someone has started drinking, and the only question that needs to be answered is, how much? There certainly is no information about the fact that it is illegal for your 10 year old to purchase alcoholic beverages before reaching the age of 21, or that alcohol is a drug or that alcohol can be deadly. The very image that Anheuser-Busch uses to advertise their products, in this case one with great appeal to young people, is carried over into these so-called "moderation messages."

Second, and very disturbing for organizations concerned about preventing alcohol-related problems, the companies that produce these products are setting themselves up as deliverers of a health message at the same time they are dependent upon sales of their products to people with alcohol problems. Over 50 percent of the alcoholic beverages sold each year are bought by the 10 percent of drinkers with the most severe alcohol problems. The American public deserves and needs more than a subtle pro-drinking message in sheep's clothing from beer barons worried that the public is catching on to the fact that their product is America's leading drug problem.

Debate on Banning Alcohol Ads

I'd like to briefly comment on a study that was released by the Leadership Council on Advertising Issues. This report is a self-serving, misleading, political document.

To counter criticism about the way alcohol and tobacco companies are targeting minorities, this report predicts the demise of minority media under a scenario that has never been proposed: namely the banning of all alcohol advertising in magazines and newspapers. To my knowledge, there has never been such a proposal.

Cooking up worse than worst-case scenarios behind closed doors, then analyzing them and reporting the likely elimination of minority media as we know them today, is intellectually dishonest and simply a scare tactic. The problems that are facing commercial television have little to do with the specter of changes in regulations regarding beer advertising. To forecast a decline in the quality of commercial television, again under a scenario that no one is proposing, is utterly irresponsible.

In 1984 and 1985, Congress was considering a bill to require equal time for health and safety messages about alcohol. In the House, the bill was championed by Representative John Seiberling of Ohio. The Association of National Advertisers characterized Mr. Seiberling's bill as a ban on alcohol advertising.

> *"Alcohol and tobacco producers . . . utilize selected advertising techniques to reach minority markets."*

An analysis of the impact of a ban then, produced by a Wall Street brokerage firm and reported in *Advertising Age* on March 11, 1985, differed substantially from the Leadership Council on Advertising report.

In an article headlined "Beer ad ban won't hurt nets," L. F. Rothschild, author of the report, described networks even more dependent on beer advertising than today—18% of network sports revenues in 1983 were derived from beer and wine advertising, compared with 15% in 1990. Further, according to Mr. Rothschild, an imposed ban would severely crimp the marketing efforts of beer advertisers, not the revenues of the networks. That's because the networks obtained sports advertising revenues from a broad variety of sources, including companies like General Motors, Ford, and IBM. Clearly there will be a period of adjustment to any changes in alcohol advertising policies, but the draconian nature predicted is simply inconceivable.

> *"Alcohol-related problems . . . are now spreading to Latina women."*

And what about the alcohol advertising policies of some of the cable networks that make the advertising/media business today so different from what it was 20 years ago when tobacco ads left the nation's airwaves? Nick-at-Night doesn't allow ads for alcoholic beverages before 10:00 p.m. The Family Channel doesn't allow any alcoholic beverage advertising at all. Even MTV says that generally they don't allow beer ads during the day. Alcoholic beverage producers are understandably concerned about advertising controls. The American public is fed up with all of their ads. In a November 1989 poll for the *Wall Street Journal*, 60% of those surveyed favored requiring equal time for health and safety messages; almost half of those polled wanted to ban them altogether, along with the retired athletes and other celebrity pitchmen. When it comes to warnings, 67% favored requiring warnings about the dangers of drinking.

The Public Wants Ads to Be Restricted

When the Roper organization asked if alcoholic beverages should be advertised on TV, 63% favored restricting beer advertising, 33% to after 9:00 p.m., and 30% favored eliminating it altogether. The Bureau of Alcohol, Tobacco, and Firearms conducted its own public opinion survey on warning labels for a report to Congress and found that nearly one-half of those surveyed felt that alcoholic beverage advertising greatly influences under-age people to drink alcoholic beverages.

When Dr. Koop issued his recommendations on curbing drinking and driving crashes, he stated, "certain advertising and marketing practices for alcoholic beverages clearly send the wrong messages about alcohol consumption to the wrong audiences . . . they send the message that drinking is a normal and glamorous activity without negative consequences."

The marketing practices of alcoholic beverage producers are the best their money can buy. For the sake of our nation's health, the policies that regulate those marketing practices should also be the best that we can muster. Obviously, reforming alcohol advertising practices alone will not eliminate all of the health problems associated with drinking and smoking. For alcohol, we need a comprehensive program that includes sharp increases in alcohol excise taxes, expanded prevention and treatment programs, and better consumer information about legal drugs.

I would like to share some information about the growing support for alcohol advertising reforms, as well as some specific proposals.

We have joined with 30 organizations to form the Coalition on Alcohol Advertising and Family Education. Among the members of this new coalition are the American Academy of Pediatrics, the American Public Health Association, the American Academy of Family Physicians, the American Medical Association, the National Council on Alcoholism and Drug Dependence, and the National Coalition to Prevent Impaired Driving. We have come together to promote the following policies regarding alcohol advertising:

1. Equivalent time for health and safety messages to balance broadcast and cable advertisements of alcoholic beverages.

2. Appropriate limitations on alcohol advertisements that target youth. This would include a) restrictions on sponsorship of youth-oriented events, such as rock concerts and sporting events, and b) an alcohol-free viewing and listening period in the broadcast and cable media.

3. Restrictions on the promotional activities of alcohol companies on college campuses.

4. Rotating health and safety warnings in all alcohol advertisements.

These organizations are working together because they share the belief that alcohol advertising reforms are long overdue. . . . In addition, the Center for Science in the Public Interest would urge [the consideration of] the following recommendations:

> *"The companies that produce these products . . . are dependent upon sales of their products to people with alcohol problems."*

• Requiring the Federal Trade Commission to monitor and publish periodic reports on alcohol advertising practices the way it presently monitors tobacco advertising practices.

• Eliminate product placements in movies. We share concerns about the placement of products like alcohol and tobacco in movies. Something should be done about the fact that Miller beer appears 20 times in the 100 minute long movie, *Bull Durham*.

At a minimum, the new warning required on containers should appear at the end of films, and viewers should be advised that the beer was shown as a paid advertisement.

• Ask the Media Partnership for a Drug-Free America to include alcohol and tobacco. If these concerned organizations don't respond to requests to expand their mandate, Congress and the President should allocate revenues to finance similar counter-ads about smoking and drinking.

Alcohol Advertisements Encourage Teens to Abuse Alcohol

by Antonia C. Novello

About the author: *Antonia C. Novello was surgeon general of the United States from 1990 to 1993. She is now working for UNICEF (United Nations Children's Fund), which provides aid and development assistance to children and mothers in developing countries.*

I am pleased to have the opportunity to talk about underage drinking and what I have found to be its key issues and its potential solutions.

I have been working on this issue since September of 1990, when I launched what I now realize was a fact-finding mission on my part. I toured the country talking to community leaders, to teachers, to kids and to everyone about the problems of underage drinking.

What I learned in that month has served me well and certainly underscores the basis of all our teen drinking prevention efforts. That is, prevention works best if the message that our youth gets at home is the one he gets at school, is the one he gets in the community and is the one that he gets from his peers. If this clear and consistent message cannot be provided, second best is to have clear and consistent messages from the parent, reinforced by messages in the school.

I also began to learn then, and I relearn every time I look at the issue, how pervasive underage drinking is and how it is truly the mainstream drug used that plagues our communities and our families.

Mixed Messages Hinder Progress

I began to learn then and I relearn every day how pervasive also are the mixed messages we constantly send our children about alcohol. I agree with Dr. Mason, our Assistant Secretary of Health, when he says we have made tremendous progress in the illicit drug war, and that is because we are forever sending non-

From Antonia C. Novello's testimony before the U.S. House of Representatives Select Committee on Children, Youth, and Families, November 15, 1991.

mixed messages.

I can tell you that at this stage of the game we are losing the one on alcohol because we are allowing mixed messages to go on and on.

Our health message is clear. The use of alcohol by young people can lead to serious health consequences far beyond those well known about drinking and driving—the likes of absenteeism, vandalism, date rape, truancy, theft and random violence, to name a few. But that message directly conflicts with the enticing drumbeat of ads that say drink me and you will be cool, drink me and you will be glamorous, or drink me and you will have fun.

> *"The use of alcohol by young people can lead to serious health consequences."*

Since September of 1990, I have conducted a very carefully thought-out campaign to try to deal with this issue, and I can tell you that it has culminated in the invaluable series of reports by the Inspector General, Dick Kusserow.

Prior to those reports I have gotten involved, and I can tell you I took the following steps to bring the issue of underage drinking to the American public:

In the fall of 1990, I helped launch the Office of Substance Abuse Prevention's "Pienselo"—an alcohol prevention campaign that was targeted to Hispanic youth, because, as you well know, 90 percent of the billboards in our communities have a picture of alcohol—Halloween advertising was being used by the alcohol industry at that time.

I regret to add that, although my press conference on alcohol advertising occurred just after Halloween, brewers still ran Halloween campaigns with the likes of Elvira and the likes of others, very similar to what they did in 1990.

In January of 1991, I held a press conference on Cisco, calling for the repackaging of this fortified wine that looked like a wine cooler, but we knew it was equivalent to five shots of vodka.

In spring of 1991, I held a press conference on Spring Break promotional activities on college drinking where I asked the industry to please remove all their ads from the places where they were, and I can tell you that it did very well in Miami Beach, but it didn't do very well in Padre Island.

I can also tell you that, together with the Treasury's Bureau of Alcohol, Tobacco and Firearms [BATF], we have worked to do research, to try to assess the effectiveness of the current warning label.

Why and What Teens Drink

In June of 1991, I released the first set of reports from Inspector General Kusserow—"Youth and Alcohol: Drinking Habits, Access, Attitudes and Knowledge" and "Do They Know What They Are Drinking?"

And the studies showed that at least 8 million American teenagers use alcohol every week, and almost half a million go on weekly binges of five drinks in a row, confirming earlier surveys by the National Institute on Drug Abuse. Junior and senior high school students drink, every year, 35 percent of all wine coolers and 1.1 billion cans of beer, or 102 million gallons.

Many teenagers, as many as 4 million of those who drink, are using alcohol to handle stress and to handle boredom, and many of them drink alone, breaking the old stereotype of party drinking and peer pressure.

Labeling is a big problem. Two out of three teenagers cannot distinguish alcoholic from nonalcoholic beverages because of the way they appear similar on the store shelves.

And the idea of designated driver has to be looked upon again. Although 92 percent of the adolescents know that drinking and driving is dangerous, 7 million of them still bum rides with their friends, even though they know they are drunk.

Teenagers lack essential knowledge about alcohol too. Very few are getting clear and reliable information about alcohol. They don't know the minimum age; 5.6 million do not know the minimum age for purchasing alcohol, and, worse, almost 2 million do not even know that a law exists.

Alcohol intoxication affects 2.6 million teenagers who do not know that a person can die from an overdose of alcohol. And one-third believe that coffee, taking a shower or getting fresh air can actually sober you up.

> *"Many teenagers . . . are using alcohol to handle stress and to handle boredom, and many of them drink alone."*

Eighty percent of teenagers do not know that one shot of whiskey and one can of beer have the same equivalence of alcohol. And at least 55 percent do not know that a can of beer has the same amount of alcohol as four ounces of wine.

Two-thirds of the teenagers who drink, or an equivalent of 7 million, walk into a store, buy the alcohol, and there is no one else to supervise it. And on top of that, 3.4 million of them on the other side of the counter sell it to them without any supervision.

And as we learn, because of the 1935 Federal Alcohol Administration Act, it is against the law, since 1935, to label beer or malt liquor with the content of alcohol. . . .

The Vulnerability of Teens

Concern over alcohol advertising arises because most alcohol advertising goes beyond describing the specific qualities of the beverage. It creates a glamorous, pleasurable image that may mislead the youth.

In September 1991, a poll was done by the Wirthlin Group that showed that 73 percent of respondents in the United States agree that alcohol advertising is a major contributor to underage drinking. And this goes very much with the feeling by all older Americans that the industry is on the wrong track. Also, one of the reasons for which they felt that the industry was on the wrong track was that the alcohol ads target the youth. This finding bolsters the 1988 BATF poll in which 80 percent of the American respondents believe that alcohol advertising influences underage youth to drink alcoholic beverages.

I am very concerned. I am extremely concerned. I cannot help but think of the young people that I see every day that have been involved in accidents, and, really, looking to the way by which injuries really put them in total disadvantage, relevant to their peers. For me, that is devastating. And as I have said, the truth of the agony that drinking brings to youth is quite different from the fantasy and the fun that is depicted in the ads.

And let me be very clear. The kinds of ads that appeal to our young people are appealing to some degree to many of us. And, in that sense, it is different, because our young people in their search for identity, their doubts about their own popularity and their doubts about their own sexual attractiveness—in that awkward moment which is adolescence they are particularly vulnerable.

And that is the part that worries me, because, according to recent research, I can tell you that there are four types of ads that attract youth, and those are the ones that make lifestyle appeals, the ones that have sexual appeals, the ones that use sports figures in them which are heroes or heroines, and those where risky activities are depicted as if there was no risk at all. . . . Those are the ones where we have the skiing, the boating race, the one that goes into mountain climbing. Many people look at this and believe that it is okay to do this in the presence of drinking, without realizing that there are so many consequences attached to the risk.

A Complex Problem

The answers on how to limit advertising appeals to youth are not as simple as I suspected. There are many problems here. We found that when you look into the government and the industry control, it is a profoundly complicated problem, and probably, as you say, that is why not many people have gotten involved in the past.

But this is a time in which the surgeon general is a public health official. She is a public health person, and for that it makes it a little bit more different, because we look into the problem with objectives, goals, time limits, and, most importantly, what is the problem and how to approach it in steps. That is what I have done all the time.

But I can tell you, not only do we have a fragmented and indirect control of the Federal and state level, but the existing voluntary guidelines of the industry are unenforceable as well.

> *"Alcohol advertising is a major contributor to underage drinking."*

In spite of this, several things are clear. First, we all have a role to play if we are going to solve this problem. And, most importantly, if we are truly committed, then we will make a difference, but if we are just speaking like we have spoken for many years in the past, then the problem will continue, and then at the end of 20 years we will all be responsible for not having taken the window of opportunity.

Federal Regulations Are Ineffective

Let me summarize the report's findings and tell you the key points. Federal jurisdiction is fragmented among several agencies, BATF, FTC [Federal Trade Commission], and even the FDA [Food and Drug Administration].

Federal regulations do not specifically prohibit alcohol ads that appeal to youth. The primary goal of BATF and FTC regulation on advertisement is to ensure that consumers receive truthful and accurate information about products.

And the BATF's enforcement authority is limited, because without state regulations that mirror the BATF regulations, BATF has no ability to regulate malt beverage labeling or advertising. Also, unlike vintners and distillers, brewers are not required to obtain permits from BATF, and, therefore, BATF lacks an important tool of enforcement.

States have difficulty adopting legislation to control alcohol advertising. And pressure on state legislators from vested interests can be barriers to regulating alcohol advertising.

> *"I have called upon the industry to voluntarily give up these kinds of ads."*

And alcohol industry standards do not effectively restrict ads that appeal to youth, and they are unenforceable. They do not specifically address the types of ads the public is concerned about, and the codes are strictly voluntary.

The network enforcement is based on negotiation with advertisers. And while the networks negotiate with the advertisers over the standard, they must also attract advertising revenues to be able to stay in business.

A case study of five ads found that the current regulations and standards have not deterred advertisers from using the ads that appeal to youth.

All Must Be Involved

So what are the solutions?

As you know, I called for the industry's voluntary elimination of alcohol advertising that appeals to youth on the basis of lifestyles, on the basis of sexual appeal, on the basis of sports figures, and on the basis of risky activities, as well as the advertising with the more blatant youth appeals of cartoon characters and those that have youth slang.

This requires action by all of us. As I said earlier, in order to win the war for the children, we must do away with mixed messages.

I have called upon the industry to voluntarily give up these kinds of ads, ideally by adhering to voluntary codes that are clear and workable, but practically by each manufacturer simply refusing to use these kind of ads.

I call upon states to continue their efforts to limit advertising, and I urge communities to provide the grass root support that makes such limits a reality. And I call upon communities generally to adopt and support creative prevention programs such as the one that I see in Roanoke, Virginia, which is excellent, and also Project STAR that I see in Kansas City.

I urge schools to make alcohol education a part of the curriculum from the earliest grades to college, and I can also tell you that the curriculum must include not only the teaching about alcohol but also teaching resistance education and risk avoidance techniques.

And finally, I urge families, the parents and the children, for once and for all, to talk about alcohol, talk to each other about the ads, and talk to each other about how to distinguish truth from fiction.

For my part, I have invited a small group of CEOs from the most important parts of the industry to meet privately with me to discuss what they can do to eliminate these ads and what we can do together to protect the health of the young people. I am pleased to say that their ready acceptance gives me hope that we might be on the right track. . . .

Only through the efforts of you, the schools, the parents, the communities, the industry—throughout the country—is the only way in which we will find lasting ways by which we can solve this problem, because we are not only saving the lives of kids, but the quality of those lives, and I believe that today that is the most precious thing that we have to look forward to, the protection of the children.

Alcohol Advertisements Should Be Banned

by Jean Kilbourne

About the author: *Jean Kilbourne, an international lecturer and filmmaker, is a visiting scholar at Wellesley College in Massachusetts and a member of the board of directors of the National Council on Alcoholism and Drug Dependence. Her films include* Still Killing Us Softly: Advertising's Image of Women *and* Advertising Alcohol: Calling the Shots.

"Absolut Magic" proclaims a print ad for a popular vodka. "Paradise found," headlines another. "Fairy tales can come true" says a third.

All these ads illustrate the major premise of alcohol advertising's mythology: Alcohol is magic, a magic carpet that can take you away. It can make you successful, sophisticated, sexy. Without it, your life would be dull, mediocre and ordinary.

Everyone wants to believe in happy endings. But as most of us know, the reality of alcohol for many people in our society is more like a horror story than a fairy tale. The liquid in the glass is definitely not a magic potion.

We are surrounded by the message that alcohol is fun, sexy, desirable and harmless. We get this message many times a day. We get it from the ads and, far more insidiously, we get it from the media, which depend upon alcohol advertising for a large share of their profits. Thanks to this connection, alcohol use tends to be glorified throughout the media and alcohol-related problems are routinely dismissed.

A Product and a Drug

Alcohol is related to parties, good times, celebrations and fun, but it is also related to murder, suicide, unemployment and child abuse. These connections are never made in the ads. Of course, one would not expect them to be. The advertisers are selling their product and it is their job to erase any negative aspects as well as to enhance the positive ones. However, when the product is the nation's

"Deadly Persuasion" by Jean Kilbourne. Reprinted with permission from the Spring/Summer 1991 issue of *Media&Values*, published by the Center for Media and Values, Los Angeles, CA.

number one drug, there are consequences that go far beyond product sales.

Most people know that alcohol can cause problems. But how many realize that 10 percent of all deaths in the United States—including half of all homicides and at least one quarter of all suicides—are related to alcohol? The economic cost to the nation exceeds $100 billion a year. At least 13,000,000 Americans, about one out of 10, are alcoholic—the personal cost to them and their families is incalculable.

The tab for alcohol use doesn't end there. More than $2 billion a year—a sizable chunk of the over $90 billion the industry takes in annually—goes to prime the advertising and promotion pump and keep drinkers' money flowing freely. Problem drinkers and young people are the primary targets of these advertisers.

Of course, industry spokespeople disagree with this claim. Over and over again, their public statements assert that they are not trying to create new or heavier drinkers. Instead, they say they only want people who already drink to switch to another brand and to drink it in moderation. However, the most basic analysis of alcohol advertising reveals an emphasis on both recruiting new, young users and pushing heavy consumption of their products.

Indeed, advertising that encouraged only moderate drinking would be an economic failure. This becomes clear when you know that only 10 percent of the drinking-age population consumes over half of all alcoholic beverages sold. According to Robert Hammond, director of the Alcohol Research Information Service, if all 105 million drinkers of legal age consumed the official maximum "moderate" amount of alcohol—.99 ounces per day, the equivalent of about two drinks—the industry would suffer "a whopping 40 percent decrease in the sale of beer, wine and distilled spirits."

Young Prospects

These figures make it clear that if alcoholics were to recover—i.e., stop drinking—the alcoholic beverage industry's gross revenue would be cut in half. I can't believe that industry executives want that to happen. On the contrary, my 15-year study of alcohol advertising makes me certain that advertisers deliberately target the heavy drinker and devise ads designed to appeal to him or her. As with any product, the heavy user is the best customer. However, when the product is a drug, the heavy user is often an addict.

Not all problem drinkers are alcoholics. Youthful drinking is frequently characterized by binges and episodes of drunkenness, making

"We are surrounded by the message that alcohol is fun, sexy, desirable and harmless."

young people a lucrative market for alcohol producers. According to the 1989 National Institute on Drug Abuse survey of high school seniors, 33 percent of students reported that they had consumed five or more drinks on one occasion within the previous two weeks. This group is vulnerable to ad campaigns that present heavy drinking as fun and normal.

Media sell target audiences to the alcohol industry on a cost-per-drinker basis. "*Cosmopolitan* readers drank 21,794,000 glasses of beer in the last week. . . . Isn't it time you gave *Cosmopolitan* a shot?" proclaims an ad aimed at the alcohol industry.

The primary purpose of the mass media is to deliver audiences to advertisers. It's worthwhile taking a closer look at how some of the common myths alcohol advertisers have created do this.

#1. Drinking is a risk-free activity. Ads featuring copy like "The Joy of Six" imply that it is all right to consume large quantities of alcohol. Light beer ("great taste") has been developed and heavily promoted not for the dieter but for the heavy drinker. It is "less filling," and therefore one can drink more.

Ads like these tell the alcoholic and those around him or her that it is all right, indeed splendid, to be obsessed by alcohol, to consume large amounts of it on a daily basis and to have it be a part of all one's activities. At the same time, all signs of trouble and any hint of addiction are erased.

Every instance of use seems spontaneous, unique. The daily drinking takes place on yachts at sunset, not at kitchen tables in the morning. Bottles are magically unopened even when drinks have been poured. All signs of trouble and any hint of addiction are conspicuously avoided . There is no unpleasant drunkenness, only high spirits. Certainly alcohol-related problems such as alcohol-impaired driving, broken marriages, abused children, lost jobs, illness and premature death are never even hinted at.

> *"If alcoholics were to recover—i.e., stop drinking— the alcoholic beverage industry's gross revenue would be cut in half."*

#2. You can't survive without drinking. "It separates the exceptional from the merely ordinary" is how a Piper champagne ad puts it. By displaying a vibrant, imbibing couple against a black and white nondrinking background crowd, the advertiser contrasts the supposedly alive and colorful world of the drinker with dull reality. The alcohol has resurrected the couple, restored them to life.

Alcohol Portrayed as One of Life's Essentials

In general, such advertising is expert at making the celebration of *drinking itself*—not a holiday, festivity or family event—a reason for imbibing ("Pour a Party." "Holidays were made for Michelob.").

At the heart of the alcoholic's dilemma and denial is this belief, this certainty, that alcohol is essential for life, that without it he or she will literally die—or at best be condemned to a gray and two-dimensional wasteland, a half-life. These ads, and many others like them, present that nightmare as true, thus affirming and even glorifying one of the symptoms of the illness.

#3. Problem drinking behaviors are normal. A shot of a sunset-lit bridge,

captioned "At the end of the day, even a bridge seems to be heading home for Red," is actually advertising not just Scotch, but daily drinking. Often symptoms of alcoholism, such as the need for a daily drink, are portrayed as not only normal, but desirable. A Smirnoff ad captioned "Hurry Sundown" features a vampirish lady immobilized in a coffin-like setting awaiting the revivifying effects of a vodka gimlet.

> *"Ads . . . tell the alcoholic and those around him or her that it is all right, indeed splendid, to be obsessed by alcohol."*

Slogans presenting drinking as "your own special island," and "your mountain hideaway" capitalize on the feelings of alienation and loneliness most alcoholics experience. Such ads seem to encourage solitary drinking, often one of the classic indicators of trouble with alcohol. They also distort the tragic reality that problem drinking increases—rather than alleviates—those feelings of isolation. Alcohol lies at the center of these ads, just as it is at the center of the alcoholic's life.

#4. Alcohol is a magic potion that can transform you. Alcohol advertising often spuriously links alcohol with precisely those attributes and qualities—happiness, wealth, prestige, sophistication, success, maturity, athletic ability, virility and sexual satisfaction—that the misuse of alcohol destroys.

For example, alcohol is linked with romance and sexual fulfillment, yet it is common knowledge that drunkenness often leads to sexual dysfunction. Less well known is the fact that people with drinking problems are seven times more likely to be separated or divorced.

Targeting the Powerless

Such ads often target young people, women and people of color, since members of these groups often feel powerless and are eager to identify with "successful" groups in our society. These ads sometimes connect "prestige" beverages with the aura of the rich and powerful or the goals of women's liberation.

Ads and products aimed at young people deserve special mention in these days when many preteens start drinking in junior high school. Cartoon and animal characters such as Spuds MacKenzie, Anheuser-Busch's canine mascot, are not as innocent as they appear. In one Christmas campaign, Spuds appeared in a Santa Claus suit, promoting 12-packs of Bud Light beer. In the summer of 1990 he was cavorting with ninjas, drawing on the popularity of the *Teenage Mutant Ninja Turtles* movie, a big hit with younger children.

Ads that portray drinking as a passport to adulthood, coupled with transitional products such as high-proof milkshakes and chocolate sodas, can be very successful lures for young drinkers.

#5. Sports and alcohol go together. Alcohol consumption actually decreases athletic performance. However, numerous ads, like a Pabst Blue Ribbon poster showing a speeding bicyclist with a bottle of beer on her basket, wrongly imply

that sports and alcohol are safely complementary activities. Others feature sponsorship of a wide range of sporting events or endorsements by sports stars.

#6. If these products were truly dangerous, the media would tell us. Most media are reluctant to bite the hand that feeds them by spending $2 billion annually on advertising and promotion. Media coverage of the "war on drugs" seldom mentions the two major killers, alcohol and nicotine. From the coverage, one would assume that cocaine was the United States' most dangerous drug. However, while cocaine, heroin and other illegal drugs are linked with about 20,000 deaths a year, alcohol contributes to at least 100,000 and cigarettes more than 390,000—or more than 1,000 a day.

Although many media feature occasional stories about alcoholism, they usually treat it as a personal problem and focus on individual treatment solutions. Reports that probe alcohol's role in violence and other chronic problems are rare, while the role advertising plays in encouraging its use is almost never discussed.

#7. Alcoholic beverage companies promote moderation in drinking. The current Budweiser "moderation" campaign says, "Know when to say when," as opposed to "Know when to say no." In the guise of a moderation message, this slogan actually suggests to young people that drinking beer is one way to demonstrate their control. It also perpetuates the myth that alcoholics are simply people who "don't know when to say when," irresponsibly engaging in willful misconduct, rather than people who are suffering from a disease that afflicts at least one in 10 drinkers.

Ads Encourage Denial in Alcoholics

Most of these programs are designed to encourage young people not to drive drunk. Although this is a laudable goal, it is interesting to note that few of the alcohol industry programs discourage or even question drunkenness *per se*. The tragic result is that many young people feel it is perfectly all right to get drunk, as long as they do not get behind the wheel of a car.

In any case, we might be better off without programs designed by the alcohol industry to promote ideas about "responsible" drinking that in fact subtly promote myths and damaging attitudes. For example, one program by Miller beer defines moderate drinking as up to four drinks a day. Copy for a Budweiser program called "The Buddy System" defines drunkenness as having "too much of a good time." Doesn't this imply that being sober is having a bad time, that being drunk and having a good time go together? Even the industry's "moderation" messages imply the advantages of heavy drinking.

"We must stop supporting the denial that is at the heart of the illness that alcohol advertising both perpetuates and depends upon."

One of the chief symptoms of the disease of alcoholism is the denial that there is a problem. In general, as a society we tend to deny the illness and to support the alibi system of the alcoholic. Advertising encourages this denial.

It may be impossible to prove conclusively that alcohol advertising affects consumption, but it clearly affects attitudes about drinking. The ads contribute to an environment of social acceptance of high-risk drinking and denial of related problems. In addition, media dependence on alcohol advertising discourages full and open discussion of the many problems associated with alcohol.

A major comprehensive effort is needed to prevent alcohol-related problems. Such an effort must include education, mass media campaigns, increased availability of treatment programs, and more effective deterrence policies. It must also include public policy changes that take into account that the individual acts within a social, economic and cultural environment that profoundly influences his or her choices. Such changes would include raising taxes on alcohol, putting clearly legible warning labels on the bottles and regulating the advertising.

Steps to Combat Alcoholism

Above all, we must become fully engaged in the struggle to solve alcohol-related problems. We must stop supporting the denial that is at the heart of the illness that alcohol advertising both perpetuates and depends upon both in the individual and in society as a whole.

What can be done? We can investigate the extent to which the media are influenced by their dependence on alcohol advertising. We can consider the possibility of further restricting or banning all alcohol advertising, as some other countries have done. We can insist on equal time for information commercials in the broadcast media. We can raise the taxes on alcohol and use the extra revenue to fund programs to prevent and treat the illness and educate the public. We can become more aware of the real messages in the ads and work to teach their implications and consequences to those we love and care for.

Alcohol Advertisements Do Not Encourage Alcohol Abuse Among Teens

by James Sanders

About the author: *James Sanders is a former president of the Beer Institute, which represents the interests of American brewers and beer suppliers.*

The old lawyer's adage says if you don't have the facts on your side, argue the law; if you don't have the law on your side, then argue the facts. And if you don't have either on your side, just argue.

When it comes to beer advertising, Surgeon General Antonia Novello is just arguing.

She mistakenly contends that beer advertising is the major factor in alcohol abuse, that it somehow convinces young people to drink and indulge in risky behavior. Accordingly, Dr. Novello has called for a voluntary ban on most of our industry's advertising.

But Dr. Novello is wrong about advertising's impact and thus wrong to ask us to withdraw our ads. Here's why.

No Tie Between Ads and Abuse

Advertising does not cause abuse. This is proven by years of government and private research, the most instructive of which are two recent studies.

In a report to Congress the Department of Health and Human Services said, "Research has yet to document a strong relationship between alcohol advertising and alcohol consumption." Dr. Novello works for HHS.

And Dr. Novello released a federal study that polled young people on why they drink. In the surgeon general's own words, "Teenagers claim not to be too influenced by alcohol advertising."

For some reason, Dr. Novello persists in blaming ads for alcohol abuse, despite her own research and that of her agency.

James Sanders, "Do Alcohol Ads Send a Bad Message?" *The Washington Times*, December 1, 1991. Reprinted with the author's permission.

Beer advertising does not cause people to drink. If the purpose of our advertising is to encourage nondrinkers to drink, then it is a dismal failure. Since 1970, beer advertising expenditures have increased dramatically, yet per capita consumption among adults has remained virtually level, and in fact declined during the 1980s.

Instead, advertising creates brand preference among adult beer drinkers. Brewers are fighting very hard for a share of a mature, level market.

> *"Teenagers claim not to be too influenced by alcohol advertising."*

Brewers advertise responsibly and under tight supervision. All beer ads on TV have been through a very demanding review and approval process. Ads must be reviewed by company lawyers, they must conform to company and industry ad codes, and they must meet the networks' standards and practices guidelines—before hitting the air.

Ultimately, the Bureau of Alcohol, Tobacco and Firearms and the Federal Trade Commission have regulatory authority over alcohol advertising and the power to remove any ad.

Industry Promotes Responsibility

Regardless of advertising's impact, though, the fact remains that we don't want underage people to buy or consume our products. We can't say it any plainer, which is why we've worked so hard to discourage underage consumption. Our most recent national campaign against underage drinking has been lauded by alcohol beverage officials coast to coast, and by the surgeon general herself.

More than anything else, this debate needs a little common sense that, coupled with solid research, tells us that parents and peers are by far the most important factors in a person's decision to drink.

A 1991 Roper poll of children aged 8-17 years old shows that 60 percent believe parents have the greatest influence on whether they drink alcohol, while only 2 percent cited TV ads. Then again, anyone who's raised a child probably could have guessed these results.

Knowing this, the brewing industry has for years devoted many resources to educating parents and their children on making the right decisions about alcohol. Happily, statistics indicate these and other programs are working.

A 1990 survey by the National Institute on Drug Abuse reported that 57 percent of high school seniors reported having a drink in the last month, down from 72 percent in 1980.

In the 1980s the number of fatalities involving young drivers (15-19 years old) and alcohol declined by 39 percent, according to the National Highway Traffic Safety Administration.

The brewing industry is committed to seeing that these statistics continue to improve through real solutions that promote education and awareness.

Alcohol Advertisements Do Not Encourage Minorities to Abuse Alcohol

by Jeffrey G. Becker

About the author: *Jeffrey G. Becker is vice president for Alcohol Issues, a division of the Beer Institute, the trade association representing U.S. brewers and suppliers.*

Marketing products differently to different consumer segments is a time-honored tradition among businesses. In today's marketplace, it is the unenlightened business that refuses to acknowledge the rich cultural diversity that exists between men and women and between various ethnic groups. And it is that business which is destined to fall behind its competitors.

Some 80 million adult Americans drink beer, and they do so responsibly. A sizable portion of those responsible beer drinkers are minorities, and they are therefore a legitimate group to which America's brewers market their products. Doing so is good business.

America's brewers have long acknowledged and valued this cultural diversity. Indeed, we were among the first industries that featured African-American actors, for example, in our advertising—a move warmly endorsed by civil rights organizations.

Antialcohol Activists Are Wrong

Still, there are some people who, because of their opposition to all alcohol consumption, criticize specialized advertising for specific consumer segments. In attacking this practice, these antialcohol activists mistakenly—yet purposefully—link advertising with alcohol abuse, and therefore claim that special marketing efforts must necessarily result in abuse by a particular market seg-

From Jeffrey G. Becker, "Advertising and Abuse: No Link," *Business and Society Review*, Fall 1992. Reprinted with permission.

ment. They are wrong.

A significant body of research shows no link between advertising and alcohol abuse. In fact, few credible researchers can draw any connection between advertising and consumption at all.

This has been widely echoed. The Department of Health and Human Services, in its 1990 report to Congress, stated that "research has yet to document a strong relationship between alcohol advertising and alcohol consumption." Instead, advertising influences brand choice by those who already drink. If advertising were

> *"It is . . . patronizing for some to allege that minorities cannot be exposed to advertising designed with specific appeal."*

meant to "create" new drinkers or generate increased consumption, it has been a dismal failure. Over the past decade, advertising expenditures by the brewing industry have skyrocketed—but the per capita consumption of alcohol has remained level.

A Condescending Attitude

Advertising does not cause abuse. Americans know this intuitively, which is why it is so patronizing for some to allege that minorities cannot be exposed to advertising designed with specific appeal. They imply that African-Americans are unable to view a television ad or read a billboard and make their own decision. It is condescension of the worst sort.

Common sense tells us the same. As Benjamin Hooks, former head of the National Association for the Advancement of Colored People, noted, "Buried in this line of thinking, and never really mentioned by these critics, is the rationale that blacks are not capable of making their own free choices and need some guardian angels to protect their best interests."

It is entirely appropriate for brewers to advertise their products to their consumers, and entirely inappropriate to blame alcohol abuse on this marketing. People have every right to debate the tastefulness of any type of advertising but we must recognize that this subjective, emotional argument is quite distinct from questioning the impact of advertising as proven by research.

America's brewers take very seriously our role in promoting the responsible use of our products. Over the years, we have invested an overwhelming amount of resources to develop creative, effective programs that address the issue of alcohol abuse. We can offer no higher expression of our corporate social responsibility than to promote safe, responsible, and legal consumption.

Censoring Alcohol Advertisements Would Not Decrease Alcohol Abuse

by Howard H. Bell

About the author: *Howard H. Bell is the former president of the American Advertising Federation (AAF), an organization of advertisers and those who wish to promote the rights of advertisers.*

[There is] a mutual concern over growing threats around the world to the freedom to advertise.

In many instances, we are dealing with more than threats—we are dealing with the reality of freedom lost or substantially limited.

We know that an attack on advertising freedom in any nation of the world is an attack on advertising everywhere. When the defense of that freedom fails in any country, advertising freedom is weakened everywhere. That is precisely what is occurring today at an alarming rate.

Protecting the Freedom to Advertise

My responsibility in the United States is to carry out the mission of the tripartite American Advertising Federation to protect the freedom to advertise legal products and services truthfully.

In today's environment in the U.S. and around the world that is an increasingly difficult task—especially for unpopular and disfavored product categories such as tobacco and alcohol.

Truthful commercial speech, advertising, has been constitutionally protected by the U.S. Supreme Court since 1976.

Nevertheless, critics argue that the harmful aspects of tobacco and alcohol use or abuse should deprive their advertising, however truthful, of the same legal status of other types of advertising. They point to actions reflecting this view in other parts of the world.

From Howard H. Bell's speech to the Latin American Congress of the International Advertising Association, Fall 1991. Reprinted from *Editor and Publisher*, December 14, 1991. Reprinted with the author's permission.

Some anti-tobacco legislators in the U.S. Congress have sought to avoid a possible direct collision with advertising's constitutionally protected freedom by turning away from proposed outright bans to content control of tobacco advertising itself. . . .

A Dangerous Precedent

We consider [attempts to control advertising] to be a blatant act of censorship, the effect of which is to make such advertising virtually impossible.

In fact, such content control results in a de facto ban of all such advertising, and it sets a dangerous precedent for advertising of all product categories. It clearly violates the free speech protection afforded advertising by our highest court.

Despite its obvious flaws, the proponents of such content restrictions are not deterred, nor are they interested in understanding facts about the advertising process, how it works and how it does not work. . . .

If tobacco advertising is number one on the legislative hit list around the world, alcohol advertising is not far behind.

In the U.S. Congress there is legislation pending in both the House and Senate to mandate rotating health and safety warning messages in all alcohol beverage advertising.

Again, we have an attempt to interfere with the content of advertising

> *"Attacks on alcohol advertising . . . are based on the false premise that there is a cause-and-effect relationship between advertising and the use or abuse of such products."*

despite the fact that such information is now contained on the labels. However, many critics and lawmakers in the U.S. confuse labeling and advertising to our detriment.

Clearly, if warning messages are required in broadcast ads, it would make such advertising in limited-time segments virtually unworkable.

Once again a de facto ban on certain kinds of advertising could be the result, however unintended.

There are also proposals to restrict advertising and promotion of alcohol beverages on college campuses, and to phase out the tax deduction for alcohol advertising, as proposed for tobacco advertising.

Like the case of tobacco advertising, individual states in the U.S. also are targeting alcohol advertising, including outdoor, for restrictions.

These attacks on alcohol advertising, as on tobacco, are based on the false premise that there is a cause-and-effect relationship between advertising and the use or abuse of such products.

There is a special concern expressed for our young people in the use of both alcohol and tobacco—all of us share that concern, but . . . young people are category non-users and are not targeted in the advertising.

At the time of the tobacco advertising ban in Australia in 1990, its proponents said this was their only target. Now they are calling for a ban on alcohol advertising. France has now passed a ban on alcohol advertising, and it includes sponsorship of events.

The single European market is designed to promote free and open competition among member countries comprising over 320 million

> *"Young people are . . . not targeted in the advertising."*

people. Actually, many of the proposals of the European Commission in Brussels may inhibit free market competition by restricting advertising which is so essential to that competition.

The European Commission has issued a directive adopted by the European Parliament to ban all tobacco advertising. The commission is considering a similar directive for alcohol advertising. . . .

A Smaller World

The list of issues impacting the freedom to advertise is endless, with new proposals in one country rapidly spreading to others. In this era of advanced worldwide communications, our global village is shrinking further while the problems we share are expanding. . . .

This is not a time for Europe to impose restrictions on the very process that contributes to economic stability and prosperity.

This is not a time for the rest of us to sit back and let it happen.

There are many individual associations and organizations concerned about global restrictions on the freedom to advertise.

Certainly the IAA [International Advertising Association] is a major player in this arena, albeit often lacking in the financial resources and support it deserves to carry out its mission.

What is not happening is coordination among all the groups that have a stake in advertising freedom around the world.

A conference of the leaders of such groups under the auspices of the IAA would be desirable. It would provide a forum in which to assess the current global regulatory climate for advertising, and provide an opportunity to consider strategies and initiatives that could be undertaken jointly to respond positively. . . .

Self-regulation is another area where coordination of activity is critical. The IAA reports in this area are excellent and the move toward a Pan European self-regulatory mechanism as an alternative to EC regulation is encouraging. To the extent that we can develop, promote, and adopt international advertising standards of self-regulation, we will provide a viable alternative to directives of governments to control the advertising process.

Another positive response to advertising critics and regulators is to point out and dramatize the invaluable role of advertising in helping communities and governments solve pressing social problems.

In fact, the AAF believes that a global awards competition to honor the best of public service around the world would be an excellent vehicle to focus the spotlight on this contribution of advertising to the public good. . . .

We are not defending merely the right of advertisers to promote legal products truthfully. We are defending the right of consumers to receive information about product benefits and prices, vital information to make informed, free choice buying decisions that can contribute to a strong global economy. What could be more important to the nations of the world than that?

If we are going to be successful in defending advertising freedom around the world, we must be better organized and coordinated on a global basis.

Carla Michelotti, senior vice president at Leo Burnett and chair of the AAF legal affairs committee, speaking on this subject at the recent AAF law and business conference, said, "We, the advertising community, must start to talk to each other and work together to fight these ad ban proposals and legislation around the world. To the extent the proponents of ad bans communicate, so must we."

Chapter 4

Do Adult Children of Alcoholics Benefit from Recovery Groups?

Adult Children of Alcoholics (ACOAs): An Overview

by Daniel Goleman

About the author: *Daniel Goleman is a staff reporter for the* New York Times *daily newspaper.*

Many popular assumptions about children of alcoholics are being questioned by new research, posing a challenge to the hugely popular therapy movement directed at them and other "adult children" of problem families.

Although proponents of the movement say they have scientific support for their views, critics are unconvinced.

Childhood Experiences

The therapy is based on the idea that the childhood experiences of "adult children of alcoholics" or "ACOA's," have left them with unique emotional patterns and problems. These include, for example, feeling different from others, putting up a false front, being reluctant to stand up for themselves and failing to enjoy life as much as they would like.

But a new study has found that most people feel this way. The researchers charge that these and other basic beliefs of the ACOA movement are so vague or true of so many people that almost everyone identifies with them. In short they are so universal that they are devoid of therapeutic usefulness. These researchers say these statements, which seem more specific than they are, are similar to those used by fortunetellers or astrologers; they call them "Barnum statements," after the huckster P. T. Barnum.

Proponents of the movement concede that more research is needed on the adult children of alcoholics. But they say scientists studying the transmission of alcoholism from generation to generation have ignored the clinical experience of therapists who treat children of alcoholics.

"Only recently has there begun to be research directed by the ACOA outlook," said Dr. Claudia Black, a psychologist who is director of a treatment center for children of alcoholics in Cerritos, Calif.

The proponents cite positive results from a new study, one of the few designed specifically to test a major idea of the movement, that children of alcoholics are drawn to help partners who exploit them.

"The reason there's not yet enough research on adult children of alcoholics is that academics have focused on things like the role of genetics in alcoholism, or on the 20 percent of children of alcoholics who have the worst problems and so can be easily studied because they are in a hospital or in jail," said Dr. Black, who has written several books on the subject.

Ruse in Testing Traits

But many researchers remain skeptical. "Most of the beliefs popularized by the ACOA movement have never been tested scientifically," said Dr. Kenneth Sher, a psychologist at the University of Missouri, who is the author of *Children of Alcoholics: A Critical Appraisal of Theory and Research*, published in 1991 by the University of Chicago Press.

It was Dr. Sher, with Mary Beth Logue, a graduate student, who conducted a study to test whether basic tenets of the ACOA movement owed their appeal to their being Barnum statements. First they combed the popular literature to identify key propositions about the traits of children of alcoholics. They then used an experimental ruse to test whether those traits would be seen as better fitting themselves by 112 sons and daughters of alcoholics than by 112 men and women whose parents were not alcoholics. The participants, all college students, were recruited for what they were told was the validation of a newly developed personality test. After responding to questions in the test, the students were shown a personality profile that was purportedly based on their answers.

The profiles were actually either from popular descriptions of the traits of children of alcoholics or statements taken from previous research on the Barnum effect, such as "You have some personality weaknesses."

About two-thirds of the men and women said the descriptions fit them well, regardless of whether the statements were from the list of traits of adult children of alcoholics or from the known Barnum statements.

> *"Most of the beliefs popularized by the ACOA movement have never been tested scientifically."*

"A lot of people resonate with the popular descriptions of children of alcoholics because they are universal truths or vague enough," Dr. Sher said. But, he added, because these personality traits do not distinguish children of alcoholics from most other people, they have little use in making diagnoses or specifying what kind of treatment would be most effective.

"It's a legitimate concern that some clinical claims about adult children of alcoholics are so broad they seem to apply to everyone," said Dr. Timmen Cermak, a psychiatrist at Genesis, a San Francisco treatment center that specializes in the problems of adult children of alcoholics.

"But whenever there is a new clinical entity, like child abuse, you have to focus on the most general truths to raise public awareness; then you can start looking at the complexities," added Dr. Cermak, whose book *Evaluating and Treating Adult Children of Alcoholics* (Johnson Institute) was published in 1991.

> *"People who are children of alcoholics are vulnerable to manipulation by self-centered partners."*

"There's another way to see it," said Luvon Roberson, director of public information at the Children of Alcoholics Foundation in New York City, commenting on Dr. Sher's study. Those people who are not children of alcoholics who agree with the statements "may simply be from other kinds of dysfunctional families," she added.

One of the few direct experimental tests of concepts from the popular ACOA movement seems to support the idea that people who are children of alcoholics are vulnerable to manipulation by self-centered partners.

The study involved 48 women, half of whom had a parent who was alcoholic. This experiment also involved a ruse: the experimenter, a young man, had a confederate, a young woman who pretended to be a participant as each group of four went through the procedure.

At one point the male experimenter left the room, pretending to have to get some missing forms. While he was gone, the confederate told the group that he used to go out with her roommate. Then, for half the groups, the confederate added that the experimenter was "the neatest guy" who used to help her roommate with everything from homework to laundry. For the other half she said, instead, that the experimenter was "the biggest jerk" who "used" her roommate "for everything from doing his homework to doing the laundry."

When the experimenter returned, he claimed to need volunteers to help him on another project, and asked the women if they would be willing to help him on it. When the experimenter was described "as a jerk," daughters of alcoholics volunteered twice as much time helping him as did women who did not have an alcoholic parent.

The "Chic Neurosis"

"Frankly, I was very surprised the results were as strong as they were," said Dr. Jeff Greenberg, a psychologist at the University of Arizona, who did the study with a graduate student, Sue Lyons. Indeed, in the article reporting their study they refer to codependency, the theory that children of alcoholics are drawn to mates who share destructive traits with their own parents, as "the chic neurosis of our time." They note that the theory has been largely ignored by scientists studying children of alcoholics.

"Before we did the study I would have thought the Barnum effect explained away the whole ACOA model, but now I think there's at least a grain of truth to it," said Dr. Greenberg, who published the results in the December 1991 issue of the *Journal of Personality and Social Psychology*. . . .

Dr. Greenberg believes the study reveals in at least some children of alcoholics what the psychoanalyst Karen Horney called "morbid dependency," in which children who have had an exploitive, manipulative parent learn to get love by meeting that parent's self-centered demands. As adults they "get the same warm feelings when they meet the demands of a manipulative partner," he said.

Eliminating this "co-dependency" is a major part of the movement. In fact, critics of the movement say co-dependency plays too large a role.

"The adult children of alcoholics movement has looked to a simple construct, co-dependency, to explain everything," said Dr. Ralph Tarter, a psychologist in the psychiatry department at the University of Pittsburgh medical school, who has done extensive studies of the children of alcoholics. "It just doesn't fit with most of what we know scientifically. It's ideology, not fact."

"In our own research," he said, "we find differences between children of alcoholics and others on personality traits like aggressiveness and impulsivity in boys, but not dependency."

Genetic Theory Disputed

One widespread belief about alcoholism, that it is largely a genetic disorder, was dealt a blow by research on 356 patients in treatment for alcoholism and their twins. The study found that environmental factors are far stronger than genes in alcoholism in women, and in men who develop drinking problems in adulthood.

There was a strong genetic influence only among men who developed drinking problems before the age of 20, according to a report by Matt McGue, a psychologist at the University of Minnesota, in the February 1992 issue of *The Journal of Abnormal Psychology*. Dozens of studies have shown that this group of "early onset" alcoholics are more likely to be hyperactive, have learning problems, get in trouble with the law as teenagers and use street drugs.

Still, "most children of alcoholics end up having a good social adjustment," Dr. Tarter said. "Even these troubled children of alcoholics have few common, unifying psychological factors that set them apart from anyone else who has had a disadvantaged childhood. That's where the evidence departs from the ideology of the movement."

But Dr. Sher said children of alcoholics had greater impulsivity, rebelliousness, a propensity to take risks, low self-esteem and a tendency to depression, especially in women, according to evidence from dozens of studies reviewed by him.

ACOAs Develop Unhealthy Relationships

by John Bradshaw

About the author: *John Bradshaw is a counselor, theologian, management consultant, and public speaker. He is perhaps best known for his television series "Bradshaw On: The Family," and his book* Bradshaw On: The Family—A Revolutionary Way of Self-Discovery, *from which this viewpoint is excerpted. Bradshaw's views on dysfunctional alcoholic families are considered fundamental to understanding adult children of alcoholics.*

After 17 bitter years of long-suffering alcoholism, I put the cork in the bottle 21 years ago. In many ways the last thing I would have believed as a child was that I would become an alcoholic. I cried myself to sleep many a night because of my father's drinking and his abandonment. I lay in bed frozen with fear waiting for him to come home at night, never knowing what exactly was going to happen. I hated alcoholism and all it stood for. I obsessed about his drinking day in and day out. At 30 years old, after studying for almost 10 years to be a priest, I wound up in Austin State Hospital on a voluntary commitment for the treatment of alcoholism!

As paradoxical as it seems, *many* a child of an alcoholic becomes an alcoholic. And if they don't become an alcoholic, they marry an alcoholic or a person with some other compulsive addictive personality disorder.

This paradoxical pattern of adults who grew up in alcoholic families has focused on the truth of "families as systems" more than any other single factor. Some 10 years ago one adult child after another began to realize that there were commonalities in their lives that seemed to have less to do with them and more to do with their families of origin. Led by Robert Ackerman, Claudia Black, Sharon Wegscheider-Cruse and Janet Woititz, the Adult Children of Alcoholics (ACoA) became a movement, which at this moment is continuing to sweep the country. With the Adult Children's movement the family systems concept took a giant step forward.

During the first decade of my recovery from alcoholism, I knew nothing of the Adult Children's phenomena. I had dabbled intellectually with family systems. I had incorporated the work of Virginia Satir, Jay Haley and Ronald Laing into my adult theology classes at Palmer Episcopal Church in Houston. But I never got the connection with my own alcoholic family of origin. I thought that my addiction to excitement, my people-pleasing and approval-seeking, my overly developed sense of responsibility, my severe intimacy problems, my frantic compulsive lifestyle, my severe self-criticalness, my frozen feelings, my incessant good-guy act and my intense need to control were just personality quirks. I never dreamed that they were characteristics common to adults who as children lived in alcoholic families.

My compulsivity was a problem that was having life-damaging consequences. I was working, buying, smoking and eating compulsively. Even though I was recovering from alcoholism, I was still acutely compulsive. I was still an addict. This realization led me to seek further treatment for my still addicted personality.

It has been due to the work in chemical dependency and especially the ACoA movement that has helped me understand the nature of compul-

> **"Many** *a child of an alcoholic becomes an alcoholic."*

sivity and how it is set up in dysfunctional family systems. The fact that there are common characteristics of children who grew up in alcoholic families betrays an underlying structure of disorder. I've outlined some using the first letters of the phrase *Adult Children of Alcoholics.*

A   *Addictive, compulsive behavior or marry addicts*
D   *Delusion and denial*
U   *Unmercifully judgmental on self or others*
L   *Lack of good boundaries*
T   *Tolerate inappropriate behavior*

C   *Constantly seek approval*
H   *Have difficulty with intimate relationships*
I   *Incur guilt whenever you stand up for yourself*
L   *Lie when it would be just as easy to tell the truth*
D   *Disabled will*
R   *Reactors rather than actors*
E   *Extremely loyal to a fault*
N   *Numbed out*

O   *Over-react to changes over which you have no control*
F   *Feel different from other people*

A   *Anxious—Hypervigilant*
L   *Low self-worth and internalized SHAME*
C   *Confuse love and pity*
O   *Overly serious*

H   *Have difficulty finishing projects*
O   *Overly dependent and terrified of abandonment*
L   *Live life as victims*
I   *Intimidated by anger and personal criticism*
C   *Control madness*
S   *Super-responsible or super-irresponsible*

From this checklist it's clear that as children of alcoholics, we are not just re-acting to the drinking of the alcoholic. What we're reacting to are the relational issues, the anger, the control issues, the emotional unavailability of the addict. These traits are a response to the trauma of the abandonment and ensuing shame that occurs in alcoholic families.

For the children this shame is primarily rooted in the broken relationship with their parents. Our index of traits shows that most of the problems ACoAs have are relationship problems. These traits also give us a clue to understanding the roots of compulsivity. The World Health Organization's definition of compulsive/addictive behavior is "a pathological relationship to any mood-altering experience that has life-damaging consequences."

Common Traits

The propensity for *pathological relationships* is rooted in and set up by the parental abandonment. Let us look at our index of traits.

A. Addictive, Compulsive or Marry Addicts—You are or have been in an active compulsive/addictive pattern of behavior. You are or have been in a relationship with a compulsive/addicted person.

D. Delusion and Denial—You are in a fantasy bonded idealization of your parents. You idealize your non-addicted parent. You minimize and deny your feelings and the impact on your life and/ or your children's lives of a relationship you are in.

U. Unmercifully Judgmental on Yourself and Others

L. Lack Good Boundaries—*You* take an aspirin when your spouse has a headache. You don't know where your feelings end and others begin. You let everyone touch you or let no one touch you. Your opinion is the same as [that of] whoever you are with.

T. Tolerate Inappropriate Behavior—You guess at what normal is. In your relationships you are now tolerating what you said you would never tolerate. You believe that your childhood was more or less normal.

> *"The alcoholic family is a compulsive family."*

C. Constantly Seek Approval—You are a people-pleaser and will go to almost any lengths to have people like you. In your primary relationships, you drive others crazy with your need to know where you stand.

H. Have Difficulty with Intimate Relationships—You confuse intimacy with enmeshment and contact with conformity. You believe that if you love someone, you will both like the same things. You are attracted to destructive relationships, and are turned off by healthy, stable, caring people. You sabotage any relationship that starts to get too close.

> *"Someone compared living in an alcoholic family to living in a concentration camp."*

I. Incur Guilt When You Are Autonomous—You feel guilt whenever you stand up for yourself, act assertive and ask for what you want. You feel guilty that you are in recovery and the rest of your family is not.

L. Lie When You Could Tell the Truth—You find yourself lying for no good reason when it would be just as easy to tell the truth. Or you are just the opposite. You adhere to the letter of the truth.

D. Disabled Will—You are compulsive, impulsive, stubborn, grandiose, overly dramatic, controlling and have difficulty making decisions. You try to control what cannot be controlled.

R. Reactive Rather Than Creative—Your life is one reaction after another. You over-react—you say things that are not relevant, feel things that are disproportionate to what is going on. You spend so much time worrying and reminiscing over others' behavior, you have no time for your own.

E. Extremely Loyal to a Fault—You stay loyal even in the face of evidence to the contrary or you are loyal to no one.

N. Numbed Out—You are psychically numb. You deny your feelings. You don't know what you feel and wouldn't know how to express your feelings even if you did know.

O. Over-react to Changes Over Which You Have No Control

F. Feel Different from Others—You never feel like you really belong. You always feel self-conscious. You are secretly jealous and envious of other's seeming normalcy.

A. Anxious and Hypervigilant—You are always on guard. You have an intense level of nameless fear and catastrophic expectation. You have a feeling of impending doom. You are jumpy and easily startled. You enjoy your vacations most after they are over and you are showing the slides!

L. Low Self-worth and Internalized SHAME—You feel defective as a human being. You cover up with roles like Caretaking, Super-responsible One, Hero, Star, Heroine, The Perfect One. You are perfectionistic, controlling, power-seeking, critical and judgmental, rageful, secretly or openly contemptuous, gossipy and backbiting.

C. Confuse Love with Pity—You are attracted to weak people. You go to great lengths to help pitiful-looking people. You enter relationships with people you can fix. You mistake pity for love.

O. Overly Rigid and Serious or Just the Opposite—You are somber and rarely play and have fun. Life is problematic, rather than spontaneous. You are perfectionistic and super-responsible. Or you are irresponsible and never take things seriously enough.

H. Have Difficulty Finishing Things—You have trouble initiating action. You have trouble stopping once you've started. You never quite finished important things, like getting degrees.

O. Overly Dependent, Clinging and Terrified of Abandonment—You stay in relationships that are life-damaging, severely dysfunctional and damaging to you. You have trouble ending anything. You stay in a job that has no future. You are possessive, suspicious and cling to the relationships you are in—spouse, lover, children, friends.

L. Live Life As a Victim—You have been physically, sexually, emotionally abused. You live in a Victim Role, finding yourself victimized wherever you are. You are attracted to other victims.

I. Intimidated by Anger and Personal Criticism—You are manipulated by anger and criticism. You will go to great lengths to stop someone from being angry at you or critical of you. You will give up your needs to stop their anger or criticalness.

C. Control Madness—You fear losing control. You control by being "helpful." You feel frightened when you feel out of control. You avoid anyone or any situation where you can't be in control.

> *"Physical, sexual and emotional battering are commonplace in alcoholic families."*

S. Super-Responsible or Super-Irresponsible—You take responsibility for everything and everyone. You try to solve others' problems even when they don't ask for help. Or you take no responsibility and expect others to be responsible for you.

From this index, researchers began to see just how dysfunctional one becomes simply by living in an alcoholic family. This index helps to focus the causes for compulsive behavior.

Alcoholic and Compulsive

The alcoholic family is a compulsive family. Everyone in the system is driven by the distress caused by not being able to get his needs met. Someone compared living in an alcoholic family to living in a concentration camp. And like survivors of a concentration camp, ACoAs carry what has been compared to post-traumatic stress symptoms. In fact, if one takes a list of the disorders experienced by war veterans or any other severe trauma victims, they will find that a large number of the post-trauma symptoms match a large number of ACoA characteristics. Children who live in alcoholic families, if untreated as children, carry these characteristics of post-trauma stress into later life.

Because of the chronic distress in an alcoholic family, every person in that family attempts to adapt to the chronic stress. Each becomes hypervigilant, anxious and chronically afraid. In such an environment, it's impossible for anyone to get his basic human needs met. Each person becomes co-dependent.

The major consequence of this chronic stress is abandonment. Along with the actual physical abandonment by the alcoholic, the neglect of the child's basic needs is another form of abandonment. There is no one there for the child. There is no mirroring to affirm the child's preciousness and no one the child can depend on. If Dad's the alcoholic, Mom is addicted to

> *"The children . . . look like and talk like adults, but there is within them an insatiable little child who never got his or her needs met."*

Dad—Mom is co-dependent. She can't be there for her children's needs because she is also an addict.

As addicts, both parents are needy and shame-based. It is impossible for two needy, shame-based people to give love and model self-love.

The normal child has healthy narcissistic needs, but there is no way these needs can be met in an alcoholic family. So each child turns inward to a fantasy bond of connection with their parents (delusion and denial) and ultimately to self-indulging habits and pain killers.

A third form of abandonment comes from abuse. Alcoholic families foster every kind of abuse. Because alcohol lowers inhibitions and knocks out the rheostat between thoughts and expression, physical, sexual and emotional battering are commonplace in alcoholic families. Some estimates say that two-thirds of ACoAs are physically violated. Some 50% of incest fathers are alcoholic.

Alcoholic families are severely enmeshed. Enmeshment is another way the children are abandoned. As the alcoholic marriage becomes more entangled and entrapped, the children get caught up in the needs of both their parents, as well as the needs of the family system for wholeness and balance. Nature abhors a vacuum. When the family system is unbalanced, the children attempt to create a balance.

In my family my dad was never there. By about age 11, he was for all practical purposes gone. I was the oldest male. The system needed a husband. I became my mother's emotional husband (Surrogate Spouse). My mom did not decide this, the system demanded it. I also became my brother's "Little Parent" since the system needed fathering. At 13 I was giving him an allowance.

The Scapegoat and the Lost Child

In another family I worked with as the drinking husband's alcoholism intensified, the oldest daughter became Mom's Scapegoat. Mom had been pregnant with her at the time of her marriage. In fact, she was the reason Mom and Dad got married. As Mom realized Dad was an irresponsible alcoholic, she turned her anger onto the girl child.

Another child was not planned. He was the accidental third child in a very dysfunctional marriage. He felt the emotional abandonment in the womb. He became a "Lost Child" in the family. Literally the parental message he got was "Get lost, child, we can't handle another child."

Parental Inconsistency

In alcoholic families the discipline is modeled by *unself*-disciplined disciplinarians. The rules of the poisonous pedagogy offer justification for a lot of the so-called discipline. Very little of it is really discipline. It comes out of the parents' irritation and rage about their own life. Most of the time it has nothing to do with the child, i.e., it doesn't come from his behavior or help the child improve. Punishment occurs frequently and is usually inconsistent. The parents model this inconsistency.

What all this adds up to is that the children, who need their parents' time, attention and direction for at least 15 years, do not get it. They are abandoned. Abandonment sets up compulsivity. Since the children need their parents all the time, and since they do not get their needs met, they grow up with a cup that has a hole in it. They grow up to have adult bodies. They look like and talk like adults, but there is within them an insatiable little child who never got his or her needs met. This hole in the soul is the fuel that drives the compulsivity. The person looks for more and more love, attention, praise, booze, money, etc.

The drivenness comes from the emptiness. And since one cannot be a child again and cannot go back and have a mom or a dad, the needs cannot be filled *as a child*. They *can* be dealt with as they are recycled in adult life. But they can only be dealt with *as an adult*.

ACOAs Suffer Emotional Problems

by William H. Crisman

About the author: *William H. Crisman is an ex-priest and psychotherapist who works with families of alcoholics in Tacoma Washington.*

I teach an eleven-week course on Adult Children of Alcoholics (ACOA). Ostensibly, the students who take the class do so as part of their training to become counselors and therapists, but what meets the eye is not all there is. There's a truism around Twelve-Step recovery meetings that nobody, absolutely nobody, comes to a meeting by accident. The same holds true for ACOA classes. Simply by counting raised hands, I've found out that over 90 percent of my students are adult children from alcoholic or otherwise dysfunctional families.

There are actually good, logical reasons for this, which will become clear as we continue. What's more important for me to point out here, however, is the kind of presumptions I can make as a teacher when I face these students. Every quarter, even though the faces and names change, it seems as if the people, the persons behind the faces, are the same.

ACOAs Dismiss Their Problematic Childhoods

And this is what I can presume: These are a group of tough survivors, master tacticians and practitioners of the arts of manipulation, avoidance, and strategic retreat. To a person, they will be far more adept at living in the world of the intellect, of their heads, than that of the gut and feelings. The majority of them will be "people pleasers" so attuned to me as an authority figure that they'll have learned to dance to any tune I might wish to play—long before I even realize I've a song in the offing. They will intuit any weakness or insecurity in me with uncanny accuracy. A few of them will be angry, raw, and ready to debate anything at the drop of a hat. A couple of others will be so skillful at camouflage and blending in that I'll never be able to learn their names. Some will be irresistibly cute, and others will have such an air of strength and security about them that my first intuitive response (I, who am no slouch at being a very big Big Daddy myself) will be to feel like a little boy again when I'm around them. Finally, I can presume that each one of those survivors, in his or her own way, will be convinced, no matter what kind of hell his childhood might have been, that it wasn't really all that bad. "After all, I only did what I needed to do to get through it, and I *did* survive . . . didn't I?"

> *"Most of us probably find ourselves relating in friendship and love with chemical abusers, codependents, and other ACOAs."*

The infallible sign that you've got a chemical abuser on your hands is the claim "I can handle my drugs." The equally infallible byword of ACOAs is "It really wasn't that bad." So, for the whole first half of the course I deliberately choose to challenge my students with the proposition that it *was* that bad—and worse. I tell them I'm going to draw stark pictures, and use shocking stories, and employ the most pointed logic I can devise to make that point. I tell them I intend to offer not only a short, intellectual education about what happens in the families of abusers, but an emotional one as well. I tell them I intend to get a rise out of them (anger, fear, revulsion, or resistance), and when I do, I shall consider that I've done my job. And what's more, I tell them that if they find themselves going through emotional upheaval of some sort as the course progresses, they're responsible for their own feelings; I'm not.

The class proceeds, and the pressure begins to grow. Usually, about the fifth or sixth week of the session, when we begin to explore the kinds of sexual battering children of alcoholic families have to endure, all hell breaks loose. (Talking about sex can do that.) Some cry, one or two might disappear permanently from class, and invariably I will be attacked for the inadequacy of the approach I'm employing to show why such abuse almost inevitably happens in the families of the chemically dependent.

All of a sudden, the name of the game is "uproar," yet the students don't even know they're in uproar to avoid their memories and their pain.

This academic mayhem only underscores the point I'm raising with them. I plainly told them what I was going to do before I did it; I reminded them of what I was doing as I did it; and I explained what had happened after I'd done it. And yet . . . uproar. Inescapably, they have become *emotionally* aware of the intense power of their childhood programming and are no longer able to examine their defenses dispassionately or academically. All of a sudden, it's that bad . . . again. . . .

Stifling Emotions

Existential psychologists tell us there are two kinds of fear, a healthy one that energizes us for self-protection and a "neurotic" kind that paralyzes us in the

153

face of danger. A healthy person walking down a jungle path can take off like a world-class sprinter when he rounds a bend and comes face-to-face with a hungry tiger. But the neurotic who chances upon the same tiger is so rooted in place by his fear that he's likely to go catatonic (literally unable to run, unable to distance himself) as the cat ambles up to begin munching. Blandly put, he has no ability to set boundaries and thus protect himself.

We ACOAs tend to be case studies in the latter category of fear. In childhood, I got the message, from my addictive stepfather, "Shut up, kid, or you'll get something to cry about!" I learned quickly that he meant what he said, and so, equally as quickly, honed my ability to stifle my tears and fear. Since even something so minor as a pouty look got the same parental reaction, I soon learned that no expression whatsoever of grief or pain was allowable. "Stuffing it" became my automatic reaction and practice.

Likewise for laughter: Addicts and alcoholics are paranoid; they "know" whom their children are laughing at. So anything louder than a muted giggle didn't "wash" during childhood: It was too dangerous.

It's obscene enough that parents would disallow their children the opportunity to experience and express their feelings at any time, but the far uglier travesty was that they forced us to begin and to practice emotional

> *"The closer we ACOAs get to those we come to like and love, the more we find ourselves becoming emotionally unavailable and defensed."*

muteness habitually, as a lifestyle. In short order, most of us became self-policing. Masters as we are of the emotional preemptive strike, we learned to disallow ourselves the feeling and expression of those emotions Mommy and Daddy didn't like. That way, we not only pleased them but also beat them at their own game by denying them the chance to get angry at us. . . .

Adult Relationships

As adults, most of us probably find ourselves relating in friendship and love with chemical abusers, codependents, and other ACOAs. Popular myth to the contrary, emotional "like" is attracted to emotional "like," because we most easily and naturally relate to the kind of people with whom we have been trained to relate, namely the members of the first community to which we belonged, our family. That fact strands us in a fascinating emotional pickle: The closer we ACOAs get to those we come to like and love, the more we find ourselves becoming emotionally unavailable and defensed.

To survive in their families, they had to become so paranoid, so alert to others, that they became almost able to read their parents' minds. So did we. ACOAs are hypersensitive: We can scope out a blow-up three days ahead of time; we have a sixth sense for danger and threat. The more vulnerable we were to somebody—Mommy and Daddy, for example—the more attuned to and paranoid about their moods we had to be.

But for all of that, mind reading remains an "almost" rather than an accomplished skill. We're good at it, but we're not divine; we can't do it perfectly all of the time. Besides, this kind of paranoia is like the arms race: The better you become at sniffing me out and deciphering the defenses I've deployed around my feelings, the more sophisticated I'm going to get at blotting out the traces of my emotional hiding places. It's a programmed-in, progressive, automatic process. Being vulnerable just isn't an acceptable option; experience has taught me it's too dangerous.

Between a Rock and a Hard Place

The consequences of this emotional "two-step" to a relationship are murderous. If those we love can't experience where we hurt, or why we laugh, or what words scrape our feelings raw, how can they know how to care for or love us? How can they know our boundaries or our limits? And since they are in the same boat, how can we know theirs?

Even more, if we have become so skilled at emotional nonexpression, how can we know our own boundaries and limits? . . .

Healthy persons (I think there are a few) don't need to rationalize in order to give themselves permission to get angry when they're trespassed upon, nor do they need much intellectual processing before they run from a hungry tiger on the jungle trail.

> *"For us ACOAs sex gets subordinated to survival."*

But we ACOAs do. We hear childhood admonitions like "You shouldn't feel that way," and "Don't get angry with me, young lady!," and "Quit sniffling and grow up!," and "Big boys don't cry!"

Consequently, we learned to live in our heads because our hearts were declared off-limits. In our childhoods, all we could call our own were the fantasies and rationalizations we nurtured and protected in our secret minds. And to the extent we made our brains into our homes, we neither laugh nor cry, we can't celebrate or grieve, we experience neither sorrow nor joy. We were so repressed that we became depressed, without feeling. We know how to figure things out, but we've no feel for where we end and the other begins; we have no feeling for life. . . .

Sexual Power Plays

If we talk of feelings and joy and if we talk about grief, we have to talk of love and sex. . . .

As with every other aspect of our lives, for us ACOAs sex gets subordinated to survival. It could not be otherwise. The core of our childhood trauma had to do with the betrayal of love, trust, vulnerability, and intimacy. Because the lesson of that betrayal happened so early in our lives, and because it struck so deeply to the emotional root of our beings, we tend to live with the very real expectation that anyone who professes love for us will betray us as Mommy and Daddy did. Worse, since Mommy and Daddy did the betraying and since Mommy and Daddy can't do any wrong, we expect and believe that people who love us *should* betray us. Mommy and Daddy did it that way, so, later in our lives, if somebody were to love us and yet *not* betray us, we'd have the very real suspicion their love was phony. And there's a final wicked twist: Since

> *"We tend to live with the very real expectation that anyone who professes love for us will betray us as Mommy and Daddy did."*

Mommy and Daddy are our unavoidable role models (even if we hate their guts), we've probably become expert at "loving by abandoning," too.

Thus, in the erotic arena, we tend to play the game of sex as Mommy and Daddy played the game of love with us. We had no choice but to love them and be dominated by them; what they wanted set the ground rules. We got love and attention by being pleasing to them, by manipulating them in the ways they wanted to be manipulated. We learned to set up situation after situation in such a way that they had no choice but to give us the kind of attention we wanted from them, for we did our best to leave them no choice but to be pleased with us. In short, we learned how to seduce. If they wanted cute, we gave them cute. If being "adult" got us love, we somehow grew into maturity before we were four.

Later on, when we actually do grow up and fall in love, we just transfer all those well-oiled, people-pleasing, manipulative, seductive skills. If our beloved ones want tender and sensitive, they get romanced to a *T*. If they want earthy, they get the best of our sexual technique. And it's all aimed toward one goal: to so entrap and enmesh them that they'll never be able to even think of letting go.

Since those beloved others are probably as ACOA as we, they're most likely barraging us with all their seductive skills at the same time. It can get to be quite a battle of one-upmanship, and the name of the game quickly transmutes from "Loving" to "Winning."

Loving Like Mom and Dad

The key to understanding it all is the realization that both parties in this romantic dance are so intent, so focused, on possession and control of the other that they lose ownership of themselves. Each has to become dominated by the other just as they were dominated by Mommy and Daddy—that's the *only* way to love and be loved, remember. When you look at a bare-bones outline of the situation, the self-contradictory insanity of it all comes clear: We have to be so controlling in our seductions that they have no choice but to love us as we want to be loved; yet somehow they have to be so powerful that they dominate us totally enough to do whatever they want, else we cannot believe in their love. Freud once called the process of falling in love a ". . . temporary psychosis," but this game is ridiculous. . . .

There's another set of factors that goes into our programming about what it means to love, and it's even more depressing. Today, I am willing to make the flat assertion that there is no such thing as an ACOA who has not been sexually abused.

The logic here is simple and unavoidable. It is impossible for chemically dependent parents and their spouses to be "present" to their children's emotional development. Sexuality is an emotional phenomenon, and so here (as in all other areas of their emotional lives) the children start on the bottom—and it goes downhill from there.

Usually, most parents, even when drunk and depressed, can see the unavoidable. They can see a boy's first crop of whiskers and hear his cracking, deepening voice. They can see that their daughter is starting to develop breasts. But what's happening beneath the child's surface—the urges, feelings, questions, attractions, confusions—that's a different story. These mommies and daddies can give to their children's feeling lives no more than they can offer to their own, chemical poisoning and emotional shutdown.

Notice here that we haven't even dug into the all-too-frequent cases of incest, rape, and intended sexual shaming that so many children from chemically abusive families suffer.

Possession and Abuse

You see, the games of sex and love can be—indeed, should be—wonderful to play. As ACOAs, however, we have little choice but to play by the only rules we know, surviving and winning by giving no quarter. Instead of cherishing and loving, we learned to possess and abuse. Since we cannot respect ourselves, there's little chance we can respect another—even our beloved.

Equally, if we cannot love ourselves and healthily celebrate our sexuality, there's no way for us to tell or signal a partner about our truest sexual drives, sensitivities, and boundaries. Inevitably, we practice our sexual/love lives as we do the other dimensions of our lives. We never ask what our partner needs . . . that would expose our vulnerability (or our stupidity). We continue to "hope against hope" . . . because everybody knows that eventually Prince Charming will show up. We devote ourselves completely to making our partner's life work . . . because we have no value if it doesn't. We fantasize the excitement of a one-night stand into the stuff of white picket fences and fiftieth wedding anniversaries . . . because, God forbid, we must never see ourselves as human, or lusty, or anything but the embodiment of the most ideal of moral values. . . .

> *"There is no such thing as an ACOA who has not been sexually abused."*

Because we are programmed to believe, think, and behave in ACOA ways—

that is, be people of denial—we do excellently at survival and horribly at life. When it comes to simple living, simply being ourselves, we are guaranteed failures because they stole from us our abilities to laugh and cry and be compassionate. We are bound to "screw it up"—to be, as Alva delicately puts it, "Lying, cheating SOBs with no self-respect."

Right now, you may be thinking, He's trying to duck responsibility for his own behavior, or He's trying to excuse his weakness. (In all honesty, there's probably even a corner of my well-tuned alcoholic/codependent/ACOA, guilt-programmed brain that's whispering the same thing.) But, "'Tain't so." Being responsible means exactly what the word says, "able to respond." More, if that "ability to respond" is going to have any worth to our lives, it must be able to distinguish between truth and falsehood.

Living Out Somebody Else's Anger

Only when I own my truth that I am a drunk can I stop being victimized by my alcoholism; only when I do my own truth can I stop victimizing others by my chemical abuse. The same is true for my codependency and ACOA patterns. The key to being genuinely responsible is the discovery and acceptance—ownership of the *facts* of my life. Nothing else works.

> *"We ACOAs live a lifestyle that's 'shame-based.'"*

And what is my "ACOA truth" that I need to see and accept if I'm going to be responsible? Just this: I am a failure at life, but I didn't program myself. I may have been following the flow of my ACOA belief system of denial for years now, always setting myself up to be a victim, abusing and victimizing others, being addicted to my role, manipulating and conning my way through life. And, as I become aware of what I'm doing, I may find I've much to grieve and make amends for. I may have many tears to cry over it all. But (and this "but" makes all the difference), those tears will be hypocritical and ultimately empty if I do not come to know that the first one for whom I need to cry is me. I must grieve for the child I was, that child who had to choose as he did and become what he was told to be . . . or die.

There's a corollary that follows from all of this—about the grandiosity of ACOA egos and their guilt. You see, if I'm guilty of all that, I must be wonderfully powerful and important. If I'm that guilty, I'm that special (of course, there's nothing an ignored, abandoned child longs for more than someday, somehow to become "that special" to someone—anyone). It would be comical if it weren't so tragic. The guiltier I feel, the less I esteem myself; but also, the guiltier I feel, the more powerful, important, and special I can see myself to be, the bigger ego I can have. It's a dilemma, but the odds are I'll choose specialness over self-esteem any day. I don't know how to do otherwise.

The next facet of ACOA guilt I want to discuss is a doozy. The guiltier I feel about myself, the more I will blame others. We do to others what we're already doing to ourselves. That's the human way.

And the opposite is true: If I am being accepting and compassionate toward others, it can only be because I am being accepting and compassionate toward myself first. (What Christ told us in the Great Commandment of Love, "Love the Lord, your God, with all your heart . . . and your neighbor *as yourself*," was much less a command to change than a description of how we humans already do our humanity.)

A Shame-Based Life

John Bradshaw has a term for it; he says we ACOAs live a lifestyle that's "shame-based." What else could children believe when they got the message from Mommy and Daddy that they were worth only being ignored or battered? Since the belief was instilled so early in our lives, it underlies almost all we think and do and feel; it's the deepest "riverbed" guiding our course.

But, inevitably, if I constantly sit in judgment on myself, I have no choice except to do the same for everyone else. We ACOAs are infamous for our perfectionism and resentments, for our tendency ". . . not to get mad but to get even." Even those of us who play caretaker and Hero do that: Implicitly and explicitly, we set standards and impose expectations that allow nothing less than perfection in ourselves and others. Woe betide our friends or ourselves if those standards and expectations are not met! We keep them in their place with explosions, abandonment, and passive-aggressive stabs in the back; ourselves we punish with depression, even more impossible demands, and gut-corroding guilt.

G. K. Chesterton was a recovering alcoholic who possessed one attribute that's absolutely anathema to chemical dependents, codependents, and ACOAs still into the practice of their diseases: a sense of humor about himself. He loved to take ordinary sayings and turn them inside out so that their wisdom spoke once again with freshness. One of his epigrams *always* hits "emotional pay dirt," especially in ACOAs: "If it's worth doing, it's worth doing poorly." When I drop that line in group-therapy sessions, the explosion is guaranteed. That it even "might" be okay for a human being *not* to do anything per-

> *"We ACOAs are infamous for our perfectionism and resentments."*

fectly is a possibility anyone driven by ACOA demons finds awful to contemplate. Yet Chesterton's logic is impeccable: What's better, to live poorly or not to live; to make love poorly or not to love at all; to see the beauty of this world dimly, or not to see at all? The laugh's on us because, in our guilt and shame, about ourselves we cannot smile at all—or be gentle in the smallest way.

Recovery Groups Can Help Adult Children of Alcoholics

by Lily Collet

About the author: *Lily Collet is the pseudonym of a Mill Valley, California, writer whose work has appeared in the* New Yorker, Mother Jones, *and the* Washington Post, *among other publications.*

My Father's drinking began in the brownstone college town to which he returned in 1944, after a shell exploded above his foxhole in Italy. "There were probably about a dozen of us, all wounded veterans," he wrote to me, four years ago, in his spidery hand, on six sheets of legal paper, documenting a lifetime of heavy drinking but rejecting the label I'd just found for him: *alcoholic.* "We regularly went to a club in the evenings and drank steadily for a couple of hours, perhaps into the evening, perhaps late into poker games that lasted to breakfast time. There was one awful morning that I woke up totally disoriented, not merely as to time or place, but as to who in fact I was."

He was writing in response to a letter from me that recalled our family's unhappiest years and pleaded with him to join Alcoholics Anonymous. "On the whole, I resist the interpretation that things in the family began to go wrong because of booze," he replied. "My memory is that I became insanely ambitious for you and let the love go out of our relationship—prior to, and simultaneous with, beginning to drink more regularly. While it did not originate the problem, it sure as hell could not have helped. . . . I know that booze is not the central issue, and I am going to lick it."

Fury at the Alcholic

I put down the letter in a fury and stared out the window. For years I'd lived with a sense that I had failed my father. Now the tables were turned: he was the one on the hot seat. His letter had left out the worst things—the under-the-influence interrogations at the dinner table, the time he visited my mother in the hospital and was so drunk that he pissed in the bedside chair. After years of a blind suffering I could not name, I had an explanation and I did not plan to lose it in subtle distinctions.

The year was 1985. I had never before thought of my father as *alcoholic*. But a new psychological label had become a social movement and stampeded into the national consciousness. It was the skeleton key to my family closet, an Archimedean leverage point from which I planned to

> *"Children of alcoholics learn not to trust, not to think, not to feel."*

move my whole world. My pain was no longer my fault, or even my father's—it was the fault of a "family disease" that had infected and affected us all.

No matter that no therapist had given me permission to define myself as an Adult Child of an Alcoholic, or that there was no such diagnosis in the DSM-III. No matter that some theorists were bemoaning the return of "disease" as a metaphor for soul-pain, or that many family therapists would have questioned the centrality of alcohol in our family's unhappiness. After all, I was part of a generation that had been questioning authority since the Vietnam War.

What mattered more was that newspaper articles and a few women therapists with little standing in any psychological establishment—psychoanalyst Alice Miller and alcoholism counselors Claudia Black and Janet Woititz—were speaking truths about my childhood that I'd never heard from "anointed" therapists steeped in Freudian drive theory, Transactional Analysis, Reichian therapy, or Ericksonian hypnosis. I was part of a lay movement and a consumer revolt against the "experts" to whom our parents had given so much power.

A Generation of Drinkers

We members of the baby boom weren't the first generation to grow up with alcoholism, but we were the first to transform a private and shameful history into a huge grass-roots movement and a therapeutic and literary market. We were primed for it in the '50s and early '60s, the era of Old Fashioneds, cocktail parties, and the suburban Daddy who drank his way home on the train. "The fathers of the baby boomers were members of a 'wet' generation for whom drinking was a symbol of generational rebellion," said Robin Room of the Alcohol Research Group at the University of California at Berkeley, pointing to the influence of the hard-drinking "Lost Generation" of writers, heavy wartime drinking, and the prosperity of postwar America.

Nobody talked about "children of alcoholics" then—just as nobody talked about incest, child abuse, domestic violence, or post-traumatic stress disorder. When I was 12, my best friend Janet was a little adult who cooked her meals out of cans. Her mother once "fell asleep" on the couch with a cigarette, started a fire, and was inexplicably angry when Janet told about it at show-and-tell. At our house, nothing seemed so obviously amiss. Yet my father seemed to fade away, while my mother grew anxious, lonely, and larger-than-life. I never did my homework, my middle brother wet his bed until he went to boarding school, my youngest brother—who is now a heavy drinker—developed asthma, would not eat, and tormented our Siamese cat.

In the early '60s, our worried parents packed the family off to the respected Judge Baker Guidance Center in Boston; my brother played checkers with his therapist and my parents were told not to let us kids crawl in bed with them on Sunday mornings. Nobody even raised the question of my father's quietly increasing drinking. Nobody gave us the tools to think of him as alcoholic, or even to see his private relationship with alcohol as part of our family dynamics.

For years after I left home, my scattered worries about my father's drinking lay jumbled in some emotional back closet. The first light went on in 1977, when my first boyfriend returned to town from his isolated homestead in the tropics. I had always known that his mother was alcoholic, but now I discovered what it had done to him. When we were kids, it seemed his crazy family had simply made him stronger. He had gotten into Harvard while raising three younger siblings and ferrying his suicidal, drunken mother to psychiatric hospitals and emergency rooms. At 30, his hidden wounds were surfacing. He spent weeks playing Pachelbel on my phonograph, going to Alateen meetings for teenage children of alcoholics, and crying.

> *"ACOAs are like the army of soldiers that sprang up overnight in the old myth."*

The second light went on in 1983, at my bridesmaids' dinner. I looked at the beautiful faces around me in the candle light: Susan, an elegant magazine writer sometimes paralyzed with self-doubt; Lisa, a workaholic graphic designer; Adrianne, a technical writer with a young baby, abandoned by a man in A.A. who was as old as her alcoholic father had been when he died; Sara, passionately involved with a series of emotionally abusive men. We all confessed we had mothers or fathers with drinking problems.

A Group for Listening

Two years later, I found myself on my way to the Monday Night Meeting for Adult Children of Alcoholics, sponsored by Al-Anon. We met in a Methodist church basement on the seedy fringe of San Francisco's Castro district. It was a day-care center during the day, and when the big chairs were taken, we sat in concentric circles on tiny wooden toddlers' chairs with our knees up. There were usually more than a hundred of us, mostly baby-boom age and mostly white. There were business suits, T-shirts and jeans, and sometimes a fresh-faced young girl with a black-and-white mohawk and a scorpion tattooed on her wrist. There, surrounded by children's drawings and alphabet cards, we read aloud the 12 Steps of Alcoholics Anonymous.

Every week a volunteer spoke for 10 minutes, following a simple format: "what it was like" growing up; what grown-up crisis brought him or her into "the program," and "what it's like now," after "working the Steps." Then the meeting would be thrown open to the floor. There was no therapist and no boss. The meeting was free—although most of us put a dollar in the basket. We identified ourselves by our first names only, and didn't mention our jobs or outside status symbols. "Crosstalk"—commenting or giving advice—was forbidden.

> *"The Adult Children are angry—and many are angrier at anxious and angry non-alcoholic mothers than they are with their warm, alcoholic fathers."*

We listened to everyone. An ex-junkie, ex-con, ex-hustler told us one night that he'd been conceived in a barn and spent his childhood sleeping in bathtubs in abandoned buildings. Now he worked in an ice cream parlor and went to Narcotics Anonymous and Al-Anon meetings. "I'm practicing abstinence from my family," he said.

The details of the stories changed, but not the underlying feelings of denial and shame expressed, often for the first time. One woman used to rip the American Airlines labels off her father's luggage because she was afraid someone might think the AA stood for Alcoholics Anonymous. Her father, a successful businessman, passed out one night in a restaurant with his face in a plate of spaghetti. A huge table full of relatives went on as though nothing had happened. The woman, then 10 years old and afraid her father would suffocate, walked over with a studied casualness, lifted his head, wiped off his face, and leaned him back in his chair. "I learned that if nobody was willing to face up to the fact that a man's head was in the spaghetti, then the truth must be dangerous," she said. "I've since learned that the truth doesn't kill. Silence kills."

The ritual form of the meeting, from the opening welcome to the closing circle where we all held hands, came from Al-Anon, the group founded in 1951 by wives of alcoholics. But the content of the people's sharings, I later learned, was quite different. "Regular" Al-Anon was more inspirational, more peaceful, and less psychological than our Monday Night Meeting. Its members were more likely to share little successes—accounts of relinquishing control to a "higher power," or of "lovingly detaching" from the alcoholics in their lives. In "regular" Al-Anon, beginners were subtly encouraged, by example, to stop ventilating rage and grief within two or three months. Instead, they listened to old-timers share, learned to take responsibility for making their own lives happier, and found sponsors (mentors) to help them "work the 12 Steps" in a systematic way.

Memories, Not Victories

In our ACOA group, the process of "working the Steps" took much longer, and sometimes never happened at all. Some old-timers spoke of detachment, and hanging up nicely on drunken 3 A.M. calls. But many of us shared memories of the past, not victories of the present. For my first two years I cried once during almost every meeting. I betrayed the family secrets: I told of being hit so hard that my father left red palm prints on my thighs; I admitted I had been depressed for years.

What little theory we had was a melange of self-help literature, the 12 Steps, and the facts of our own lives. We heard "children of alcoholics learn not to trust, not to think, and not to feel." We used Al-Anon slogans: "'No' is a complete sentence," and "There are no victims, only volunteers." We heard the "three C's"—"you didn't cause it, you couldn't cure it, and you couldn't control it," and the "three A's"—"awareness, acceptance, *then* action." In telling their life stories, people used concepts borrowed from psychoanalyst Alice Miller and spoke of "re-parenting the inner child," and trying to break out of cycles of isolation and over-responsibility. It was safe to recall almost any victimization of childhood: incest, beating, pulling your unconscious brother in out of the snow. It was safe to admit having done almost anything in adulthood: working in the sex industry, attempting suicide, falling in love with addicts and alcoholics, staying for years in jobs you hated. It was less easy to do what Al-Anon pamphlets encouraged—to describe little victories of "experience, strength, and hope" and to "keep the focus on ourselves," rather than blaming our alcoholic relatives or trying to figure out why they did what they did.

A Tidal Wave of ACOAs

As we psychologically oriented baby-boomers poured into Al-Anon in the early 1980's, one or two new meetings for ACOAs were registered at Al-Anon headquarters in New York every day. This tidal wave of newcomers, new to the traditions of Al-Anon, shook—and continues to shake—the organization. "Al-Anon is trying to stay very firm," said an anonymous spokeswoman at the headquarters recently. "All of a sudden, your ground gets shook up and I'm hoping everybody is patient enough."

The Adult Children are angry—and many are angrier at anxious and angry non-alcoholic mothers than they are with their warm, alcoholic fathers. "When I was first in Al-Anon, I was angry, too, and expressing it is important," said the Al-Anon spokeswoman, herself both the child and the spouse of alcoholics. "But later I realized that harboring it wasn't any good for me, and things smoothed out."

> *"The ACOA movement's poignant insights have literally struck home for some therapists."*

We ACOAs are like the army of soldiers that sprang up overnight in the old myth. The tremors from this army are being felt in therapists' offices across the country. A spiritually based lay movement is challenging a secular, psychological priesthood. "It's a grass-roots movement that has revolutionized mental health and nobody's adjusted to it," said Stephanie Brown, the founder of the Stanford Alcohol Clinic, and the author of a widely respected academic book on treating adult children of alcoholics. "Patients are diagnosing themselves, and saying they want a treatment designed for them. They're often more informed than the therapists. It's terrorizing both the chemical dependency and the mental health fields, because it reveals big holes in theory and practice in both worlds. The chemical dependency counselors have no theory or practice of long-term development; the rest of the mental health field is splintered and overspecialized and often unaware of the special dynamics of chemical dependency. There's no longer any single theory or treatment that will do the trick."

An Influential Movement

Like a 900-pound gorilla, the ACOA movement cannot be ignored, and it is forcing the creating of bridges: between individual and family therapy; between family therapists and chemical dependency counselors; between MFCCs [Marriage, Family, and Child counselors] and LCSWs [Licensed Clinical Social Workers]; between once anti-psychological 12-Steppers and often anti-spiritual psychologists.

Some principles of family therapy have been brought to a mass audience, and at the same time the ACOA movement's poignant insights have literally struck home for some therapists. "Suddenly I had a language," said a family therapist who had grown up in a home where Daddy passed out under the Christmas tree. She had never thought of him as alcoholic until she attended an experiential workshop on alcoholic family roles in 1976. "In a funny way, learning I had lived with alcoholism gave me a perspective on myself that allowed me to feel less sick," she said.

> *"Like a 900-pound gorilla, the ACOA movement cannot be ignored."*

Some therapists have responded with caution, hostility, or even envy. Others—of widely ranging competence and experience—have jumped on the bandwagon advertising themselves as ACOA specialists. And a growing group have found a middle ground: they encourage clients to join 12-step programs and are fashioning ways for the two forms of healing to support each other.

Jo-Ann Krestan, a family therapist based in Brunswick, Maine, and coauthor, with Claudia Bepko, of *The Responsibility Trap*, believes that 12-Step groups provide a sense of mutual helping that therapy can't. "Shame has to be healed, not in isolation, but in community," she said. "And therapy is not about mutuality. No matter how egalitarian you are, the therapist has the power." Bepko added that the emotional work encouraged by the ACOA movement must often be done before Adult Children can take on more cognitive forms of therapy. Bepko, trained as a Bowen-style family therapist, found that Adult Children often do not respond well at first to the Bowen approach's non-emotional coaching to change family patterns of interaction. "When people begin to realize they have been affected by alcoholism, they go through a period of being very angry, feeling a lot of grief and experiencing themselves as victims," she said. "Often it's not possible to do the coaching until they have a chance to sit with those feelings, feel them, and work them through. Then they're ready to move to a more cognitive level and change some of the family patterns and dynamics."

Some family therapists—like psychiatrist David Berenson of Mill Valley, California—live with a little cognitive dissonance. "The systems theorist part of me doesn't like the labelling, but the clinician within me finds it's very helpful to send people to a program where they can relate to people's stories," said Berenson, who routinely recommends clients to 12-Step programs if they qualify. "The label can be very helpful as a way to begin experiencing emotions—and then later it's necessary to take the label off. And then there's the practical issue," he said with a smile. "I like to combine 12-Step programs and therapy, but the truth is, it cuts down on the number of therapy sessions. Nevertheless, I prefer it, because it also cuts down on transference. People get many of their needs for emotional and social support met, so all of their emotional intensity is not channeled into the therapy session. I can be more of a consultant, and their sponsor does more of the direct helping."

Some Caution Advised

Some therapists who are enthusiastic about older 12-Step groups like A.A. and Al-Anon are nonetheless cautious about the newer groups for ACOAs. Janet Woititz, a chemical dependency counselor and author of the best-selling book *Adult Children of Alcoholics*, recommends that her clients spend a year in A.A. or "regular" Al-Anon before attending groups targeted for ACOAs. "If the ACOA groups spend their time returning to the traumas of childhood and blaming parents, they are counterindicated," she said. Tarpley Richards Long, an LCSW in private practice in Washington, D.C., has had clients attend a single ACOA meeting and never go back. "There are some meetings, usually the ones connected with Al-Anon, that adhere closely to the 12-Step program and use solid common sense expressed in workable, day-to-day language," she said. "Then there are ACOA splinter groups that are almost like leaderless psychotherapy groups, where people stand up and talk about how they've been harmed by their parents, and give long, wrenching descriptions of incest. The antidote for people who have difficulty with feelings is not to flood them with feelings but to be gradual and very cautious."

> *"In Al-Anon I found acceptance, a community of peers, a priesthood of all believers, help freely given in a society otherwise dominated by the market economy."*

After 18 months in my Monday Night Meeting, I found myself a sponsor and systematically worked the 12 Steps. At first, the steps seemed pious and irrelevant: *I'm trying to work out my pain. What does making lists of my faults or figuring out who my "higher power" is have to do with anything?* I did them only because I was still desperate. In practice, it boiled down to this: I tried to refrain from the busybody quality that was hurting my new marriage and to express what I needed without blame. I admitted that I couldn't do it alone. I straightened out my relationships by admitting my faults, and paying my

> *"I've wanted alcoholic family issues to have a serious hearing within family therapy."*

debts, and I accepted help from a Higher Power whom I defined simply as a "force of rhythm and meaning" in the universe.

Sometimes I still cried at meetings, and yes, once in a while meetings were a ritual blame-a-thon for us all. But for me, those years of grief and rage—as I reinterpreted my family history, putting alcohol back into the picture—were necessary ones. I had had "a normal response to an abnormal situation." My father's cruelty came not because I deserved it, nor from gratuitous meanness. It was the striking-out of a man who was often under the influence of alcohol, hung over, or desperately trying to keep his drinking under control. This explanation—this new myth, if you will—allowed me to admit what had happened to me without giving up my love for him, or his for me.

A Meaningful, Anonymous Community

In Al-Anon I found acceptance, a community of peers, a priesthood of all believers, help freely given in a society otherwise dominated by the market economy. There was someone there to hear me as long as I needed to grieve. In a culture where we hardly know how to talk to each other any more except in the language of television commercials and bumper stickers, we members of the Monday Night Group found a way to speak of what holds meaning. In a culture where real community is scarce and families are broken, we were a real community, albeit an anonymous, instant one, reconstituting each week and then dissolving into the night. In a culture with an exaggerated sense of human perfectibility and the efficacy of human will, we had a metaphor—"disease"—that allowed us to face our problems and get help from each other without blaming ourselves, or others, for our limitations.

Problems with ACOAs

We borrowed the disease metaphor wholesale from Alcoholics Anonymous, which describes alcoholism as a progressive, fatal disease that can never be cured, but only arrested through abstinence. This metaphor is now widely applied—to compulsive spending, sex, gambling, overeating, and "codependence"—and there are Anonymous groups to match. Participants say the metaphor works: they stop searching for causes and get group support to change unwanted behavior. I visited a Debtors Anonymous meeting once, and I heard more sanity about American compulsive consumerism than I have ever heard anywhere. But there are limits to the accuracy of the metaphor. Abstinence—the solution for alcoholics—obviously cannot be practiced 100 percent when it comes to eating, having relationships, or taking care of others. In the absence of a subtle and well-articulated theory integrating the existing body of psychological knowledge with the realities of life in alcoholic families, the popular movement has cobbled together psychological models populated by black and white stick figures.

The Press and Mental Health

"The popular press is at the vanguard of the movement," said Brown of Stanford. "The media has defined a clinical mental health population by lifting denial, but it stopped there. Practitioners and patients are getting hooked into assuming they can read self-help books and change a lifetime of development, which is absurd." Brown is particularly impatient with the buzzword "codependence," first used to describe partners "addicted" to rescuing and caretaking alcoholics, and then extended to ACOAs with similar low self-esteem. Codependence theorists now call the behavior epidemic. They describe a fairly universal set of human weaknesses, including the compulsive practice of self-denial, dishonesty, and what used to be a virtue—putting another's needs before your own.

"Professionals have failed to grapple with the realities of people's lives."

"Codependence is a global term describing a reactive, submissive stance to a dominant other—something that is part of all human behavior but is now being perceived as entirely negative," said Brown. "There's such a thing as healthy dependence—being able to rely on someone else to do what they say they'll do in a partnership, for example. The codependence label is anti-needy, anti-dependent; it's very isolating and it reinforces all the problems Adult Children bring from their childhoods. It encourages rejecting others, being unkind and ungiving, and it's antagonistic to good, healthy altruism. I was walking down the street with a colleague and when I leaned over to pick up a piece of paper she told me I was being codependent. Multiply that attitude exponentially and you have a ludicrous and inhuman world."

For Jo-Ann Krestan—a strong believer in A.A. and Al-Anon—the lens of codependency can discourage people from negotiating changes in their relationships. "I had a client who was trying to renegotiate the rules of her relationship and get her needs met. Her partner got angry, and punished her by withdrawing," Krestan said. "At their respective meetings of Codependents Anonymous, both were told, 'What do you expect? You can't get water from a dry well!' That's ignoring a systems view of change—of course, the first reaction is negative. You've got to hang in there past that first reaction."

Krestan is also alarmed by what she sees as a tendency of the mass movement and its gurus to offer an implied promise that there is a sanctuary, somewhere, from the pain, limitation, and imperfection associated with being human. "I've seen people clutching checklists as if they were Bibles," she said. "I've spoken at conferences where I've been overwhelmed by the pain in the room, and I didn't want to be one

> *"What I have seen in myself and others is healing, something magical that I can't even try to explain."*

more broken promise," said Krestan, who is frustrated by what she calls a "lunatic fringe" that has over-globalized the insights of addiction theory.

"I've wanted alcoholic family issues to have a serious hearing within family therapy, and that was beginning to happen," says Krestan. Now there's a backlash, and why wouldn't there be? I'm worried by simple solutions—that if you do 'recovery' right you can have it all; that the child within will be healed, and the adult will have no pain; that relationships are not work; that parents or partners are to blame and you don't have to take personal responsibility." To Krestan, even the most precious label of the movement is a contradiction in terms. In the long run, Krestan said, "You cannot be an 'Adult *Child.*'"

For some therapists, the label "Adult Children" conjures up images of people living forever under the volcanoes of their childhoods, feeling condemned and defined by their pasts. Says Michael Elkin, a Boston therapist and former heroin addict who wrote *Families Under the Influence*, "If you identify yourself as a survivor of incest or abuse, you are making an existential and self-hypnotic statement that defines you by the most destructive thing that ever happened to you. In the short term, it's important to say it, but you can get stuck there—just as it's important to express your anger, but if you're still doing that six months later, you've got caught. We all want to feel like victims. Self-righteous indignation is the hardest drug to beat."

A Grassroots Movement

Such excesses within the ACOA self-help movement may tempt some therapists with limited training in addiction to dismiss it. But the grass-roots movement—with all its limitations—shows that professionals have failed to grapple with the realities of people's lives. "The reason this is a grass-roots movement—just like the movements around sexual abuse and domestic violence—is that as professionals we've been sitting on our hands for years, not being helpful," says Lori Dwinell, a Seattle-based psychiatric social worker specializing in grief, depression, and alcoholism. "Some family therapists say 12-Step programs are a cult. But what infuriates them is that it's not *their* cult, not *their* special language being spoken. The issue is control. Self-help movements can do harm as well as good, but they are a reality of the contemporary scene. The people involved are fairly sophisticated shoppers. If you don't speak their language—or more importantly, let them speak it—they'll go somewhere else, to someone less snooty about how they frame their problem."

I recently called my old sponsor on the phone. Raised in Morocco, Australia, and all around the world by an alcoholic, pot-smoking father, he joined the Monday Night Meeting at 22, lonely, depressed, and afraid to pursue his ambition to act. He is 27 now and on the brink of qualifying for Artists' Equity; he rarely goes to the Monday Night Meeting anymore. "I got lots of awareness and acceptance, but I wasn't getting any action," he explained. "I'd pray for knowledge of God's will for me, and then I would sit and wait for something to happen. I didn't get that it was up to me." I asked him whether he thought that ACOA meetings were keeping people stuck. "The program works. People will grow up and get out of the victim role if they do the Steps—but not all of them do," he said. "ACOA is like a hospital ward or a recovery room. The point is to get better and go out in the world, not to live in the hospital forever."

When I drop into the Monday Night Meeting these days, I find that many of my old companions have gone on, and in their place are newcomers first coming to terms with their family alcoholism. Sometimes I hear people talking as though their problems were simply choosing "bad" people—addicts, alcoholics, abusers—and that once they "recover" they will find mythical "good" people who will treat them well. But on the whole, what I have seen in myself and others is healing, something magical that I can't even try to explain.

I see my father now not so much as an alcoholic but as someone who has moved in and out of alcoholic activity all his life. He has never stopped drinking, but he hasn't drunk himself into the grave or the mental hospital in the inexorable progressive way that A.A. literature describes. (He may, if my mother dies before him, and if he does, I'm sure I'll find myself back in "regular" Al-Anon.) In any case, I'm less preoccupied with it, and once in awhile, when I hear that familiar slurred and absent tone on the phone, I don't prolong the call. I finally quit a job I'd kept for years because I was afraid my father would disapprove if I left. I'm happier in my own life, my marriage is happier, and I do more of what I want these days. Two years after I wrote my father those angry, grieving, and accusatory letters—two years of Al-Anon, some bitter fights, a few family therapy sessions with my parents, and individual therapy with someone supportive of 12 Step programs—I was ready to make a week-long visit home.

My father wrote to me afterwards—a brief letter, on two sheets of white stationery, shortly after he and my mother dropped me off at the airport limousine. "Imagine my surprise last Monday, the day after taking you to the limo, when I discovered a turning point—that a visit from a truly benign being gave me a week of unalloyed and quite exceptional pleasure," he wrote. "The being was not exactly a stranger, but she was, in some way difficult to describe, new, with a competent and generous interest in what I was doing. . . . We ached the afternoon you left, but now we remember simply with joy."

The Recovery Movement Harms ACOAs

by Steven J. Wolin and Sybil Wolin

About the authors: *Steven J. Wolin is a clinical professor of psychology at George Washington University in Washington, D.C., an investigator at the university's Center for Family Research, and the director of the center's family therapy training. He has conducted research projects on the importance of family rituals and the prevention of alcoholism from generation to generation. He and his wife and collaborator Sybil Wolin are the authors of the book* The Resilient Self. *They provide training and consultation on substance abuse and mental health.*

The "Challenge Model" is an alternative to traditional psychiatric thinking, conventional wisdom, and a popular psychology which stress that children growing up in adverse circumstances suffer lasting emotional consequences. I call this gloomy prediction the "Damage Model." It's a prophecy of doom, a kind of pseudo-scientific version of the ancient admonition that the sins of the father will be visited upon the sons, The Challenge Model, which originates in a growing literature on resiliency and 20 years of my own research on non-alcoholic adult children of alcoholics, presents a more balanced, and much more optimistic, point of view.

Both models start with the observation that troubled families can inflict considerable harm on children. In the Damage Model, children are passive; they are without choices to help themselves. As a result, their inevitable fate is to be wounded and to grow up as damaged adults.

In the Challenge Model, the family is not only a destructive force, but it's also an opportunity in the lives of its children. Survivors are wounded in the Challenge Model, too, and they are left with scars as adults. But they also are challenged by the family's troubles to experiment and to respond actively and creatively. Their preemptive responses to adversity, repeated over time, become incorporated into the self as lasting resiliences.

Jacqueline overcame a childhood that would be called grinding by anyone's standards. At age two, she was dropped off by her parents at a foster home. A year and a half later, Jacqueline's foster father murdered his wife, whereupon Jacqueline was transferred to a second family. After two years, Jacqueline's mother showed up without explanation, took her away from that foster family, and kept her with two more children of unknown origin for the next four years. Jacqueline's mother was promiscuous and had a string of lovers in and out of the house, some of whom abused Jacqueline. The family was so poor that Jacqueline remembers making dinner for the four children out of a can of Campbell's soup and a pot full of water.

When Jacqueline was 10, her mother dropped her off once again, this time in a Methodist orphanage, where she remained until she was 17. "This was no teary goodbye," says Jaqueline. "She was glad to be rid of me, and I was glad to be free of her." In comparison to home, she says the orphanage was like a great recreational facility. Popular psychological theories could predict that Jacqueline could have folded in despair, developed an anti-social, problem-ridden personality or, at the very least, been left with some type or relationship disorder that would have constricted her life seriously. None of this happened, although Jacqueline did not escape unharmed.

As a child, Jacqueline excelled in school, and was a leader among her peers, respected mostly for her integrity. Against all odds she remained optimistic about her future, found pleasure in her friendships, and a love of the outdoors. As an adult, now, she describes herself as the "parent to my children that I never had, and a loyal friend." She is married to a man that she describes as "my greatest fan, my best friend, and terrific fun in bed." Jacqueline is the alumni chairwoman of the orphanage reunion committee.

Childhood Pain

Jacqueline is keenly aware, despite her successes, of the lasting pain of her childhood. She suffers from bouts of depression and withdraws into herself. In addition, on many mornings, Jacqueline has trouble getting out of bed. Her morning blues, and the tendency to plummet, symptoms easily traced to her past, brought her into therapy with me. However, I must point out that while she was concerned enough to seek help for herself, she was equally proud. She said, "I've pulled myself out of the fire, I've been tested, and I've prevailed. I just want to feel better. I just want life to be a little easier." I saw my job as her therapist to support her pride while addressing her pain.

> *"Survivors . . . are challenged by the family's troubles to experiment and to respond actively and creatively."*

Jacqueline's story revolves around an interplay of vulnerability and resilience; stamina and sadness, discouragement and determination. These contrasts of light and dark weave through the life histories of resilient survivors and are the core of the Challenge Model.

I have identified a number of objectively describable resiliencies, and traced their development across time. The survivors I talk to described how they were emboldened by adversity, and undertook deliberate measures to protect themselves. For example, they deliberately and consciously chose spouses who were strong and they married into non-alcoholic families; they put distance between themselves and their parents; they were spurred on by ghastly memories of holidays with Mom and Dad to establish strong, healthy rituals in their own generation.

> *"Rituals are the time when we weave the web of group and family identity."*

Now for all of us, rituals are the time when we weave the web of group and family identity. And for the healthy offspring of alcoholics, rituals in the new generation have the added significance of compensating for the past, reinforcing healthy self-images, and reaching out towards a hopeful future.

Seeing this strong positive influence of the challenge frame of mind on healthy adults from alcoholic homes, I laid the foundation for the Challenge Model. I expanded my interest and strengths to other disabling conditions that affect families, and with my wife and co-author, Sybil Wolin, began a series of interviews with resilient adults who had grown up in less than minimal, expectable caring environments. The stories of how they saved themselves added three new findings.

Recalling Triumphs Nurtures Pride

First, for these resilient adults, the process of completing our resiliency assessment lit a special spark they had not felt before in therapy. The door to pride was opened by answering detailed questions on how they had endured; how they worked themselves into a friend's home, earned a niche in the adult world with a job, cultivated a talent, and made links to the community by joining the Scouts and other youth organizations. In recalling their triumphs, no matter how small, the survivors I interviewed began to see themselves in a new light: not as damaged merchandise, but as brave, resourceful, determined people.

Secondly, these interviews showed me a way of reaping the benefits of the resiliency assessment in my clinical practice. Cautiously at first, I experimented with a Challenge Model approach. In addition to addressing the wounds, I asked patients about the times when they elevated themselves above the hardship of their lives. Initially, most patients responded with strenuous objections, saying that I "just didn't understand how badly they felt, how they hurt." For example, one resilient survivor shot back at me, "What do you know about pain? You look like you had a mother who loved you." But, I persisted, and after a while, I saw that many patients gradually shifted attention from their pain to their resilience, and discovered considerable pride and esteem as they went along.

In Challenge Model Theory, pride drives the engine of change. In damage model therapy, with its exclusive emphasis on the hurts of the past, shame all too often jams the gears.

Our third finding may be the most important. Sybil Wolin and I systematically have described resilience by grouping the characteristics of successful survivors into several clusters. And we've traced these clusters across developmental stages, from childhood through adulthood.

For example, one resiliency cluster is a cognitive factor. Some young survivors, some as young as five or six years old, develop a hunch that something is seriously wrong with their troubled parents. Their awareness is usually sensory at first, coming in the recognition of a drunken father's key rattling and missing the lock, or the icy prickly feel of a mother's skin, signaling the onset of withdrawal depression. Later on, in adolescence, these sensory impressions sharpen into a clear understanding of the trouble that is brewing at home.

Resilient children know who lines up with whom in family feuds, and they can read the hidden ominous messages behind seemingly innocent remarks. Often, they can put a name or a precise description to the family's illness. As adults, then, resilient children expand their sensitivities and understanding into permanent and protective growth producing parts of the self. To summarize just this one factor, the initial sensory impressions of resilient children refine and diversify into empathy, introspection and clear thinking, and an ability to tolerate and intellectually manage life with all its complexities and ambiguities.

Damage Model Runs Wild in Recovery Movement

Over the past 10 years, the Damage Model has slipped out of professional hands, where it did have shortcomings enough, and into the popular culture, where it has gone wild. I'm referring to the recovery movement. Its leaders are offering a noisy commotion of advice for the alienated, the forlorn, and the frightened. We are witnessing an explosion of books, videos, self-help groups, inpatient treatment programs, and media coverage at "liberating people from the harm of the past," making no mention whatsoever of people's strengths, completely bypassing our capacity for resilience. I believe the recovery movement and its lopsided counsel of damage have become dangerous.

> *"The survivors I interviewed began to see themselves . . . as brave, resourceful, determined people."*

When the recovery movement began to take shape, I welcomed its appearance. Bringing an invisible group to professional and public attention for the first time, the movement described the daily hardships and long-term effects of having an alcoholic parent. Before long, the movement also attracted and helped children of other troubled parents, who, like alcoholics, were unable to provide an acceptable home life for their families. And I welcomed this expansion of the movement, too.

But then recovery got out of control, and spread across our country like wild-fire, turning us into a nation of emotional cripples. So-called experts now warn that 96 percent of the population is suffering the effects of growing up in so-called "dysfunctional" homes. Everyone who found their parents wanting in any way were welcomed into the fold, and encouraged to inspect themselves for signs of damage. An amazing number of people responded, and recovery obliged by pumping out a host of illnesses and addictions that by earlier standards were mere habits—some good, some bad. Everywhere we're finding people talking freely about being in the grips of compulsive shopping disorders, sex and food addictions, jogging addictions, and most severely, in the unmanageable urge to please other people.

Glorifying Frailty

We are being virtually flooded with news about co-dependency, the wounded inner child, and intimacy impairments. Here's my quarrel with the recovery movement: it glorifies frailty, it lumps trivial dissatisfactions with serious forms of mental illness, and, worst, it portrays the human condition as a disease.

In a recent satire of co-dependence, Elizabeth Crystal derides the reckless abandon of the popular co-depen-dence literature. Crystal states, "We

> *"The recovery movement and its lopsided counsel of damage have become dangerous."*

learn of parents who routinely tell their children, 'Later, maybe.' Or, 'you kids play outside or something.' We're told the terrifying tale of Anne, who could not once remember sitting in her father's lap. And of course, this is not to be confused with homes where there is too much sitting in father's lap. There is little hope that you will escape co-dependency if your parents didn't get along, since the disease will strike if your parents exercised any of the following options: divorce, separation, fighting, or remaining together for the sake of the children."

Playing on a childish wish to escape the burdens of being a grown-up, the movement calls people "adult children" and encourages them to wear their illness or addiction as a badge of honor. They declare themselves insufficiencies at their parents' feet.

In the recovery movement, sickness is de rigueur and attributes like fortitude, perseverance, health, and resilience are taboo. For the survivors of troubled families, the fad is lethal, as the very strengths that enable children of hardship to prevail are being twisted around, labeled as illnesses, and identified as the cause of lifelong pathology.

"You sir—you say you protected your brothers and sisters when your father went on his drunken rampages. You made meals when your mother was locked up in her bedroom. Perhaps you imagined that you had done a good job. Not so fast. Your behavior has left a permanent scar and you are now neck deep in the

175

syndrome of over-responsibility.

"You, madam, you avoided a family blow-up by making good on a promise to your mother when your father copped out. Perhaps you think well of yourself for being so compassionate. Wise up. You're in denial, and doomed to a pattern of placating others for the rest of your life.

> *"The recovery movement . . . glorifies frailty."*

"And you? You say you cut the family tension with a good joke. You think you have a great sense of humor. Forget that. You're a compulsive clown. You're damaged goods, all of you, the experts are saying, 'and the sooner you get to a recovery group, the better.'"

How can we stop the self-anointed experts who are claiming that emotional illness has reached epidemic proportions in our society? Please join me in objecting to the modern-day voices of doom—on the professional and popular front—that are threatening to drown out our awareness of the human capacity for strength and resilience.

We don't stand a chance without a convincing alternative to the Damage Model. We need research to show how children can be strong in the face of hardship, studies equal in number to those that show why we fall sick, and we need a Diagnostic and Statistical Manual with a listing of diseases. We need to endorse the Challenge Model, speak out against the damage uproar, and legitimize the case for strengths by developing a vocabulary of resilience.

The Recovery Movement Encourages ACOAs to Unfairly Blame Their Parents

by Melinda Blau

About the author: *Melinda Blau is a writer and contributor to* American Health *magazine.*

Barbara and her mother are trying to work out their conflicts in a family therapy session. Recovering from the most recent of many love affairs gone sour, Barbara is convinced her shattered romances are the result of an abusive childhood. Her anger is palpable. "How do you have a good relationship?" she asks the therapist, her eyes narrowing as she leans forward in her chair. "If you grew up in a house where relationships were good, you learned that. I'm 44 years old and I'm reading books like *Toxic Parents* to learn what healthy is about!" The "toxic parent," 75-year-old Evelyn, seems willing to make peace with her daughter. But Barbara has another agenda: "Without some resolution of the past, I can't go forward," Barbara asserts. "Part of this has to do with my mother . . . obviously. Whether she will take any level of responsibility and make it easier for me is questionable." Barbara sees herself as the victim. "It's very painful. The way I feel has to do with things done to me—not because of who I am as a person. I'm dealing with it on several levels. I'm going to a therapist. I'm also starting to go to ACOA." The mother looks confused. Her daughter is speaking a foreign language. "AC-what?" she asks. "Adult Children of Alcoholics and other dysfunctional families," Barbara explains authoritatively. She makes it clear that there was "absolutely no alcohol" in her house— but her childhood was nonetheless "dysfunctional." The mother inhales deeply and sighs. She asks innocently, "I'd like to know—how many *functional* families are there?"

These two generations are worlds apart. The mother, a child of the Depression, was taught to put others' needs first, to repress her feelings, and silently endure life's hard knocks. In contrast, Barbara flaunts her distress; she is low on compassion.

Blaming parents for what they did or didn't do has become a national obsession—and big business. Like Barbara, increasing numbers of people are now referring to themselves as "Adult Children," a curious

> *"Blaming parents for what they did or didn't do has become a national obsession—and big business."*

metaphor. With self-help groups and a spate of books such as the best-selling and pointedly titled *Toxic Parents* to guide them, plus magazines and TV talk shows eager to air dirty laundry, Adult Children are definitely front and center on the American scene.

The movement began about 10 years ago with survivors of extreme abuse: children of alcoholics and drug abusers or victims of incest and physical or mental violence, who very early in life learned the unwritten credo—don't feel, don't think, and don't trust. What once was survival for the child became a way of life for the adult. "I lived in constant terror," recalls a 34-year-old incest survivor whose parents were alcoholics. "One time, on the way home from a restaurant, my father was speeding recklessly, shouting, 'I've met my Maker, and I don't care who I take with me!'"

But the scope of the movement has grown enormously. It now includes a cadre of parent-bashing Adult Children eager to tell their parents "It's your fault that we love too much or not at all and never the right person; that we don't trust ourselves or anyone else; that we are 'afflicted and addicted' (as a *Newsweek* cover story declared); that we are divorced, drunk, desperate, and— pardon the jargon—'dysfunctional.'" These Adult Children are looking for the Answer—and many think their parents are *it*.

If you believe some experts, 90 percent of us are suffering from the ravages of childhood. And salvation, say gurus such as Susan Forward who lead these flocks of Adult Children, lies in the recovery movement. You must face the reality of your chaotic childhood and reclaim your life by looking at the pain you've never been allowed to talk about, much less feel.

Stuck in the Pain

But other therapists are concerned. "The whole new 'wounded child' mythology has given people a language for talking about pain, grieving over it," notes family therapist Jo-Ann Krestan, co-author of *Too Good for Her Own Good* (Harper & Row, 1990). "But there's really no such thing as an 'Adult Child.' That's a description of where you came from, not a diagnosis of who you are today."

Certainly, the Adult Child movement will help many people exorcise childhood demons of shame and isolation. It will also help them understand that what happened to them as children wasn't their fault and that as adults they need no longer be victims. They don't have to stay stuck in the problem—they can do something.

But as the media and the burgeoning self-help movement continue to encourage Adult Children to stand up and be counted, many experts now ask: Will those same people get stuck in the solution? In therapy, Barbara dumps her sorrows on her mother; other Adult Children assemble to flesh out forgotten images from painful childhoods. But there may be little talk of forgiveness, much about blame, and, sometimes, fantasies of revenge. Will chronic angst simply be transmuted to chronic anger? And if parent bashing is the prescription, what are the long-term effects of that "medicine" on succeeding generations? How will the children of these Adult Children view *their* parents? . . .

Adult "Children"

The mere fact that adults are labeling themselves "children" implies that there's some resistance to actually growing up and facing adult responsibilities. Landon Jones, the journalist whose book *Great Expectations* (Coward, McCann & Geoghegan, 1980) tracked this generation through 1980, also suspects it's in keeping with the baby boom mentality. "All of their life stages have been prolonged—their childhood and adolescence—and they stayed in college and were single longer," says Jones. "Now they're approaching middle age, when one of the tasks is to come to terms with your parents. But they're not ready to accept who they really are."

The children of the Me Generation had the time and money to indulge themselves in the pursuit of perfection. When their dreams began to shatter, say the experts, the boomers began to point a finger at their parents. After all, it must be *someone's* fault.

"When you look at the 'recovery movement,' you see a mass audience turning childhood into an illness you recover from," says Ronald Taffel of New York's Institute for Contemporary Psychotherapy. "They even have networks and support systems to keep it going. These obviously serve a useful purpose—but only if parent bashing doesn't become an end in itself."

If the fitness movement belonged to the '80s, then "recovery" may well be the hallmark of the '90s. An influx of alcoholic and addicted boomers doubled Alcoholics Anonymous membership between 1977 and 1987. Al-Anon, AA's companion program for families of alcoholics, now has more than 19,000 groups nationwide; and scores of me-too groups, like Cocaine Anonymous and Shopaholics, have been created to accommodate boomers who didn't drink but found other ways to soothe inner discontent. But none responded to the grass-roots call for self-help in greater numbers than the

"Adult Children are looking for the Answer—and many think their parents are it."

179

unhappy adults who called themselves Adult Children.

Although ACOA's original focus was on alcohol, the Adult Child movement now reaches out to all kinds of suffering adults. ACOA's growth has been staggering—at last count, from 14 Al-Anon-affiliated ACOA groups in 1981 to more than 4,000 meetings nationwide today, many of them independent of Al-Anon.

"A man called me and said, 'I'm an Adult Child, and Dr. So-and-So said I'm one of the worst cases he's ever seen.' I cracked up," recalls Marianne Walters, director of the Family Therapy Practice Center in Washington, D.C. "I told him I'd see him, but as an Adult Person. I'm concerned about these typologies—not that they don't resonate with some truth. But if you're so self-absorbed and only understand yourself this way, you don't take as much responsibility for your own behavior, for others, or for the world you live in."

Many therapists encourage clients to attend programs like AA and Al-Anon as an important adjunct to treatment and a safe place to share feelings. After all, the 12-step structure calls for admitting you're powerless over the problem—whether due to your own behavior or someone else's—and then, with group support, looking honestly at your own contribution.

But some Adult Child meetings, which tend to be "younger" than the more established 12-step programs, may encourage just the opposite: blame.

"I went to ACOA meetings for about a year—but week after week people just dumped." Karen, whose mother was alcoholic, is referring to the litany of complaints common to many of these meetings. One of her resentments was that her parents had refused to send her to college: "I carried that around for years." Her brothers were sent to college, her parents went to Europe, but "poor" Karen had to go to a local junior college. "I'd share it at meetings, but I'd leave feeling worse," she says.

> *"Adults . . . labeling themselves 'children' implies that there's some resistance to actually growing up and facing adult responsibilities."*

"In ACOA groups, people definitely have to get through the anger and denial," says Michael Elkin, a family therapist at a school for disturbed adolescents in Stockbridge, Massachusetts. "But that's only the first step in the process—it's where people have to start. Hopefully, they'll move past the blame. However, some people get stuck—they misuse the program."

Family therapist Jo-Ann Krestan also sees some people using "recovery" in much the same way they used drugs or other substances—to avoid their real feelings. "They think if they can only do recovery 'right,' they won't have to feel uncomfortable," she says. "But if you really begin to look at your own choices, at who you are, it's going to be uncomfortable."

Karen decided to go through the pain. A counselor at an ACOA rehab she attended encouraged her to write letters to each of her parents, telling them everything she was angry about. "When I had to read them aloud and talk about my part, I realized I always blamed them when I failed."

Karen, a recovering alcoholic, now takes full responsibility for her choices as an adult. "Sure, there was a lot of anger over my mother's drinking, and for years I blamed my own drinking on her. It made it easier for me. She did inappropriate things to me as a child, such as making me her confidante and telling me about her sex life, but I was never physically abused. There is no fault, no blame. Millions of people grow up in the same kind of household I did, and they don't all drink. It was easier to blame than to take responsibility for my own lifestyle."

> *"Forgiveness is the only place peace comes from."*

Equally important, Karen now also understands the context of her own mother's life. "This was the early '50s; my father traveled, my mother was young and knew nothing about having a child. She was lonely. There were no support groups then."

Good Intentions, Bad Results

Had Karen read California therapist Susan Forward's *Toxic Parents* (Bantam, 1989), she might have gained no such insight. Nor would she have been interested in hearing a basic truth about many supposedly "abusive" parents: Most never intended to hurt their children.

Even Alice Miller, the Swiss psychoanalyst who unwittingly inspired much of the popular focus on the "inner child," stressed that the issue is not culpability. In her book *The Drama of the Gifted Child* (Basic Books, 1981), Miller wrote: "Many parents, even with the best intentions, cannot always understand their child, since they, too, have been stamped by their experience with their own parents and have grown up in a different generation."

Therapist Marilyn R. Frankfurt of the Ackerman Institute for Family Therapy in New York City agrees that parental attitudes of the earlier child-centered Not-Me Generation are totally foreign to today's Me Generation. "Those earlier mothers," she says, "were told they had to shape their children and make them conform to cultural expectations. But often they had no emotional attention from their own parents. Despite this, they didn't complain. Now they're being held responsible for how their children feel.

"We're imposing ideas on the past generation that don't apply," says Frankfurt. "These Adult Children act as if their parents knew all of this and chose not to act."

But Forward offers no such compassion in *Toxic Parents*. Relentlessly presenting case after case of manipulative, selfish parents, she tells readers it's not their fault. That's fine, but as Frankfurt points out, "Forward also implies, 'Someone's got to be responsible.' The author even goes so far as to warn readers not to be fooled by comments like 'We did the best we could' or 'You'll never understand what I was going through.' She says that's the parents' problem."

Forward declined several requests to be interviewed for this article, but it's clear she has tapped into a ripe market. Although drawing its examples from the extremes—people who were terribly abused—the book *Toxic Parents* seems to appeal to anyone along the continuum of an "unhappy childhood."

Understanding and Insight

Though Krestan doesn't support the idea of blaming parents, she does agree with Forward on one point: "Adult Children need to acknowledge what's theirs and what belongs to their parents—and get through the grieving process. Forward's book will certainly help validate those negative shameful experiences that people have had." Krestan adds, however, "You have to get good and Goddamned angry, but that doesn't constitute healing. It's not helpful to confront and cut off."

Janet Woititz, author of the landmark work *Adult Children of Alcoholics* (Health Communications, 1983) and an unofficial "grandmother" of the Adult Child movement, points out that an understanding of our childhood "gives us insight into who we are and what gets in the way of our achieving healthy relationships in adulthood—but that's all. If we get stuck in blame, it develops a smoke screen so that we don't have to make changes ourselves.

"Books can just offer awareness," she stresses. "Looking at our parents is step one. Then we have to look at ourselves and what we're doing to the next generation."

Without doubt, there are abusive parents who will fully brutalize their children, but most are themselves victims. As Michael Elkin puts it, "Toxic parents have toxic kids who become toxic parents and so on. In the end, forgiveness is the only place peace comes from. That doesn't mean overlooking the pain and harm—it means understanding that you have emerged from it."

Psychologist Augustus Napier, director of the Family Workshop in Atlanta and author of *The Fragile Bond* (Harper & Row, 1988), which discusses intimacy in marriage, is also opposed to "making parents the villains."

People have a right to their anger, he says, but in some cases there's a kind of excuse-making going on for the purpose of gaining sympathy. "I help patients express their feelings about the past without having them actually take it out on the parent. My work honors both generations."

"Life is basically unfair," says Betty Carter, director of the Family Institute of Westchester, New York. "Our families are dealt to us like a deck of cards. So it's to your advantage to come to terms with the hand you were given. It's understandable that the person is furious about whatever happened—and I empathize and try to get him or her to ventilate the feelings. But anger and blame poison them." Forgiveness

> *"Until you can see your parents as human beings you can't see yourself as a human being."*

is important, adds Carter. "I don't mean an intellectual gloss-over; I mean a forgiveness of the heart that comes out of a very long journey."

"If you continue to blame your parents, you'll feel all right for a while, but it's no way to live. You then use blame to resolve other problems," psychologist Ronald Taffel observes. When his clients get into relationships, he says, many try to solve problems by blaming or disengaging altogether. "We need to try to see what our parents were up against," he suggests. His reason is simple: "Until you can see your parents as human beings you can't see yourself as a human being."

The Movement Matures

The baby boomers are now referred to as the Sandwich Generation—caught between the needs of their children and needs of their aging parents. Baby boom chronicler Landon Jones suggests parent bashing may be just an evolutionary step toward the Me Generation's finally accepting the burden of middle age. Indeed, there are signs the Adult Child movement is in transition.

The publication—and instant popularity—of Dwight Lee Wolter's book, *Forgiving Our Parents* (CompCare Publishers, 1989), mirrors a hopeful trend. Wolter, 39, in recovery as an Adult Child for five years, says he couldn't have written the book earlier. "But I finally walked around angry at my parents long enough.

"I'm not talking about the fact that my daddy wouldn't let me go to Harvard. Mine is an open-and-shut case of child abuse," says Wolter, referring to an anecdote in his first book: One day when he forgot to walk his dog, to teach young Dwight a lesson, his father shot the dog. "The question no longer is: 'Who is to blame?' or 'How could they do such things?'" Wolter writes. "The question is: 'Who has been hurt and how can we get (him or her) back on track?'"

And as Adult Children mature, moving from anger and blame toward forgiveness and acceptance, they might also teach society a valuable lesson about being human. In Wolter's words, "As we begin to forgive our parents, we begin to forgive ourselves. And we begin to forgive the world for not being perfect either."

The Recovery Movement Promotes Self-Centeredness and Irresponsibility

by Wendy Kaminer

About the author: *Wendy Kaminer has written numerous articles on politics, law, and culture. She is the author of the books* A Fearful Freedom, Women Volunteering, *and* I'm Dysfunctional, You're Dysfunctional, *from which this viewpoint is excerpted.*

Instead of a self-help section, my local bookstore has a section called recovery, right around the corner from the one called New Age. It's stocked with books about addiction, psychic healing, and codependency—the popular new disease blamed for such diverse disorders as drug abuse, alcoholism, anorexia, child abuse, compulsive gambling, chronic lateness, fear of intimacy, and low self-esteem. Codependence, which originally referred to the problems of women married to alcoholics, was discovered by pop psychologists and addiction counselors during the 1980s and redefined. Now it applies to any problem associated with any addiction, real or imagined, suffered by you or someone close to you. Now this amorphous disease is a business, generating millions of book sales, support groups, expensive treatment programs, and an annual recovery conference in Scottsdale, Arizona. Codependency "has arrived," according to the First National Conference Report issued in 1989; experts laud recovery as a national grass-roots movement.

Bad Habits Have Become Addictions

Codependency is advertised as a national epidemic, partly because every conceivable form of arguably compulsive behavior is classified as an addiction. We are a nation of sexaholics, rageaholics, shopaholics, and rushaholics. What were once billed as bad habits and dilemmas—Cinderella and Peter Pan complexes, smart women loving too much and making foolish choices about men who hate them—are now considered addictions too, or reactions to the addictions of others, or both. Like drug and alcohol abuse, they are considered codependent diseases. If the self-help industry is any measure of our state of mind in the 1990s, we are indeed obsessed with disease and our capacity to defeat it. All codependency books stress the curative power of faith, introspection, and abstinence. It's morning after in America. We want to be in recovery.

> *"You don't have to be a therapist . . . to wonder about a society in which people are so eager to call themselves addicted and abused."*

Almost everyone—96 percent of all Americans—suffers from codependency, experts assert, and given their very broad definitions of this disease, we probably do. Melody Beattie, best-selling author of *Codependent No More* and *Beyond Codependency*, defines codependency as being affected by someone else's behavior and obsessed with controlling it. Who isn't? Anne Wilson Schaef, author of the best-selling *When Society Becomes an Addict* and *Co-Dependence: Misunderstood—Mistreated*, defines it as "a disease process whose assumptions, beliefs, and lack of spiritual awareness lead to a process of nonliving which is progressive."

That some readers think they know what this means is a tribute to what George Orwell considered reduced expectations of language and the substitution of attitudes and feelings for ideas. It is enough for Schaef to mean that codependency is bad and anyone can have it, which makes this disease look more like a marketing device. Codependency offers a diagnosis, and support group, to virtually anyone with a problem who can read or listen to a tape cassette. . . .

Group Thinking

Consumers are free not to buy codependency books, and they determine their own degrees of participation in support groups, which are generally open to an anonymous public. No one is required to speak, and direct responses to anyone's testimony or comments on anyone else's problems are generally discouraged. The groups are supposed to be nonjudgmental, and you are supposed to talk only about yourself.

Yet, listening to recovering codependents describe their struggles in the same jargon and the same prefabricated phrases, you hear the voice of the crowd. Of course, speaking a common language is part of what holds a group together, and one measure of the success of any cultural phenomenon is the extent to which its language enters the vernacular. You knew the counterculture had peaked, for instance, when middle-aged, middle-class people started talking about the far-out things they were into. Today, people in line at the supermarket talk about their dysfunctional families.

Maybe it is possible to use someone else's jargon to convey your own thoughts. Maybe the jargon shapes the thought. But if the relationship between language and thought is a mystery, it's clear that recovering codependents not only use the same specialized language but often say the same things, partaking in the same popular attitudes toward addiction, abuse, and their own victimization.

I guess it is possible that their unanimity of opinion is evidence of its truth or, at least, its utility. "Why question what works?" I'm often asked. ("By their fruits ye shall know them.") A lot of people say they've found the answers in recovery, as well as support, self-esteem, and what experts might call a lifestyle system. "It saved my life," some declare in dramatic defense of recovery, and if that's true I'm happy for them.

But without questioning their right to choose their gateways to salvation, I can question their judgment as well as prevailing claims about the general efficacy of twelve-step groups. No one really knows just how well recovery works. People who are helped by twelve-step groups may have been helped by other treatments and sets of beliefs, and the actual success or failure rates of disease model treatment programs, like AA, have been credibly questioned by other "experts in the field," [as Stanton Peele states]. But you don't have to be a therapist, M.D., or any other certifiable expert in drug or alcohol abuse and other bad behaviors to wonder about a society in which people are so eager to call themselves addicted and abused.

Convincing People That They Are Weak

Whether alcoholism is an inheritable disease or a learned behavior is a controversy about which I have no opinion. (I do doubt, however, that absolutely everyone who drinks habitually or in excess is the victim of her genes.) Some drugs are indisputably addictive, and the Narcotics Anonymous meetings I've attended clarified for me the uses of support. (What I've occasionally heard recovering addicts describe is support that includes some active intervention.) Smoking may be addictive for some people, but many have given up cigarettes by exertions of will, without the aid of any program. Some people eat, shop, have sex, or twirl their hair compulsively, but I doubt it's helpful to convince them that they're powerless to stop. Practicing overeaters, shoppers, and twirlers, like drugs addicts, are even warned against trying to stop eating, shopping, or twirling on their own: a belief in self-control is a symptom of codependency and the "perfectionist complex." Exaggerating every foible, bad habit, and complaint, taking our

> *"Recovery encourages invalidism."*

behavior out of our control, and defining us as adult children, recovery encourages invalidism. Calling the recovery process self-help doesn't change the way it tends to disempower people.

It is an odd program in self-esteem that rewards people for calling themselves helpless, childish, addicted, and diseased and punishes them for claiming to be healthy. Admit that you're sick and you're welcomed into the recovering persons fold; dispute it and you're "in denial." Thus the search for identity is perversely resolved: all your bad behaviors and unwanted feelings become conditions of your being. Instead of a person who smokes, you are a nicotine addict. Instead of a person who is sometimes depressed, you are a sadness addict. (Feelings can be addictive too, we're told.)

The popularity of these diagnoses reflects, in part, a natural preference for a treatable disease—codependency—over the undefinable sense of unease from which everyone must sometimes suffer. Codependency experts stress that *disease* is *"dis-ease,"* with the ersatz profundity of adolescents discovering that *God* is *dog* spelled backward; but unlike the adolescents, the experts miss their point. Identifying codependency with what some might consider the human condition only undercuts the claim that it is a discrete dysfunction from which people may recover.

Trivializing Real Abuse

Labeling all their problems symptoms of disease, people in recovery find not only the promise of a cure but an external cause for what ails them—the dysfunctional family (and their families in particular). Codependency experts assert that practically everyone is a victim of child abuse, defining abuse broadly enough to make the assertion true. Who among us has ever enjoyed or could ever provide always perfect parenting?

The unwillingness to tolerate, much less laugh at, the inevitable conflicts and imperfections of family life may be poignant in adolescents, but it is tiresome in adults. It also impedes efforts to address serious patterns of abuse. When the minor mistakes that every parent makes are dramatized, or melodramatized, the terrible misconduct of some is trivialized. If child abuse is every form of inadequate nurturance, then being raped by your father is in the same general class as being ignored or not getting help with your homework. When everything is child abuse, nothing is.

> *"The unwillingness to tolerate ... the inevitable conflicts and imperfections of family life ... is tiresome in adults."*

There is something niggardly and mean-spirited in the passion with which some recovering codependents point to themselves as victims of abuse, laying claim to the crown of thorns. Adult Children of Alcoholics (ACOAs) are like Holocaust survivors, suffering post-traumatic stress disorder, John Bradshaw writes offensively. Recovery gives people permission always to put themselves first, partly because it doesn't give them a sense of perspective on their complaints: parental nagging is not the equal of physical abuse and deprivation, much less genocide; vague intimations of unease are not the same as cancer. No one seems to count her blessings in recovery. I've heard no one say, "Some people suffer more than I." For all the talk about sharing and caring, in recovery there's more evidence of self-pity than compassion.

The failure to acknowledge that there are hierarchies of human suffering is what makes recovery and other personal development fashions "selfist" and narcissistic, as critics charge. That is not, however, a failure of individualism. Thinking for yourself and considering your existential autonomy does not mean losing your sense of place in society and the understanding that other people's problems may be more pressing than your own.

> *"There is something niggardly and mean-spirited in the passion with which some recovering codependents point to themselves as victims of abuse."*

The selfism of recovery is more a failure of community; at least it reflects a very shallow notion of community, which is not a group of people going on about themselves in the belief that they're all equal in their pain. Community requires an awareness of inequalities, the desire to correct them, and faith in your capacity to do so—faith that the human will can sometimes be a force for good, not just the blackened, shriveled heart of a disease. *"The will is the most dis-eased part of any adult child's co-dependence,"* Bradshaw writes, and since practically everyone is supposed to be an adult child, practically everyone must surrender the will in order to recover, which doesn't leave us with many possibilities for willful, moral actions. That recovery is extolled by its advocates as a paradigm of community and condemned by critics for excessive individualism only measures our confusion about individualism and community. It also reflects a pervasive fascination with victimhood as a primary source of identity. Acted upon, put upon, and always aggrieved, adult children, the victims of their families, are hardly models for individual or communal action. Yet this emphasis on the essential helplessness of the individual has perverse appeal. It offers absolution and no accountability, and instead of imposing the capacity to act, it confers entitlements to sympathy, support, and reparations.

The phenomenal success of the recovery movement reflects two simple truths that emerge in adolescence: all people love to talk about themselves, and most people are mad at their parents. You don't have to be in denial to doubt that truths like these will set us free. . . .

Agonizing Over Trivialities

At an Adult Children of Alcoholics meeting, people testify to their inability to "handle" mundane complications and annoyances of daily life—checking accounts that won't balance, files at work that won't be found, friends who borrow books and don't return them. They discuss the dynamics of "dealing" with bank managers, auto mechanics, and acquaintances the way I imagine foreign policy advisers discuss an upcoming summit. Should you ask your neighbor to pick up your mail when you go on vacation? How should you pose the question and initiate the "process" of negotiation? Should you be relying on your neighbor? Can you trust him with your mailbox key and will he expect a favor in return? You'd like to ask a friend who lives across town to check your mail instead, but you're afraid of appearing too needy.

How do these people get through the day, I wonder, listening to them agonize about the nuances of every trivial human encounter, thanking my higher power I'm not a therapist.

I realize that many people in recovery are genuinely unhappy and deeply confused about human relations, having been damaged, or at least dented, early on in childhood. Some people are as debilitated by inconveniences as others are by crises. Still, my capacity for sympathy is sometimes limited. The problems you hear discussed in ACOA and CODA [Children of Drug Addicts] meetings don't seem nearly as formidable as the problems of the poor and uninsured chronically ill. Listening to thirty-five-year-olds complain that they have never been understood by their parents, I find myself thinking about the Kurds.

Am I being unfair or unrealistic? As a legal aid lawyer, I represented people facing serious felony charges and people with summonses for not paying their subway fares. It may only be the equivalent of a traffic ticket, I'd remind myself when a farebeat asked anxiously about his case, but it is his traffic ticket. "They may only be imperfect parents," an ACOA might say, "but they are my imperfect parents."

> *"In recovery there's more evidence of self-pity than compassion."*

Unfortunately, that's precisely what ACOAs and other people in recovery tend not to say (at least not one of them has ever said it to me). They're more likely to complain that their parents are not merely imperfect but abusive. They're more likely to insist that their problems are not simply their problems but our problems too, the symptoms of a social disease. Virtually all American families are dysfunctional, we live in a dysfunctional society, recovery experts proclaim, effectively assuring people that virtually all their personal problems are automatically worthy of public attention. . . .

People with Real Problems

Attending several twelve-step meetings a week, listening to people talk about their parents and their PMS, I needed to listen to people grappling with more awesome problems. Of course, some of the problems you hear aired in twelve-step groups are awesome enough, like the problems of alcoholics, drug addicts, and incest victims; it's just that I find the rhetoric of recovery unrevealing and the ideology disturbing. So, as an antidote to recovery, I visited groups of Cambodian women refugees—women who were persecuted by the Khmer Rouge regime, women who survived torture, starvation, multiple rapes, and internment in concentration camps and witnessed the slaughter of their families, women who endured what I can't imagine. The Khmer Rouge is reported to have killed about one million people between 1975 and 1979, the years they remained in power.

These women are the Holocaust survivors to whom some recovering codependents, like John Bradshaw, compare themselves. Many people in recovery tell "trauma stories" and have seized upon the syndrome afflicting these refugees—post-traumatic stress disorder—and claimed it as their own. (Virtually all codependents are said by the experts to be victims of PTSD.) If some recovering codependents resent my comparing them to Cambodian refugees whose sufferings they cannot match, I'm making the comparison their movement has invited.

Metaphorical Holocausts

I'm not suggesting that we should ignore all lesser degrees of suffering and care only about greater ones or that only torture victims and targets of genocide have reason to be unhappy and the right to be heard, but they do have more reason and perhaps we should afford them greater rights. Mostly, I offer this portrait of Cambodian women refugees as a reality check, a reminder of the difference between holocausts that happen only metaphorically and holocausts that happen in fact.

Unlike many ACOAs and other people in recovery, these Cambodian survivors don't glibly proffer their stories to strangers. Their relative silence reflects, in part, a difference between Asian and American cultures: discussing emotional problems with strangers or even clinicians is not part of the Indochinese tradition. Their reticence also reflects, I suspect, the severity of the traumas they have suffered. How do you testify casually, facilely, to torture and genocide?

So, although I have sat in on several group sessions, I have only heard the individual trauma stories of these women secondhand, from their doctors and social workers. I find the details hard to remember, probably because they are so horrific and hard to absorb. For some reason, I only recall the story of a woman who watched soldiers split her husband's head open with an axe and was spared, unaccountably, after being forced to dig her own grave. The literature on Indochinese refugees includes stories like this: A woman sees her parents disemboweled; she is beaten, tossed on the bodies of her relatives, and left to die. A ten-year-old girl is interned in a work camp until she is fifteen; she is regularly beaten, tortured (once she was hung by her ankles from a tree for three days), kept in solitary confinement for months, and raped repeatedly. A man who was interned and tortured is the sole survivor of his family of forty-seven people.

> *"All people love to talk about themselves, and most people are mad at their parents."*

Survivors of the Khmer Rouge are, in general, multiple trauma victims.

"Khmer psychiatric patients in the United States have experienced an average of 16 major trauma events," according to a 1989 U.N. report: "The traumatic experiences of these patients fall into four general categories: 1) deprivation; 2) physical injury and torture; 3) incarceration, brainwashing, re-education camps; and 4) witnessing killings or torture.". . .

Real Resilience

There is more laughter and lightness in these meetings of vulnerable, impoverished survivors of genocide than in any twelve-step group I've attended, where people pursue recovery with deadening earnestness. Twelve-step groups depress me—so many people talking about such relatively trivial problems with such seriousness, in the same nonsensical jargon. The Cambodian women's groups impress and enhearten me—such resilience these women show. . . .

There are many obvious differences between professionally led groups for Cambodian refugees and leaderless recovery groups. But the structural differences (or similarities) between refugee and recovery groups are not relevant to my concern, which is this: the hierarchy of suffering that the recovery movement denies and the cult of victimization it encourages. . . .

I don't mean to minimize the struggle to begin a new life in a strange, hard country with so little resources and a history of so many losses. I have seen only a moment, barely a moment, in a long passage to recovery. I imagine that many of these women are deeply depressed and may remain so. Some have trouble sleeping and are plagued by bad dreams and need medication to maintain their equilibrium. Still, of all the groups I've visited, these are virtually the only ones that engaged me, the only ones I enjoyed and looked forward to attending, the only ones that left me with a sense of hope.

Chapter 5

How Should Alcoholism Be Treated?

CURRENT CONTROVERSIES

Chapter Preface

Alcoholism can destroy the life of an alcoholic and devastate the alcoholic's family. But it also has overwhelming consequences for society. Consider these statistics from the National Council on Alcoholism and Drug Dependence:

- In 1988, alcoholism and problems related to it cost the United States an estimated $85.8 billion in mortality and reduced productivity;
- Fetal alcohol syndrome (FAS), caused by a woman's drinking during pregnancy, afflicts five thousand infants a year; it costs about $1.4 billion annually to treat the infants, children, and adults afflicted with FAS;
- More than twenty thousand people die annually in alcohol-related car accidents.

Clearly alcoholism harms society in numerous ways, and it is in society's best interest to find effective treatments for alcoholics.

The primary goal of all treatments for alcoholism is to get the alcoholic to stop drinking and refrain from abusing alcohol in the future. The paths to this goal are diverse. Several factors—biological, social, and psychological—influence why an individual becomes an alcoholic. So treatments vary, depending upon why the alcoholic drinks and what the physician or therapist believes is the best method for recovery. Some treatments focus on the physical addiction of alcoholism. Others emphasize the alcoholic's social or psychological cravings.

Treatments that focus on the alcoholic's physical addiction rely on recent research showing a correlation between alcoholism and certain biological or genetic factors. Some researchers theorize that a chemical imbalance in the brain causes the craving for alcohol, and that treating alcoholics with antidepressants may reduce the craving. University of Texas researcher Kenneth Blum and his associates may have found a gene defect related to alcoholism. If this proves accurate, alcoholics in the future may be treated with genetic engineering.

Despite the promise of these medical advances, though, the reality is that alcoholism has a strong behavioral component. So for any treatment to work, the alcoholic must stop drinking and must stop those behaviors that lead to drinking. Alcoholics Anonymous and Rational Recovery are two support groups that help alcoholics do this. Other alcoholics benefit from one-on-one therapy with counselors, who may help patients understand the social or psychological motivations for drinking and change their behavior.

Finally, for some alcoholics the most effective treatments are those that combine medical treatment with counseling. Such treatments enable the alcoholic to more easily break the physical addiction to alcohol as they evaluate their social and psychological reasons for drinking.

Until and unless researchers find a specific biological cause and cure for alcoholism, treatments will continue to vary, depending upon the alcoholic and the therapist. The authors in the following chapter offer a variety of treatments for alcoholism.

Nutritional Therapy Can Help Alcoholics

by Susan Kissir

About the author: *Susan Kissir is a free-lance writer whose articles on health issues have appeared in the* New York Times *news syndicate,* Let's Live, Natural Health, Your Health *and other national publications.*

Alan Dalum was 37 years old and thoroughly convinced he was soon going to die.

An executive at Dispatch Communications, a Minneapolis-based radio communications company, Dalum was not dying of cancer, heart disease, or any other illness from which one can leave the world with dignity. Dalum was dying of alcoholism. As millions of Americans do every year, Dalum was drinking himself to death.

Past Treatment Programs

It's not as if Dalum hadn't tried to help himself. He had gone through two grueling, month-long inpatient stays at conventional treatment programs. Like 95 percent of all alcoholism treatment programs, these were modeled after a psychologically oriented "talk therapy" program. This method of therapy is based on the assumption that people abuse alcohol because of painful experiences in their past and that once those events and emotions are dredged up and confronted in group therapy sessions, the desire to drink will go away.

More than 600 follow-up studies have confirmed, however, that only about 25 percent of the people who complete such programs remain sober one year following therapy—a number barely higher than that for people who try to quit drinking with no therapy at all. One federally funded study of 922 men from seven such programs found only 21 percent still sober one year after therapy and just 7 percent sober by the fourth year.

Dalum was no exception to this rule. Confronting his past didn't stop the insatiable cravings, and only days after completing each program Dalum was drinking again, even though he knew he was just a few drinks away from losing

Susan Kissir, "Treat Alcoholism with Nutrition," *Natural Health*, January/February 1993. Reprinted with permission.

his career, his marriage, even his life. Dalum now says, "I truly believed that the only way I'd ever be able to stop drinking would be through death."

Just when he thought all hope of recovery was lost, Dalum stumbled across a book by Robert Erdmann called *The Amino Revolution* that discussed the importance of biochemical repair in alcoholism recovery, using nutrients and herbs. Upon learning that Minneapolis, where he lived, had one of the only programs in the country that employed such methods, Dalum decided to give Health Recovery Center's six-week, outpatient program a shot. That was in 1988. Dalum's been sober—as well as nicotine- and caffeine-free—ever since.

"With the nutrients and detox formula they started me on, I simply felt good from day one," Dalum explains. "In fact, I began to feel normal for the first time in my life. I didn't have any cravings during the program and haven't had any since. But, then, I've made some radical changes in my diet. And my life."

A Different Program

The 12-year-old, holistically oriented Health Recovery Center (HRC), which claims a 74 percent success rate (patients still sober one year later), differs from conventional programs in several significant ways. First, it focuses on uncovering and treating physiological imbalances that may be causing alcohol cravings and throwing the entire body out of whack. Hypoglycemia is a common imbalance found (studies

> *"I began to feel normal for the first time in my life."*

show up to three quarters of alcoholics suffer from low blood sugar), as is an overgrowth in the intestines of Candida albicans, a common bacteria, which can cause an array of problems. The center's philosophy is simple: Until the body begins getting the essential nutrients it needs, recovery cannot begin.

"Just as diabetics cannot be 'talked out of' their biochemical abnormalities, no amount of talk will stop the cravings, anxiety, depression, mental confusion, and fatigue that result from alcohol's biochemical and neurochemical damage," declares Joan Mathews-Larson, Ph.D., the center's founder and executive director. "And there isn't time to obsess over past traumas when you're dying of a major disease. If you go in for cancer treatment, they aren't going to want you to be in heavy therapy over your childhood—they're out to make you well first. So are we. Why do people persist in believing that the damage done by excess ingestion of alcohol can be undone with psychological methods alone?"

For Mathews-Larson, this question is deeply personal. About 20 years ago, her teenage son, Rob, began abusing alcohol and drugs. Mathews-Larson put him into the city's most respected treatment program, but shortly after completing 28 days of inpatient therapy, he committed suicide.

In response, Mathews-Larson said, "I thought, 'I can either go completely crazy,' which I was pretty close to doing, 'or I can try to figure out why this program hadn't touched the real problem at all.' I became obsessed with learning the truth about addiction and recovery."

While rummaging through her son's things, Mathews-Larson discovered the journal he'd been instructed to keep while in rehab, and she broke down crying. "He'd made lists of all his faults and defects," she says softly. "Well, no wonder he killed himself! When you talk at length about something negative you make it bigger than life. That whole philosophy is nuts. It leaves the patient with no self-worth at all."

> *"Until the body begins getting the essential nutrients it needs, recovery cannot begin."*

A few years later, armed with a Ph.D. in nutrition and a Minnesota counseling certificate, Mathews-Larson founded Health Recovery Center, Inc., an outpatient clinic devoted to the restoration of bodies, minds, and spirits that have been ravaged by alcohol.

Such restoration begins the moment a new patient walks through the door. After the staff physician takes a thorough medical history and performs the initial physical exam, the patient is hooked up to an IV solution, out of which drips high doses of ascorbic acid (vitamin C, a powerful detoxifier), calcium, magnesium, B vitamins (which help eliminate withdrawal symptoms), evening primrose oil (a natural anticonvulsant), and a full spectrum of amino acids, including glutamine (an alternative form of glucose that significantly diminishes cravings). While conventional programs frequently numb new patients with drugs like Librium and Valium to help ease withdrawals (and later must wean patients off of them), HRC's detox formula is entirely natural. Mathews-Larson says, "The sum total of it all is that people go from consuming half a quart of alcohol a day to consuming none at all—without drugs."

No Drug Detoxification

Having experienced both types of detoxification, Dalum is adamantly opposed to the drug approach, which he says made the first two programs just a useless blur. "The Librium they gave me had pretty much the same effect as if I'd had three or four cocktails," he recalls. "I couldn't comprehend any of the things they were trying to get across." Although the use of such drugs appears to have been slowly diminishing over the last several years, it remains commonplace. Of eight treatment centers contacted for this article, five admitted to at least occasional use of these powerful antianxiety drugs.

Following the IV, HRC patients are supplied with bottles of the vitamins and minerals they've been deficient in for so long, and put on a diet that's free of sugar, salt, caffeine, and, most importantly, nicotine. That is because tobacco is cured with cane, beet, and corn sugars, which may not only cause intense cravings in those with hypoglycemia (and render them incapable of getting the condition under control), but may also stimulate allergic/addictive reactions in those sensitive to sugar and corn—two of the most common hidden food allergies.

In the ensuing six weeks, HRC patients meet once weekly with a nutritionist, once weekly for individual therapy with one of HRC's five certified counselors, and daily for group sessions, at which they talk openly about such subjects as anger, humor, and insecurity. Such sessions are purposely NOT like conventional 12-step meetings, at which participants are expected to talk about the power they believe alcohol has over their lives. Rather, both the group and individual sessions focus on the here and now.

"We call it 'rational management therapy,'" explains HRC counselor Cathy Hilgart. "First of all, we make a list of the client's goals, long- and short-term, and map out ways they can achieve them. We decide together what they need to work on about themselves, whether it's their self-image, job skills, or whatever. We try to get them to do things that will make them feel good about themselves—whether it be going back to school or just learning how to say 'no' to people who take advantage of them."

In sharp contrast to the AA approach, HRC counselors try to instill in patients the belief that they are in control of their destinies—that they have power over alcohol rather than the other way around. "We try to put clients in the position where they take responsibility for their own well-being," Hilgart says.

Alcoholism and Health

Perhaps the most dramatic way the HRC program differs from more conventional programs is in its concern with the effects that food allergies and chemical sensitivities can have on alcoholics. The phrase "allergic addictive alcoholic" was first coined in the 1950s, when Theron G. Randolph, M.D., the founder of clinical ecology, discovered that sensitivities to corn, yeast, barley, and other foods commonly found in alcoholic beverages were the reason some of his patients couldn't stop drinking. In his book *An Alternative Approach to Allergies*, Randolph wrote, "The alcoholic is never completely free of his 'alcoholism' as long as he's consuming the foods that constitute his addiction." After studying a large AA group, Randolph wrote about their tendency to replace alcohol with candy containing corn sugar, and said, "This was, in fact, the standard operating procedure of the AA unit. Through practice, these individuals had found that they could relieve their craving for grain-containing alcoholic beverages by sucking on another rapidly absorbed form of grain. They had, in effect, transferred food addiction in its highest form—alcoholism—to food addiction in a less severe (and from the addict's point of view, less satisfying) form—addiction to corn sugar."

> *"No amount of talk will stop the cravings . . . that result from alcohol's biochemical and neurochemical damage."*

Mathews-Larson says the allergic addictive alcoholic is the "most frequent type of person who comes in for treatment. These people typically do have food sensitivities or other things they take into their bodies, like environmental chemicals, that produce an altered brain response." As a result, all HRC patients are sent to a clinical ecologist for extensive food allergy testing and all culprits are removed from their diets. They're also tested for sensitivities to chemicals, particularly ethanol (alcohol), the fumes from which can actually intoxicate a susceptible individual, making him desperate for the real thing, says Mathews-Larson.

"It's no accident that house painters, garage mechanics, printers, hair stylists, and others who are continually exposed to chemical fumes, sprays, and dyes in their work rank high in alcoholism and depression," Mathews-Larson says. Usually, patients are able to find ways to avoid frequent exposures to the chemicals to which they're sensitive; occasionally, however, a patient will have to change occupations in order to comfortably abstain from alcohol.

Criticisms of Nutritional Therapy

Not surprisingly, this controversial program has its critics. Michael Stoil, Ph.D., director of operations for the Washington (D.C.) Area Council on Alcoholism and Drug Abuse (WACADA), for instance, believes sugar addiction is a myth and says the only connection between nicotine and alcohol is a social one. Stoil admits some research does suggest that there *may* be something to the food allergy/alcohol addiction connection, but, he adds, "that's a long way from proving" that if you eat corn you're going to get alcohol cravings.

> *"Seventy-four out of 100 HRC patients were still 'stable and sober' one year after treatment."*

On the subject of ethanol-induced intoxication, however, Stoil believes Mathews-Larson is right on the mark. "Of course that's true," he declares. "We've got a lot of people who become affected by household solvents—not so often ethanol, but methyl alcohol."

Although this unique program has yet to prove its success rate in an independent study (Mathews-Larson and Robert A. Parker, M.Sc., conducted a study, "Alcoholism Treatment with Biochemical Restoration as a Major Component," that found that 74 out of 100 HRC patients were still "stable and sober" one year after treatment), it has had noteworthy effects on the substance abuse field. Similar programs are popping up throughout the country, such as California Recovery Systems in Mill Valley, which is modeled in part after HRC.

And there's no denying that to many HRC graduates, for whom conventional treatment had failed miserably, the nutrition-oriented program was, quite literally, a lifesaver. Terri Cox says she was seriously considering suicide when she saw a TV commercial for HRC that led her to the program. Today, Cox, 45, is two years sober. "This worked for me when I truly thought nothing could," she says. "When I really believed I could not live on this earth without alcohol and knew I couldn't live much longer with it."

Acupuncture Is an Effective Treatment for Alcoholism

by Margaret Shockley

About the author: *Margaret Shockley works in an acupuncture and alternative medicine clinic.*

In a country where the problems of alcohol and drug abuse are fought through the media hype instead of medical treatment, any innovation that promised to provide inexpensive, effective and easily obtained help would be welcome news. In countless low-income communities, just such an innovation is being hailed by detoxification and community health experts as being "the best thing to hit drug treatment since twelve-step programs," according to a San Francisco health worker.

Acupuncture, used as a basic health care technique in Asia for millennia, has found a new application in this country as a component of drug and alcohol detoxification efforts. For state and county health budgets stretched to the limit, acupuncture can be an effective and low-cost method of substance abuse treatment. For many communities of color, hit hard by drug abuse and alcohol-related illness and disease, acupuncture could literally be a lifesaver.

Widespread acceptance of acupuncture, however, is hindered by the position of the American Medical Association and federal agencies, which do not view the treatment as "real medicine." Despite some encouraging results, according to the *Washington Post*, "the federal government . . . seems uninterested in acupuncture as a drug-abuse therapy." Without support from either the government or the medical establishment, acupuncture has so far had a much more limited application than it might, had it been given this support.

Successful Programs

It is, however, being used in diverse locations, from New York City's Lincoln Hospital to the prisons in Dade County, Florida. Hospitals in Hennepin County, Minnesota, use it as a basic component of alcohol detoxification programs, as

Margaret Shockley, "Acupuncture and Alcohol in the Inner City," *The Minority Trendsletter,* Fall 1991. Reprinted with permission.

do the Bay View Hunter's Point foundation's MIRA Project in San Francisco and the Hooper Community Clinics in Portland, Oregon.

Jeaneane Fast Horse, Director of Project Recovery on the Pine Ridge Sioux Reservation in South Dakota, said that the number of clients using their services has skyrocketed since they instituted acupuncture detoxification, because it is cheap, easy and effective. Columbia Presbyterian Hospital in New York City and San Rafael Hospital in New Haven, Connecticut (a Yale University affiliate) have added successful acupuncture detoxification programs to their drug treatment efforts.

> *"Acupuncture . . . has found a new application . . . as a component of drug and alcohol detoxification."*

Patricia Keenan, O.M.D. , Clinical Director of Acupuncture services at Bay View Hunter's Point, explains that "Chinese medicine offers a safe, non-addictive, non-chemical means of detoxification from drugs of all sorts—PCP, heroin, cocaine, crack cocaine. It is extremely effective in detoxification from alcohol, as Pat Culliton's work at the Hennepin County Medical Center clearly demonstrates. Here at Bay View Hunter's Point, we treat pregnant moms, infants exposed to drugs, poly-drug abusers—you name it, we see it. And we do so effectively, with no side effects or secondary addictions like you get with methadone and other chemically-based treatments."

For initial detoxification from either drugs or alcohol, most practitioners use an "ear-needling" technique, setting four to six needles in specific acupuncture points in the ear. In most clinics, patients are first "needled" in this point, and then encouraged to relax for 30 to 45 minutes. When they're ready, the clients remove the needles themselves. Even practitioners who are enthusiastic about its results, however, admit that they really do not know how it works-just that it does.

"It made me relaxed," one crack addict was quoted as saying in a newspaper interview. "I don't get any cravings."

Young Lords Bring Acupuncture to the Bronx

Acupuncture detoxification was first used on a large scale in the U.S. in 1974 at Lincoln Clinic, in a Bronx neighborhood of New York. The clinic was established through the efforts of a political organization, the Young Lords, who were a militant African-American group similar to the Black Panthers. Originally, the clinic offered a straight methadone detoxification program. According to Mickey Malendez, an organizer with the Young Lords, "we were looking for a method to treat addicts that went beyond addicting them to new drugs."

Dr. Michael Smith, medical director at the Lincoln Center for Substance Abuse, estimates a 50 percent success rate based on urine tests given over a two-month period. These results are especially significant because most of Lincoln's acupuncture clients are referred by the court, instead of having entered the program by choice. In this kind of situation, according to Dr. Smith, successful treatment outcomes using traditional techniques are the exception.

The National Acupuncture Detoxification Association (NADA) has adopted the methods developed at Lincoln. This standardized method is administered in a group setting on an outpatient basis, and costs between $5 to $10 per treatment session. In the Hooper Center in Portland, Oregon, treatments are as little as $2 each. Many of the clinics using the NADA model are walk-in clinics associated with community clinics offering counseling, twelve-step programs similar to Alcoholics Anonymous and other forms of health care.

The Lincoln/NADA model emphasizes a non-judgemental approach to health care, where the substance abuse problem is seen as a condition requiring treatment rather than a moral failure on the part of the addict or alcoholic. One of the benefits of acupuncture is that the practitioner does not need to know what drug or drugs the client has been using in order to provide treatment.

Some infants exposed to drugs or alcohol in utero show various symptoms, such as constant restlessness, sleeplessness, ceaseless crying, poor appetite, and rigid arching of the back. Without intervention, they may face learning disabilities, dysfunctional behavior and social stigma. In the cases involving infants and children younger than six, some practitioners use the Chinese medical technique of taping small seeds of Vaccariae to one to three acupuncture points in the ear selected according to the infant's development. The baby's caregiver is then instructed to press lightly on the seeds several times daily to stimulate the points.

Used on Newborns

While it is too early to evaluate the long-term effects of Chinese medical interventions in these cases, Patricia Keenan reports marked improvement in the infants she has treated. By relieving withdrawal symptoms and reducing the dulling seen in substance affected newborns, acupressure stimulation enhanced focusing and the maternal-infant bonding. This is extremely important for mothers threatened with losing their child because of their addiction. It makes it easier for her to seek help for both herself and her child.

There is a growing body of evidence to support the claims of acupuncture practitioners. The World Health Organization (WHO), for ex-

> *"Chinese medicine . . . is extremely effective in detoxification from alcohol."*

ample, has researched and declared Chinese medicine to be effective for over 150 diseases, including asthma, arthritis, colitis, and ulcers, to name a few. It does not appear, however, that research into new treatments is on the American drug policy agenda. In a nine-billion dollar a year budget for fighting the "war on drugs," almost 75 percent is reserved for enforcement of drug laws, and 25 percent for treatment and therapy. In 1981, those percentages were reversed.

Psychotherapy Can Help Alcoholics

by Marc Galanter

About the author: *Marc Galanter is a professor of psychiatry and director of the division of alcoholism and drug abuse at New York University School of Medicine in New York City. He is the author of* Network Therapy for Alcohol and Drug Abuse, *from which this viewpoint is excerpted.*

I was recently contacted by Paul, a physician practicing at a local hospital. He was concerned that Nancy, whom he hoped to marry, was alcoholic. When they were getting to know each other, there were periods when Nancy had seemed to be unavailable in person or by phone, but it was only after they had moved in together that he realized the reason for these periods of absence. He soon became aware that Nancy went on drinking binges and sometimes did not show up the next day at the law office where she worked. She once threatened to kill herself when she was drunk.

Paul turned to her parents, but they preferred to minimize the issue, apparently not wanting to tarnish their daughter's image. He pleaded with Nancy to go to AA; she said she'd think about it.

Addiction Problems Little Understood

Nancy had been in treatment a few years with a reputable psychiatrist, who, I later found out, had tried to discourage her drinking. It was the problem this therapist had encountered that is typical of those confronted with addicted patients. Although it must have been clear that his pleas were doing little good, the psychiatrist was unwilling to speak with Paul because of the need to preserve the "integrity" of Nancy's analysis.

A few weeks after Paul and I met, Nancy herself came to see me at Paul's behest, and I tried to get her to look at her problem. She, however, said that she was quite comfortable in her analysis, and that it was offering her valuable insights. Further, she did not think it useful for me to speak directly with her doctor. When I pointed out that her continued drinking argued for additional inter-vention, or at least some visits to AA, she contended that her relationship in therapy should be enough to deal with her problems.

For many alcoholics, years of treatment have meant that they had achieved "insight" but that their drinking con-tinued. Stories of therapy like hers abound at meetings of Alcoholics Anonymous. Ironically, though, these addicted people could have been treated effectively by those same therapists if the psychology of addic-tion were more widely understood and more effective care implemented.

> *"Most mental health professionals are ill-prepared to help the alcoholic or drug abuser achieve recovery."*

Substance abuse is as great a challenge as any clinical issue that has emerged in recent decades. Addictive illness is among the most prevalent psychiatric disorders.

A major study, the Epidemiologic Catchment Area Study, shows that the life-time chance of an American developing an abuse or dependence disorder is 15 percent for alcohol and 6 percent for other drugs. These are the most prevalent disorders among men of all age groups and the most prevalent among women 18 to 24. The cost of alcohol and drug problems is greater than that of all other mental illnesses combined—$144 billion versus $129 billion in a recent year.

Most mental health professionals are ill-prepared to help the alcoholic or drug abuser achieve recovery even though addicted people and their families regularly turn to them for help. Further, few alcoholics and addicts are willing to go to Al-coholics Anonymous until they've suffered very long, and most drop out before becoming involved. How can we engage and treat these people more effectively?

Most effective addiction treatment entails either self-help, peer support, or both, and these are hard to come by in office practice. To address this strategic deficit, I have developed an approach that engages the support of a small group, some family, some friends, to meet with a substance abuser and therapist at regular intervals to secure abstinence and help with the development of a drug-free life. The evolution of this new approach did not come easily, but through careful attempts to manage many patients over the course of their rehabilitation.

Network Therapy

I call it network therapy. Family and peers become part of the therapist's working team, not subjects of treatment themselves. Such an approach is war-ranted by the unique characteristics of the substance dependence syndrome. So-cial supports are necessary for overcoming the denial and relapse that are so compromising to effective care for the substance abuser.

Nancy's resistance to seeking help for her alcoholism was typical of the way denial shows itself over the course of the disease. A few months after I saw her, she became annoyed at her psychiatrist for "pestering her" about going to AA, and dropped out of treatment. The drinking continued, and later that year she lost her job because of unreliability. Paul was ready to walk out as well, but he said he would give her one more chance if she saw me, "the doctor who said she had to stop drinking."

Nancy came in saying that her problem was that she needed "to get a handle on the depression" she had felt since losing her job. I was not about to let her ventilate her feelings in isolation, and fall into the same trap as her first therapist. I told her that since drinking played a role in her problem, it was important that we get some support for her, to help her look at her situation. I asked her to bring Paul and a friend to our next session to discuss the issue. So began her network therapy.

Two network members were certainly more revealing about the extent of Nancy's alcoholism than she had been. They described how it had often left her in awkward social situations, and feeling incapacitated in facing the next day. I encouraged Paul and the friend to voice their feelings and concerns, to soften her inclination to avoid the problem. The impact of this network session moved Nancy to acknowledge that she had a problem with alcohol. The network members helped me to prevail on her to accept the idea of abstinence.

A Support Regimen

Together, the four of us developed a regimen to support her recovery, one that included individual sessions as well as meetings with this network. To this we added AA meetings, and the network members supported her in attending the meetings during later sessions, when she expressed misgivings about them. Nancy and I continued to meet with her network while she focused on ways to protect her continued abstinence and on the psychological issues that would allow her to achieve full recovery.

She had a few slips back into drinking while in treatment and was once prepared to give it all up. Her network was behind her continued abstinence, though. We all consulted together at these times of crisis. With each slip we would work together to understand what certain drinking cues—situations and emotional states—led to the relapses. We would then plan together how Nancy could handle these cues when they came up again.

As time went on and Nancy's abstinence was secured, our network sessions were held less frequently, but were not called off, and her individual therapy continued. In network sessions, the three of us would act as a sounding board for her recovery. We also provided the assurance that if *"Most effective addiction treatment entails either self-help, peer support, or both."* Nancy slipped again, even after treatment was over, there would be a resource to draw on to secure her return to sobriety.

The nature of network support is further evident in the way we drew on one particularly meaningful relationship to bolster Nancy's abstinence. We often spoke with her sister on my speaker phone during our network sessions. Although her sister lived in a remote city, Nancy had a trusting relationship with her, and the sister had been very distressed for years over her drinking problem. This relationship was one that added strength to the bonds of affiliation that supported Nancy's recovery.

Measures to Increase Chances of Success

I call on a variety of devices that enhance the effectiveness of the network, like introducing relapse prevention techniques into network sessions, using formal written agreements, and managing medication intake. There are many tortuous turns on the road toward recovery.

Twenty years ago, I was appointed a career teacher in alcoholism and drug abuse by the National Institute on Mental Health. Expertise and competence at treating this problem was so uncommon then that the federal government was eager to support young medical school faculty members in the hope that their academic commitment would lead them to become involved. I took this mission seriously. In my searches of the literature, I found nothing on the technique of resolving a drinking or drug problem for a patient who came to the doctor's office. But soon my colleagues began to send me addicted patients to treat, and I felt obliged to do the best I could.

"There are many tortuous turns on the road toward recovery."

Since then, researchers in addiction have begun to develop a systematic understanding of how drug and alcohol dependence wreak their effects on thinking and behavior. But there are still very few descriptions of a comprehensive approach that the therapist can apply to addicted patients. Detoxification regimens, research approaches, and hospital programs are available, but they do little to clarify the day-to-day struggle that must be staged while recovery is achieved with a patient who is living in the community.

Few therapists venture beyond recommending to alcoholics that they attend AA or take a long break from job and family and go away to a rehabilitation hospital. Beyond this, psychiatrists, psychologists, and social workers simply apply their "usual" approaches to treatment and hope that they will be useful. And because "usual therapy" rarely solves these problems, it is assumed by many that hospitalization is the only safe treatment for addicted people. It is not. An astute application of what we now know about addiction can avert hospitalization for the large majority of substance abusers.

For relapse prevention, I draw on behavioral techniques that have recently emerged from psychology and physiology for managing impulses for drug-seeking, along with a supportive network for self-examination. Awareness of the relationship between addiction and symptoms of depression and anxiety is also essential; alcoholics are prone to depression and suicide. All these issues must be brought together for effective treatment.

How does network therapy fit into our evolving understanding of addiction? Addicted persons generate great conflict and resentment among their family and friends. On the one hand, persons close to the addict have long been angered by his lack of responsiveness and by a history of many disappointments that he has conferred on them. On the other, they are remorseful over his unhappiness and the losses that he has suffered.

> *"Professionals have begun to consider the orchestration of family dynamics to move the addicted person toward recovery."*

The tension between anger and guilt makes it all but impossible for individuals close to the addicted people to approach them in an objective way. They are likely to overreact at one time and castigate them, and at another time they may shrink from asserting their concerns and be overly permissive, even enabling their addictive behavior.

In recent years, professionals have begun to consider the orchestration of family dynamics to move the addicted person toward recovery. One important approach has been a technique for intervention with the reluctant substance abuser, which brings his family together to plan a confrontation designed to impress him with the immediate need for hospitalization. With aid from a professional, family members can thereby work together, spurring the patient into action. Multiple family therapy groups for substance abusers have also come into use to create a setting where a diversity of issues are melded together to neutralize individual resentments. The sense of community engendered can be supportive, and aid in achieving compliance with an expected norm of abstinence.

By themselves, therapists have only marginal potential for influencing patients outside the office. If a patient has a slip into drug abuse the therapist may not be apprised, and if he knows, he can bring little influence to bear. Therapists on their own are limited in the degree to which they can make demands on the patient's life, and the patient is free to walk away from the therapeutic situation if it is uncomfortable for him—that is to say, if it challenges a serious relapse to addiction. All these factors make the engagement and orchestration of family and friends into the therapy with a substance-abusing patient an invaluable resource, one which offers remarkable opportunity for the modification of traditional psychotherapeutic techniques to treat the substance abuser.

The Importance of Family

A social network is very important in altering addictive behavior. In the public alcoholism clinic I once directed, patients without families to support them had to be repeatedly confronted with the realities of the addiction in group therapy by their peers so as to assure that denial did not erode their capacity to deal with reality. A social network is apparently a necessary vehicle to stabilizing the cognitive components of patients' recovery, to allow them to deal with the reality they need to see, and to provide the support essential for accepting the new reality. I realized that because of the social ties in a cohesive network, a patient in a therapist's office might be reluctant to run out on his treatment.

Inpatient rehabilitation facilities, by contrast, often disrupt family and social ties while the patients are hospitalized. They also remove patients from the opportunity of learning to deal with the conditioned cues for drinking while treatment supports are greatest; the real temptations to drinking do not present themselves in the hospital.

A person's immediate network might draw on his spouse, some friends, or his family of origin, perhaps a friend from work. Components of the network are only parts of the natural support systems that usually operate without professional involvement. But, brought to act in concert, the strength of their social influence can serve as a therapeutic device.

A number of forces shape the network:

• *Cohesiveness.* Social cohesiveness has been defined as the product of all forces that act to keep members engaged in a group, and it can be an important therapeutic instrument. It is generally evident and well focused in indigenous mental healing rituals in pre-industrial societies—and among members of groups like the Moonies and Hare Krishna. Colleagues and I have actually measured the emotional well-being experienced by members of these groups and found it to be directly proportional to the intensity of their respective feelings of cohesiveness toward the group. The relationship between emotional well-being and cohesiveness apparently served as an implicit motivation for persons to stay close to the group and promoted their compliance with its expectations.

> *"In order to act out a pattern . . . that is clearly self-destructive, addicts must adopt a pattern of denial."*

Although community ties in our society are generally weak, the kinds of intimacy and social support that characterize traditional societies can potentially be generated by engaging a small network of persons close to the patient. If the relationship between cohesiveness and emotional being is harnessed within the therapeutic context, and the patient comes to experience closeness to the therapy network as a vehicle toward well-being, then the resulting social forces can move the patient toward accepting the group's expectations, as abstinence becomes the ticket to sustaining closeness.

A Stress-Free Atmosphere

The purpose of network therapy is then to create an atmosphere that will allow an alcohol or drug abuser to experience relief from distress by participating, and moving towards a drug-free outlook. After initial sobriety has been achieved, network sessions often acquire a social quality. The group becomes friendly and close-knit, and stories and even jokes may carry over from one session to the next.

• *Cognition.* In order to act out a pattern of behavior that is clearly self-destructive, addicts must adopt a pattern of denial. This denial is supported by a variety of distorted perceptions: persecution at the hands of employers, failings of his distraught spouse, a presumed ability to control the addiction if he wants. This cognitive set is not only unfounded, but it is also at variance with the common-sense views of his drug-free family and friends. Because of this, intimate and positive encounters with them in the network produce an inherent conflict between addicts' views and the views of network members. The addict must resolve this conflict, or cognitive dissonance, in order to feel accepted in the group. The network therefore creates an ongoing pressure on the addict to relinquish the trappings of denial.

A New View

Typically, addicts deal with this conflict by defensive withdrawal, but if their network is properly managed, cohesive ties in the group will engage them and draw them into an alternative outlook. Gradually, they come to accept that their distress can be relieved by a change in attitude, as denial and rationalization are confronted in a supportive way. Over time, engagement in the network allows an addict to restructure the perspective in which the addiction has been couched.

For addicts, both healthy and faulted attitudes have long coexisted in conflict with each other, and the cognitive dissonance produced by these contradictions has driven them into a defensive stance, fending off any attack on this awkward balance. On the other hand, in a proper supportive context, a constructive view premised on abstinence and on acknowledgment of the harmful nature of drug use can emerge. Addicts can experience a "conversion" of sorts, perhaps gradual, but real nonetheless.

For one woman, four members of her network quickly made clear that she was much more likable at social gatherings before she would begin drinking. Her inclination to present herself as a "happy drunk" could not sustain itself in the face of two siblings and two friends who attested to the contrary.

"No society can codify the many proprieties it expects of its members."

Attribution theory holds that under confusing circumstances, people are more open to the introduction of unfamiliar or previously unacceptable ideas from their social environments, so long as these ideas lend clarity to the context. They may attribute new meaning to an unfamiliar feeling when it is artfully introduced. Engagement into a new perspective is particularly effective when it is offered in a supportive group setting. In the case of the addict, the therapist promotes a new perspective: Abstinence may indeed be the best option for the relief of distress and reordering a disrupted life.

• *Coercion.* Every society has options for forcing reluctant members to comply with its norms of behavior. However, formal controls, such as legal restrictions, are less influential overall than the informal controls embodied in a community of mutual

> *"Acceptance of the proposed treatment modality is, for the addicted person, a strong predictor of better outcome."*

understanding, and mediated by family and friends. No society can codify the many proprieties it expects of its members.

Actions such as the withdrawal of affection, the expression of group disapproval, and the disruption of social interactions desirable to the patient can be highly coercive. More importantly, these steps need not be actually taken to enforce compliance. The implied threat of action may be enough, particularly when it is clear that the patient cannot avoid the network's judgement by being manipulative.

The network modality can convert idle threats into effective coercion. Standing alone, network members are generally ambivalent about taking action against a substance-abusing peer because they experience sorrow over his plight, as well as anger. But in the network, the therapist converts these motives into justified action, sanctioned by a professional; potentially coercive behavior is now understood to be for the patient's own good, rather than to relieve resentment.

Since network members act in concert, the impact of their interventions is much greater than if taken alone. They are now less hesitant to express disapproval over inappropriate behavior for fear that others will back off when confronted by the angry, defensive alcoholic. The cooperative tone set by the therapist encourages mutual support and conjoint action.

The natural response of disappointment alone has great coercive potential. Once a balanced network is properly established, the patient is reluctant to invoke its disapproval.

The Outcome of Treatment

Among the 60 addicted people whom I had treated for at least three sessions since 1981, the average age was 37. Most (63 percent) were unmarried, employed (72 percent) , and male (77 percent). They were dependent on a variety of substances, alcohol and cocaine the most common (42 percent).

Almost all the patients were treated with a network, rather than alone. A majority of these networks included mates (62 percent) and peers (51 percent). Parents, siblings, and children participated less often. The younger patients were more likely to have their parental families represented, although I never set up networks without someone the patient's age.

A variety of treatments was used in addition to networks. All were seen in individual therapy. Almost a third went to more than 10 Twelve-Step meetings, and this was a sizable number since alcohol was not the principal drug of abuse for most. Seven were treated with antidepressants; four of them were hospitalized because they could not maintain sobriety.

The results of treatment were gratifying. The large majority of patients (77 percent) achieved a major or full improvement. They were abstinent or had virtually eliminated substance use, and their life circumstances were materially improved and stable. Patients whose drug use was mild to moderate were more likely to achieve success (93 percent) than those with severe dependence (61 percent). Interestingly, a patient's drug of choice was not associated with relative success, nor was regular AA attendance.

The majority of patients whose primary drug was alcohol were offered disulfiram (Antabuse), observed by a network member (16 of 21), and this was associated with a major or full improvement in almost all cases (14 of the 16). On the other hand, refusal to take disulfiram was typically associated with only moderate improvement (4 of 6), probably due to the fact that these were patients who had rejected the initial proposed treatment option. In a sense, acceptance of the proposed treatment modality is, for the addicted person, a strong predictor of better outcome.

Physicians' Warnings Can Motivate Alcoholics to Seek Treatment

by Diana Chapman Walsh et al.

About the author: *Diana Chapman Walsh is affiliated with the Harvard School of Public Health's Department of Health and Social Behavior in Boston, and the Department of Social and Behavioral Sciences at Boston University's School of Public Health.*

The medical profession has been criticized for insensitivity or blindness to patients' alcohol abuse, while problem drinkers are characterized as clever deniers, adept at disguising their dependency on alcohol. As a result, many alcohol problems are believed to elude medical detection, with the loss of an important educational and therapeutic opportunity and a skewing of the alcohol treatment effort toward "too much, too late, for too few." Although many studies have raised urgent questions about how effectively the medical profession diagnoses and counsels alcoholics, it is possible that they are exceedingly difficult to detect when the object is to intervene and reduce their drinking. Moreover, few studies have assessed whether physicians' warnings have any impact on ultimate success in treatment.

Physicians and Alcoholism

In the context of a randomized trial of three alternative treatment referrals for problem-drinking workers, we asked clients being newly enrolled in an employee assistance program (EAP) whether physicians had warned them about health hazards associated with their drinking in the year before they entered the EAP. It seems reasonable to argue that alcohol abuse advanced enough to be identified in a work setting ought to be detectable by an alert physician, given the chance. We constructed patterns of drinking and help seeking, emphasizing the previous year and the previous month. Next, we followed up subjects for 2

From Diana Chapman Walsh et al., "The Impact of a Physician's Warning on Recovery After Alcoholism Treatment," *JAMA* 267 (February 5, 1992): 663-67. Copyright 1992, American Medical Association. Reprinted with permission.

years after initial intake and assessed whether the recollection of a physician's warning was independently associated with drinking outcomes.

This study asks four questions: (1) Of the 200 problem-drinking EAP clients, how many had seen physicians for any reason, in any settings, over the previous 12 months? (2) Of those who saw physicians, how many recalled being warned that their drinking was injuring their health? (3) What distinguished problem drinkers who received a physician's warning from those who eluded medical detection? (4) Is a health warning from a physician an independent predictor of success in treatment, measured at a follow-up 2 years after intake?

Methods: Study Population

The study was located in a 10,000-employee New England manufacturing plant of a *Fortune*-500 multinational industrial firm. To be eligible, employees had to be newly identified by the EAP, with a primary presenting problem of alcoholism or alcohol abuse, according to an assessment conducted by company and/or union administrators. Also excluded were any employees about to be fired or jailed and any whose alcoholism was so far advanced as to require immediate hospitalization, as well as any believed to pose an imminent danger to themselves or others. . . .

Altogether, 227 subjects (94% of all eligible) consented to participate. They were randomized to one of three initial treatment alternatives: hospitalization with Alcoholics Anonymous backup, Alcoholics Anonymous only, or a choice of treatment. For this report, we focus on the 200 subjects who were followed up by interview for a subsequent 2 years from intake: 88% of the 227 initially enrolled and randomized. . . .

Results: Subjects

The mean age of the 200 subjects was 32 years, and they were overwhelmingly male (96%) and white (90%). Just under half (47%) had family incomes below $25,000, and the majority (51%) were high school graduates without college degrees. Forty-two percent were currently married, and nearly half lived alone.

Subjects were drinking heavily and experiencing numerous drinking-related problems. They averaged 6.3 drinks a day and 61% reported a family history of drinking problems; 21% were drunk daily and another 45% weekly during the prior month, 24% reported one or more binges (periods of drunkenness lasting >24 hours) in the previous 6 months, and 26% reported 3 or more blackouts (episodes of memory loss) in the same period. Over 90% scored "alcoholic" on the SMAST [Short Michigan Alcoholism Screening Test], 77% registered "definitely alcoholic" on the RAND index, and more than

> *"The group warned by physicians . . . had significantly more abstainers . . . in the final 6 months of post-treatment follow-up."*

212

half were "alcohol dependent" on *DSM-III* and "late" or "very late" stage alcoholics according to Mulford's Iowa stages index. Other indicators of problems these respondents had ever had with alcohol included arrests for driving while intoxicated (53%), attendance at Alcoholics Anonymous meetings (54%), and prior hospitalizations for drinking (11%).

In terms of access to medical care, all respondents worked full time for a firm with a generous health benefit plan, 35% said they had private physicians, 34% were under care for chronic illnesses, and 46% had ever been hospitalized for any reason. The 148 subjects who saw physicians were not appreciably different on these intake characteristics.

Asked to think back over the year before being enrolled into the EAP, 148 (74%) of the 200 respondents reported at least one medical encounter during that 12-month period, in emergency departments or outpatient clinics of hospitals (87 respondents), the plant dispensary (70), private practices (51), and hospital beds (18). When asked whether any physician had told them in the past year that drinking was injuring their health, only 33 subjects responded yes (17% of the total sample and 22% of the 148 exposed to any physician).

Among the 148 problem drinkers who saw physicians, some had multiple encounters. All told, in the year before intake, the sample of 200 subjects tallied 534 medical encounters: 142 to private physicians, 150 to hospital outpatient clinics and emergency departments, 17 hospital admissions, and 234 visits to plant physicians. Among the presenting problems were 112 accidents, noteworthy in light of the well-established correlation between alcohol abuse and trauma. Although we did not probe whether medical warnings were issued during each encounter, if we assume (optimistically) that a once-warned patient was always warned, we still have at least 416 medical encounters over a 1-year period in which patients recalled no warnings.

> *"Many physicians are not sufficiently alert to their patients' alcohol use and abuse."*

Who Received Medical Advice?

The likelihood of a warning during the year before EAP enrollment was greatest for patients who saw a private physician (37%) or went to a hospital as an inpatient (33%). Somewhat fewer of those who visited the plant dispensary (20%) or hospital outpatient clinics (20%) or emergency departments (16%) recalled warnings. When we compared subjects who did and did not have medical contact in the year before EAP intake, few significant differences emerged. Not surprisingly, subjects who had a job accident requiring medical attention were significantly more likely to have seen physicians, as were those who reported a chronic medical condition or having a private physician.

Among respondents who did have at least one medical encounter, those who reported that a physician did warn them that drinking was harming their health were older (mean age, 36.5 vs. 30.9 years) and had been drinking heavily longer (21 years, compared with 16 years for those not warned). Greater impairment, as measured by the *DSM-III* and the Iowa stages index, increased the likelihood of receiving a health warning from a physician, as did more reporting of illness owing to drinking, of liver disease and stomach problems, of chronic illnesses, and of previous hospitalizations for drinking. Warned employees also were more likely to have been on the job for 11 years or more and to have notices from supervisors dissatisfied with their work performance. . . . Respondents who continued to drink despite serious physical illness were five times more likely to recall having received health warnings than those who did not. Liver disease increased the chance of being warned by a factor of six. Also, being older, using marijuana, and having a supervisor's notice of unsatisfactory job performance significantly increased the chance of recalling a physician's warning, independent of other factors.

> *"Patients who recalled physicians' warnings were significantly more successful in bringing their drinking under control."*

The Impact of a Physician's Warning

Finally, looking prospectively, we analyzed follow-up data on drinking outcomes for the 148 subjects who had seen physicians in the year before enrollment into the study, comparing those who did and did not recall receiving physicians' warnings.

First, . . . 2 years after enrollment into the study (at the 24-month exit interview), the group warned by physicians in the year before intake, compared with the group not warned, had significantly more abstainers (63.6% vs. 32.2%) and fewer individuals who reported monthly drunkenness (one or more episodes) in the final 6 months of post-treatment follow-up (28.1% vs. 55.7%). . . .

Employees who recalled at intake that a physician had warned them about the harmful effects of their drinking were significantly less likely to have relapsed a full 2 years later. . . . Employees reporting at intake that they had been warned were significantly more likely, 24 months after intake, to be abstaining, . . . were less likely to report one or more episodes of drunkenness, . . . and were significantly less impaired on the RAND behavioral index. . . .

A Lack of Counseling

The results of this analysis are consistent with the frequent observation that alcohol abusers are not receiving needed counseling about their drinking from physicians. Of the 200 seriously impaired workers in our sample, only 15% recalled warnings that their abuse of alcohol might be compromising their health during the year before being identified on the job. Fully 74% (148) of the workers identified on the job had seen physicians in that year, but only 22% of them recalled health warnings. That the manifestations of alcohol abuse are overt enough to bring these same heavy drinkers to the attention of intervention programs at work during the course of the year in which they have visited physicians lends further weight to the argument that many physicians are not sufficiently alert to their patients' alcohol use and abuse.

Prior Warnings

Of greater interest, our data seem to support previous studies demonstrating the therapeutic potency of a physician's timely warning to a patient with drinking problems. . . . Patients who entered treatment with a clear recollection of a prior warning from a physician that their drinking was harming their health were more likely to be abstaining and sober and were less impaired in a 24-month follow-up assessment.

Although we cannot assert that the physician's warning caused the fuller recovery (employees with better prognosis might have been more attuned to, or more strongly influenced by, their physician's advice), our data suggest that a physician's warning may have a lasting beneficial effect. This study underscores the importance of incorporating screening and interviewing strategies into standard clinical practice so that a condition that has officially been designated a "disease" will be identified as efficiently in the medical care system as it is in the employment system. . . .

In summary, the two signal findings of this study underscore the need for greater vigilance on the part of practicing physicians for opportunities to alert their patients to potential hazards associated with heavy or problem drinking. On the one hand, it is of concern that physicians issued memorable warnings to less than a quarter of patients whose drinking was so manifestly out of control that their employers intervened at work. On the other hand, patients who recalled physicians' warnings were significantly more successful in bringing their drinking under control. Although physicians may become discouraged when their advice about alcohol seems to have little immediate effect, these findings suggest that a physician's warning, in combination with corroborating messages from multiple sources, may indeed contribute to meaningful behavioral change.

> *"A physician's warning, in combination with corroborating messages from multiple sources, may indeed contribute to meaningful behavioral change."*

Antidepressants May Be Effective at Treating Alcoholism

by Marc A. Schuckit

About the author: *Marc A. Schuckit is a professor of psychiatry at the University of California at San Diego School of Medicine and the director of the Alcoholism Research Center at San Diego's Veterans Administration Hospital.*

In recent years data have begun to accumulate to indicate the *possibility* that drugs that specifically affect one brain chemical called serotonin might have some unique effect on alcohol intake behavior. . . .

Brain cells "communicate" with one another primarily through chemicals. A stimulated cell releases a neurotransmitter substance that then diffuses or travels across a small space (the synapse or synaptic cleft) and attaches to a neighboring cell. The resulting actions on the second cell occur primarily through a number of structures called receptors which are likely to cause changes in the activity of the cell membrane that subsequently result in the generation of an electrical activity as the second cell is stimulated.

How Serotonin Affects the Brain

Over the years, many brain neurotransmitters have been identified including dopamine, norepinephrine, and serotonin. The latter is associated with many effects in the brain with the results depending upon the brain area being considered. Among the predominant actions said to occur from stimulation of serotonin-rich cells are painkilling, sleepiness, and change in appetite. The latter may be especially important as there is evidence of an interconnection between eating carbohydrate-rich food, changes in serotonin activity of the brain, and resulting eating disorders. These have in turn been hypothesized to be related to important changes in mood.

As important as serotonin is to the brain, by itself it cannot cross from the

From Marc A. Schuckit, "Do Some Antidepressants Help Control Drinking Behavior?" *Drug Abuse and Alcoholism Newsletter*, April 1990. Reprinted with permission of the Vista Hill Foundation, San Diego, California.

brain to the body because of a "blood brain barrier." Therefore, the things we eat or drink can only impact on serotonin activity indirectly through providing building blocks that go into the production of serotonin, by boosting the release of serotonin from one brain cell in order to affect the next, or by increasing the production of this chemical in brain cells. Another way to increase the impact this substance has in the brain is to specifically enhance the amount of serotonin present in that space between cells, thus theoretically increasing the effectiveness of the serotonin that is on hand. This latter effect can be observed with some antidepressant drugs that act by stopping cells from reabsorbing serotonin—in other words, these drugs stop the re-uptake of serotonin back into the cells from the synapse.

A number of these serotonin re-uptake inhibiting drugs have been tested over the years. These include zimelidine (marketed in the past as Zelmid, although now withdrawn from the market), fluoxetine (Prozac), and a number of other experimental drugs that are not yet available including alaproclate and citalopram. Another antidepressant drug that has a major effect on serotonin is trazodone (Deseryl). It is these drugs that affect serotonin levels in the space between cells that have served as the major focus for animal and human research as it relates to alcohol.

Serotonin and Alcohol Intake

The control of alcohol intake is very complex. Because of the carbohydrate characteristics of beverage alcohol and the ability of carbohydrates to boost levels of brain serotonin, it has been thought for years that this specific neurotransmitter may play some role in alcohol-seeking behavior.

This contention has been supported by a variety of animal studies. It appears as if boosting brain serotonin levels by either increasing its production or by giving precursors of this neurotransmitter will result in a decreased selection of alcohol among heavier drinking animals in an experimental situation. While not all studies agree, the data from these investigations have been considered strong enough to justify further evaluations of serotonin re-uptake inhibiting antidepressants in animal models.

Most investigations indicate that there is a decrease in alcohol consumption in animals, usually rodents, pre-fed serotonin re-uptake inhibiting antidepressants. Numerous drugs of this type have been tested in these studies including fluoxetine, zimelidine, and alaproclate. There are enough differences among these agents to indicate that it is their effects on serotonin re-uptake that may be the most important in the alcohol moderating effects. This could occur directly through actions on appetite, impact on feelings of craving, or (as proposed by at least one inves-

> *"Drugs that specifically affect one brain chemical called serotonin might have some unique effect on alcohol intake behavior."*

tigator) via a decrease in the rewarding or reinforcing effects of alcohol. The overall result is that serotonin re-uptake inhibiting drugs modify drinking behavior among diverse strains of animals.

"Serotonin re-uptake inhibiting drugs modify drinking behavior among diverse strains of animals."

These data were consistent and strong enough to justify trials in humans using numerous serotonin re-uptake inhibitors. One study reported on sixteen heavy drinking men (consuming an average of six drinks per day) who were treated for two-week periods with 200 mg per day of zimelidine (a rather high dose), followed by two-week periods of placebo. The research subjects, evaluated as outpatients, were asked to carefully record their alcohol intake patterns. While on zimelidine, there was a significant decrease in the number of drinks per day as well as the number of days on which drinking occurred. The onset of these effects appeared to be fairly rapid (certainly within a two-week period), and there was no correlation between any pre-existing mood problem and the effect of the serotonin re-uptake inhibitor (i.e., people do not have to show signs of depression to respond).

Additional Results Support Theory

In a second study, healthy men aged 20 to 42 who were relatively light drinkers (imbibing one to three times per week) were given 200 to 300 mg of zimelidine on a single occasion. Two hours after taking the drug orally they were given alcohol and their reaction evaluated. The investigators report a significant decrease (as much as 20%) in feelings of euphoria for these twelve subjects compared to their response without zimelidine pretreatment. This led to the possibility that zimelidine might decrease alcohol intake in animals or people because it interferes with the positive rewarding effects observed after the drug. Finally, another study reported that citalopram (40 mg per day) resulted in a decrease in the number of drinks per day and number of days drinking for subjects.

These findings must be viewed in perspective. The antidepressant drugs, including the serotonin re-uptake inhibiting agents, are not totally safe. They have effects on diverse parts of the brain, many patients complain of side effects with some agents including anxiety and tremor, and all of these drugs are dangerous when mixed with large amounts of alcohol. Also, while the majority of data come from zimelidine, that medication has been withdrawn from the market because of serious side effects. Indeed, in the first clinical trial of sixteen subjects related above, three of the original sixteen subjects had to stop the drug because of potentially serious changes in the liver function and an additional three (for a total of six) dropped out or did not complete the protocol—perhaps related to drug side effects. In addition, there is only one relatively pure serotonin re-uptake inhibiting antidepressant available on the market at present (fluoxetine or Prozac), and this drug does not have extensive literature relating to its specific effect on alcohol intake in humans. Finally, the decrease in alcohol intake or associated euphoria reported in most studies is relatively small. This raises the possibility that the potential dangers of these drugs among alcoholics, especially if they are mixed with alcohol, might be too high in relationship to the relatively modest improvement likely to be seen with their clinical use.

Some Clinical Conclusions

I do not yet use serotonin re-uptake inhibiting drugs in treating alcoholics. Even after reviewing the data offered above, I am not certain that the magnitude of the effects clinically justifies the dangers. On the other hand, this is a most interesting class of agents and holds some promise for enhancing our understanding of the effects of alcohol. It may help us develop drugs that decrease the alcohol craving that plagues alcoholics for long periods after achieving abstinence.

All-Women Treatment Groups Can Help Female Alcoholics

by Sondra Burman

About the author: *Sondra Burman is a doctoral student at the University of Illinois, School of Social Work, in Urbana.*

There is a growing recognition that women's health care has been neglected in the areas of research and treatment. For example, the National Institutes of Health's largest study of health care among the elderly was conducted on men only. Another major NIH research project on the effects of aspirin on heart attacks enlisted 22,000 male physicians, without any participation of women. In an effort to correct this deficiency to a greatly underserved population, the NIH recently created an Office of Research on Women's Health to evaluate the research and treatment of various female maladies. The new director, Dr. Bernadine Healy, noted "Women have unique medical problems that need greater attention."

Focus on Men Ignores Alcoholic Women

Likewise, in the area of drug and alcohol abuse, the preponderance of research studies have focused on the physiological, psychological, and sociological effects of alcohol abuse on the male. These elements have been the basis for the "male model" of alcohol treatment that has typified the predominant traditional mixed-gender alcohol/drug treatment program. By overlooking or minimizing the significant differences of chemical effects and experiences of women which have been well documented, the quality of services offered, as well as women's opportunities for recovery and a better quality of life, may be profoundly hampered.

The history of women's alcohol/drug treatment has shown that women have been grossly underrepresented in programs. S. B. Blume indicated, "Although our best estimate of the ratio of males to females suffering from alcoholism . . .

Sondra Burman, "A Model for Women's Alcohol/Drug Treatment," *Alcoholism Treatment Quarterly* 9 (no. 2, 1992): 87-98 (footnotes omitted). Copyright 1992 by The Haworth Press, Inc., 10 Alice St., Binghamton, NY 13904. Reprinted with permission.

is about 2 to 1, our best current national statistics reveal a male-to-female ratio in alcohol treatment closer to 4 to 1." B. G. Reed reported that the majority of treatment programs have a 2:1 to 10:1 imbalance of men to women. Drop-out rates of women in most programs have been much higher than men's, as much as 50% in some treatment centers. This gap in reaching and treating women demonstrates a serious flaw in providing satisfactory funding and services that will motivate women to seek help and complete treatment.

Barriers to Seeking and Obtaining Effective Treatment

Significant barriers prevent women from seeking the treatment they need. Responsibility for children, lack of network supports, finances and health insurance, and the greater stigma of alcoholism applied to women are but a few of the constraints limiting women's ability to obtain treatment. Women are more likely to face opposition from family and friends to enter treatment. Physicians and social workers make relatively few referrals for women's treatment. In reporting the low arrests and conviction rates of DUI's [driving under the influence] for women, B. L. Underhill proposed that women's alcohol problems were simply not taken seriously. She elaborated, "In both DUI programs and recovery programs, enrollment of women is much lower than their male counterparts . . . [This] perpetuates the denial that women's problems with alcohol abuse exist and are as serious as men's problems."

Societal attitudes toward women alcoholics (and drug abusers) as well as toward women, in general, are often enmeshed in the treatment setting. Women inadvertently become subjected to similar consequences of gender role inequality and biases as experienced in the outer environment, with its subsequent inferior and subordinate status messages, sometimes subliminal, oftentimes overt. M. Vannicelli reported that, "[There are] negative attitudes and expectancies that women often face once they are in a treatment setting." She further explained that negative myths and stereotyped sex-role expectancies can have a detrimental influence on clinical judgments and outcomes.

Reed indicated that in programs where women are substantially outnumbered by men, gender-related dynamics and stereotyping become more problematic for women clients. She also argued that women staff should have positions with power and leadership. "This sends an important message to clients about the value of women." Serving as role models, these women exemplify a self-sufficient and equitable stance for others to follow.

> *"The history of women's alcohol/drug treatment has shown that women have been grossly under-represented in programs."*

Underhill has emphasized that programs must reinforce the importance of self-esteem and acceptance as a woman. Strategies of attack and highly confrontive techniques that are used in typical drug treatment programs are counterproductive to these goals. She pointed out that because men are often perpetrators of sexual and physical abuse, combining men and women in groups can be injurious to those women who have been previously or are currently being victimized.

"Women are far less likely to be able to find treatment programs that offer many key services that they need. In fact, in many programs, a woman's experiences there may increase her difficulties," stated [Reed]. She explained that this, in part, is due to the failure to recognize that existing treatment models were designed for men. Women sensitive programs including dual addiction treatment and education, sexual and physical abuse counseling, treatment of gynecological problems, child care services, out-reach services, family counseling, resources for vocational training and job seeking support, and women support groups are needed to attract and keep women in treatment.

A Model Treatment Program for Women

In response to public testimony regarding the level of unmet treatment needs, 5% of Federal block grant dollars were set aside in 1985, specifically for the creation of women's services. This was increased to 10% in 1989. The long-range goals are the effective functioning of women as vital members of the family and community, and healthier children and families. Considering the hazards of the fetal alcohol syndrome and the cocaine-baby phenomena, it was also acknowledged that successful treatment outcomes would have significant impacts on both present and future generations.

> *"Significant barriers prevent women from seeking the treatment they need."*

Through these block grants, funds have been appropriated to the States to improve women's services in traditional alcohol/drug programs. They also are being used to develop and implement separate women's programs that will target their special needs, concerns, and problems.

A qualitative case study of one of these programs, the Prairie Center Intensive Outpatient Program for Women (known as the IOP) in Champaign, Illinois, is being presented. From staff interviews, observations of staff meetings and group and family therapy sessions, and perusal of case records and policy standards, data was collected to describe and illuminate significant themes of the workings of a new concept in women's treatment.

The IOP was officially opened on 2 January 1990. Its goals are to provide services to women that would help them cope with life's difficulties and traumas, without the aid of mood-altering drugs. All substance abuse women are accepted into the program. Especially targeted are women who abuse alcohol and other drugs and are subsequently neglectful mothers. This program (and several other aligned programs across the State) is a new and unique concept in the treatment of women.

The IOP and similar programs were the culmination of years of preparation on the national, state and local levels in response to the increasing awareness of the gaps in treatment services for women substance abusers that was resulting in serious consequences to these women, their children and families. It was recognized that many women were not able to afford or were not being helped by traditional chemical dependency programs. Other women were resistant to seeking help or were unaware that treatment was available to them.

> *"[There are] negative attitudes and expectancies that women often face once they are in a treatment setting."*

Original and creative programs, such as the IOP, are beginning to look at women as a distinct group, with problems that need to be addressed differently from men's. These programs are targeting issues such as the physical, social, and economic effects and consequences of alcohol/drug usage on women; difficulties of single parenting; self-defeating relationships; sexual abuse and battering; female developmental stages and changes; the need for self-improvement and empowerment; job skills; and specific problems related to the recovery from alcohol/drug addiction.

The IOP Origins

Acknowledging the contributing roles of maternal substance abuse to the neglect of children, the state and federally mandated child protection agency, the Illinois Department of Children and Family Services (DCFS), joined with the Illinois Department of Alcoholism and Substance Abuse (DASA) to develop a model of treatment that would intervene and motivate women to seek treatment services. Women who could not afford to pay for treatment were provided free access to services. Others would pay on a sliding-scale arrangement.

Project SAFE

In 1986, the Department of Health and Human Services funded several pilot projects in Illinois to test a model, which came to be known as Project SAFE, an acronym for a Substance and Alcohol-Free Environment. It was designed to be an intensive outpatient counseling program for women for the purpose of substance abuse recovery, improved over-all functioning, and learning constructive parenting skills.

The model consists of a close working relationship between DCFS caseworkers and a local substance abuse treatment program. DCFS workers are trained to identify women in their caseloads who are at high risk for abuse of substances and neglect (and possible abuse) of their children. They also serve as case managers who assess women's needs and make appropriate referrals to treatment programs and other agencies in the community.

Often the court system is involved to protect children and assure their mothers' participation in treatment. In severe abuse and neglect cases, children are removed from the homes and placed in foster care. Only after the mothers' satisfactory completion of treatment would the children be returned home.

Four sites were chosen as Project SAFE demonstration models in Illinois: Rock Island, Galesburg, Dixon, and Peoria. The Prairie Center IOP is the direct result of the success of these projects.

Prairie Center was already well established as a treatment center that contracted with other agencies to provide services for substance abusers. Over 80% of its services have been state-funded. The Illinois Department

> *"The alcoholic woman . . . is still an example of a discredited, stigmatized, and disadvantaged individual."*

of Alcoholism and Substance Abuse (DASA) is the major revenue source. Most clients are from the local area and surrounding communities. Many are court ordered and on probation. Both male and female clients are accepted, although males are by far in the majority.

Prairie Center was chosen as a Project SAFE Intensive Outpatient Program for Women (IOP) site because it met the following criteria:

1. It is a DASA licensed and funded substance abuse treatment program that includes outpatient services among its various units.
2. It is located in a community that has a local DCFS office.
3. Both Prairie Center and the local DCFS agency were committed to a cooperative effort in providing women's treatment services and parenting training according to the Project SAFE guidelines.

Establishment of the IOP

After the success of the pilot studies from the other Project SAFE programs, the IOP was established at Prairie Center, in Champaign, Illinois. Funding, guidelines for staff qualifications and training, treatment standards and formats, and program evaluations are provided through the collaboration of the two state agencies, DASA and DCFS. Additionally, the facility of Prairie Center provides administrative support, organizational structure, office space, and staff support and services of their other programs (Detoxification, Residential, and Aftercare).

An integral part of the program is the effective coordination of activities of the IOP and the local DCFS office. Both work closely together to identity women and families at risk and to intervene in providing treatment. Other referral sources are: community and social service agencies, the court system, the Women's Shelter, churches, the AA community, families, and self-referrals.

The IOP all women's staff consists of a director, two substance abuse counselors, and two outreach workers. It is an 18-hour/week, six-week rotational, intensive outpatient program for women, followed by an eight-week (two-hours/session) parental skill training course. The possibility exists of an extension for those women who can benefit from more treatment. It also offers its services to women referred to the Residential program who exhibit more severely disabling problems.

Each woman is assigned a primary substance abuse counselor and outreach worker. The former is responsible for the educational and counseling activities within the confines of the treatment facility. The latter has multiple roles, that of motivator, guide, advocate, friend, role model, resource finder, and transportation manager as she "reaches out" in the community to work with clients and other supportive agencies.

Outreach workers visit the clients in their homes to make assessments, help with problems-of-everyday-living, arrange day care services, and provide transportation to the treatment program, if necessary. They also assist DCFS investigators in assessing the severity of substance abuse in prospective clients.

The total focus of treatment is on addiction and recovery, from a female perspective, as well as women's issues related to daily living. Modalities include substance abuse and 12-Step counseling and education; individual, group, children, and family therapy; special women's issue groups (sobriety and recovery, feelings, spirituality, sexuality, domestic violence, physical and sexual abuse counseling, stress management, value clarification, assertiveness training, and self-esteem), AIDS and drug education forums, and parenting classes. Community resources are obtained to assist with gynecological problems, financial aid, housing, job procurement, and other needs.

The IOP Experience

When DCFS gets a referral involving women and children (often from the courts), the IOP is notified if there is any suspicion of an alcohol or other drug involvement. An outreach worker, along with a DCFS investigator, will make a preliminary assessment, followed by an evaluation by the IOP director. The staff of the IOP also assesses potential clients from other referral sources. These assessments include a lengthy interview, a personal and familial drug history, current family status and involvement, life-style, educational and employment history, medical and psychiatric history, and present and past legal problems.

If a woman is a likely candidate for treatment, recommendations are made whether outpatient substance abuse treatment would be beneficial. If the potential client appears to be functioning adequately in her home environment and not "at risk" for destructive or abusive behaviors, she will be admitted to the IOP six-week program, followed by eight weeks of parenting instruction.

> *"Alcoholic women have difficulty seeing themselves as separate, autonomous individuals."*

When there is evidence of maladaptive functioning, with the potential for severe abuse and neglect of children and self, residential inpatient treatment is recommended. These women participate in both programs, spending mornings and evenings in residential treatment and afternoons in the IOP.

Upon admission to the program, the woman fills out a variety of forms identifying parental and personal substance usage and a psycho-social history. These forms and the initial assessments made by the DCFS and outreach workers, and the IOP director, are added to the clinic records. Many of the questions on forms which the women personally fill out are similar to those asked during preliminary assessments conducted by staff. This process serves as a double check on the data presented.

> *"Women-only groups may be more effective than mixed-gender groups."*

The IOP, consisting of an intensive four hours/day of self-examination, exploration of behaviors, thoughts, beliefs, and values, is a unique experience for these women. Most of them have never been exposed to any kind of substance abuse or mental health treatment before. Many have never had the opportunity to discuss their problems and fears in a safe, nonthreatening environment. Some are uncomfortable or reticent about self-disclosing past and present indiscretions. Many have difficulty trusting.

It is the task of the staff to change this. In order for the women to share their lives with strangers, and to listen, learn, and incorporate new ideas and information, they must be open and receptive. Gaining rapport is the first step; trust, the next. What these women must feel is an acceptance, a nonjudgmental attitude and support.

The Importance of Role Models

If the program is making a difference in their lives, they will not only internalize what is learned, they will begin to share more, see alternative means of solving problems and making decisions, accept the necessity of different lifestyles free from chemicals and destructive relationships, and begin to emulate female role models who have also experienced pain and suffering, but are living productive and satisfying lives.

There is a growing camaraderie among the women. They begin to laugh and cry together; empathize with the difficult life of addiction; express shock at some of the horror stories; and support one another to make the changes needed to get off the treadmill and be free, knowing that some may make it, fearing that some never will.

Specific patterns emerge as time passes: co-dependency, intimacy and sexuality issues, and poor self-esteem. This matches literature studies that claim these issues surface quite often amongst women. The power of messages spoken during the group process reflects the changes that are noted. "You can smile now." "You hold your head up high." "You don't seem as depressed." "You seem to be getting it together." Words of encouragement that make a difference.

As time passes, noticeable changes in behavior become evident. Comments from staff included:

> In many women, there appears to be a change in the third week. They stop the struggle and start accepting. The acting-out stops, and they start listening and re-

sponding. Instead of using drugs, they start using the IOP, their families and support systems. They begin looking for jobs and housing (away from drug sources). Their physical appearance improves. They start taking care of themselves.

This woman was so depressed, almost immobilized at first. She didn't miss a day, but seemed lethargic, without direction or a will to live. I thought she got zero out of the program. Then she got angry and exploded. The other women understood her pain and supported her. It was like a catharsis. She did well . . . got a volunteer job in a nursing home. After proving her dependability, they hired her. She went from existing to living again.

She looked like death when she came in . . . a cocaine addict. I thought there was nothing there. She existed only to use. It was three weeks before she even made eye contact. She'd bring in her baby who was only three pounds at birth (a cocaine baby). There didn't seem to be any bonding between them. With this woman, it was a gradual change, but it was happening. She found hope through others making it, and became part of the group.

These women form new attachments with each other, both inside and outside of treatment. They go to AA and NA [Narcotics Anonymous] meetings together and support each others' sobriety and existence.

Characteristics of an All-Women's Program

The following themes emerged from the analysis of the data collection:
Benefits of the IOP

1. Emphasis on recovery from all mood-altering chemicals and problems of daily living, from a female perspective.
2. Increased self-disclosure, less inhibiting participation, and "working through" of sensitive issues (sexual abuse, incest, rape, battering, domestic violence, harassment, sexism, etc.).
3. Opportunity for acquiring acceptance and pride in a feminine identity from positive associations with other women.
4. Opportunity to learn from and emulate strong women role models.
5. Promotes bonding and trust with other women; fellowship and camaraderie are experienced.
6. Provides a supportive, nurturing, empathic environment.
7. Facilitates "letting go" of destructive attachments (substances and relationships), and the incentive to overcome adversity.
8. Exhibits less "game" playing and deferring to others than in mixed-gender groups.
9. Acquires an understanding of personal, physical, social, and economic consequences of drug use and responses to experiential stressful and oppressive conditions.
10. Develops parenting skills, with specialized parenting classes.
11. Empowers women to problem-solve, make decisions, and "take charge of their lives."

12. Includes separate children's and family groups.
13. Provides Outreach services (assists with interventions, identifies potential abusers, provides encouragement for treatment involvement, provides transportation to/from treatment and other community agencies, obtains community resources and individual needs).
14. Incorporates Advocacy services (offers assistance obtaining financial and legal aid, housing, clothing, and child care).
15. Goals are abstinence, empowerment, independent functioning, and improvement in coping abilities.

Benefits/Liabilities of Female Counselors

1. Empathize and relate to women's situations and problems, leading to greater understanding of feelings and behaviors.
2. Offers support, strength, guidance, and hope through role-modeling and empowerment.
3. Over-identification and involvement can interfere with objectivity in permitting women clients to assume their own responsibility for problem-solving and decision-making.
4. May expect more from women clients, often becoming overly critical with perceived failure to progress (especially noted in recovering counselors who have overcome similar problems).

Basic Needs Must Be Met

In order for women to overcome their problems in treatment, attention must be paid to their basic needs, concerns, and problems in a society that engenders routine stresses and unequal opportunities and advantages. The alcoholic woman, who is represented in all walks of life, is still an example of a discredited, stigmatized, and disadvantaged individual. Her self-esteem and self-confidence is shaken. Supports and resources have dwindled. Family and friends often forsake her. Society condemns and segregates her, much more than her male counterpart.

She often does not have the skills to compete in the job market to maintain herself. Even her attempts at obtaining necessary treatment are thwarted by limited funds, insufficient health insurance, and a biased system. Frustration, anger, and hopelessness often maintain the cycle of substance abuse and degradation. Many of these women, traumatized by emotional, sexual and physical abuses, insufficient finances and opportunities, self-medicate to escape the pain of living with these conditions. It is well documented that women's abuse of substances is frequently precipitated and associated with specific life crises and stresses.

"All-women's programs . . . offer a viable alternative to current treatment practices."

According to G. Hamilton and J. Volpe, "Alcoholic women have difficulty seeing themselves as separate, autonomous individuals, and instead develop identities based entirely upon their relationships with others." All-women's programs offer a unique opportunity to gain a sense of self, empowerment, independent functioning, and achievement as the totality of their experiences are recognized. The socialization process which promotes gender inequality, and societal norms that guide the way an individual thinks and behaves, are challenged. Women learn from other women, sharing similar experiences and trepidations. In the case of addicted women, perhaps for the first time, there exists a camaraderie with other women and an acceptance of the assets of womanhood and their roles in society. The staff and clients have comparable goals—total abstinence and the improvement of women's conditions.

Recovery, as difficult as it may be, becomes a viable goal as plans to change the present and future are not restricted to a familiar dependency on a substance, unhealthy life-style, or unfulfilling relationship. Attempts to reduce some of the inequities of women's experiences and to develop a sense of pride and optimism where little exists become tangible goals.

A Forum for Acceptance

It is important for women to have the opportunity to learn to take responsibility for their own recovery, without distractions, before attending other groups. L. J. Beckman reported that in all-women's groups, women are more honest and self-disclosing than in mixed groups. P. Fellios has indicated that women-only groups may be more effective than mixed-gender groups by providing a forum for acceptance, nurturance, kinship, and identification which places the female client more at ease (and therefore more amenable to working on personal problems).

Most therapeutic programs agree that it is important to initially focus on the recovery process, postponing other considerations (like relationship mending or making). All-women's programs afford this process, without distractions that may interfere with primary goal-setting, problem-solving and decision-making. They offer a viable alternative to current treatment practices.

Likewise, it is also acknowledged that a reality orientation must be experienced in treatment that will provide skills that can be generalized to other environmental situations. At the proper time, male clients and staff can offer this sense of reality, providing useful information and insights from a male perspective and assisting with altering dysfunctional social skills and associations.

Therefore, it is being proposed that the ideal intervention for many women would be a completion of a woman's program prior to attending mixed-gender groups and aftercare. Given the relatively few women's programs currently in existence throughout the country, it is suggested that more women's programs be funded and implemented, thereby being available for women who choose to go that route.

Treatments Designed for Elderly Alcoholics Could Be Effective

by House Subcommittee on Health and Long-Term Care

About the author: *The Subcomittee on Health and Long-Term Care is a subdivision of the U.S. House of Representatives Select Committee on Aging.*

More than 18 million adult Americans have medical, social, and/or personal problems related to alcohol use. Alcohol use disorders are seen in persons who are drinking excessively, are experiencing alcohol-related disabilities, and who require treatment. Approximately 1.5 million Americans seek treatment for alcoholism annually. The economic cost of alcohol abuse and dependence in this Nation is projected to reach $150 billion by 1995.

Estimates of older persons in hospitals or other health care facilities who evidence illness or other serious consequences of alcohol abuse range up to 70 percent. This is in stark contrast to the prevalence of alcohol-related problems among hospitalized persons of all ages, which has been estimated at 25 percent. Most of these older patients suffer debilitating illnesses exacerbated by their alcohol abuse that result in particularly costly lengths of stay. Nevertheless, for many, an undiminished social stigma and lack of specific insurance coverage leads to inappropriate hospital stays, when treatment could be provided just as effectively in less costly settings.

Alcoholism Among the Elderly Is Increasing

While overall consumption appears to be leveling off or declining, alcohol remains the leading drug of abuse in the Nation. Findings indicate that alcohol is the drug of choice for the older adult. Late-life alcohol abuse is increasing and is recognized as a significant problem.

It is estimated that there are almost 2.5 million older adults who have prob-

From U.S. Congress, House Select Committee on Aging, Subcommittee on Health and Long-Term Care (Edward R. Roybal, chairman), *Alcohol Abuse and Misuse Among the Elderly*, 102d Cong., 2d sess., 1992. Committee Publication No. 102-852.

lems related to alcohol. Twenty-one percent of hospitalized individuals age 60 and over have a diagnosis of alcoholism. The cost of treating alcoholism in older adults is surprising. In 1990, the cost of alcohol-related hospital care for the elderly was estimated to be as high as $60 billion. It is also estimated that, of the 30,916 elderly that died of alcohol abuse in 1985, each lost 10 years from his or her life. Aside from the loss in human terms, this translates into a productivity loss of $624 million.

There are many factors that contribute to making alcoholism in the older population a "hidden problem." For example, many criteria used in screening and diagnosis of alcohol abuse and alcoholism are inappropriate for this population, leading to underestimates of the scope of the problem. Traditional measurement of alcoholism may not apply to the elderly, such as the cutoff point used to define heavier drinking, which may be inapplicable to older persons because of their increased sensitivity to alcohol. Our perceptions and attitudes towards the older adult may also serve to hide an alcohol problem. Americans have a "mental block" which prevents many from believing the elderly can have alcohol problems. Some may also have the attitude, "Why take away one of the few remaining pleasures the elderly have?" This rationalization uses age to justify a failure to provide help to our elderly. And any recovering alcoholic will tell you that alcohol, when it's being abused, is not a pleasure. A recent study found that older adults are less likely to be recommended for alcohol treatment than younger patients.

The Surgeon General's 1988 workshop on Health Promotion and Aging, and the1981 Mini-White House Conference on Aging and Alcohol both expressed the need to find effective ways to reduce the current level of late-life alcohol abuse.

Dimension of the Problem

Although the true impact of alcohol abuse on mortality is difficult to assess, chronic liver disease and cirrhosis (the main chronic health hazard associated with alcohol abuse) was ranked as the 9th leading cause of death in the U.S. in 1986, causing over 26,000 deaths. Alcohol-related health problems are diagnosed in a high proportion of older patients who have been hospitalized for non-alcohol related problems. It is estimated as many as 70 percent of older persons in hospitals or other health care facilities evidence illness or other serious consequences of alcohol abuse.

"Alcohol is the drug of choice for the older adult."

Estimates indicate that as much as 37 percent of the over-55 population has a severe problem with alcohol or medication and as many as one in five have a serious emotional problem. About 60 percent of older people are likely to be daily drinkers. One study found that 15 percent of persons over age 60 reported drinking the equivalent of 4 or more drinks daily.

The elderly population is increasing rapidly. Projections indicate that the over-60 age group will grow from its current level of 11 percent of the U.S. population to 25 percent by 2030. This increase, with associated increases in numbers of older alcohol abusers, will have serious implications for future health care providers.

Among this older age group, differences in patterns of alcoholism emerge. For example, male alcoholics make up 88 percent of the total elderly population who receive treatment. Depending on the setting, up to 60 percent of elderly men admitted to acute medical wards are active alcoholics. However, only 28 percent of the older men reported drinking alone. Solitary drinking was much more common for women.

The Female Alcohol Abuser

Female alcohol abusers have only recently become the subject of research interest. The few studies of older women suggest that they are more likely than men to start drinking heavily in later life, especially if they are single or widowed; that drinking-related problems among women are related to loss or lack of roles; and that depression may precede and possibly contribute to the onset of alcohol abuse for women. It is not unusual for family members to hide the drinking problem of their female loved ones from others. Women are also at a higher risk due to the fact that they tend to consume about two and one-half times more medications

> *"Twenty-one percent of hospitalized individuals age 60 and over have a diagnosis of alcoholism."*

than men which can lead to serious adverse drug interactions. Although sparse, the research suggests that the number of older women who are "hidden alcohol abusers" exceeds the number of identified male alcohol abusers.

Abuse Patterns

Elderly alcohol abusers generally fall into one of two categories: early onset and late onset. Early onset is considered a chronic condition while late-onset problem drinking is in response to stresses associated with aging. Little research attention is focused on late-onset alcohol abuse and alcoholism. Late-onset alcohol abuse may begin in response to stressful life experiences such as bereavement, poor health, loss of employment, retirement, or financial difficulties. It appears to be more frequent among persons of higher socioeconomic status. At least 41 percent of the people age 65 and over who were enrolled in a Mayo Clinic alcoholism treatment program reported symptoms of alcoholism that began after age 60. In another study, almost two-thirds of the elderly were there for the first time.

One reason alcoholism and alcohol abuse among the elderly is hard to detect and treat is that it is largely a hidden problem. Unrecognized by society and often ignored or denied by the elderly person him- or herself, or family members, it escapes the attention of health policymakers and counselors who might intervene and make a difference.

A Hidden Problem

Alcohol abuse and alcoholism among the elderly is a "hidden problem" for many reasons:

(1) Self-reporting of alcohol consumption is the primary source of information on rates of heavy drinking. Older adults may have difficulty with mental arithmetic and may take prescription medications that adversely affect recent memory. There are also generational differences in the perceived social acceptability of drinking. As a result, older adults may be more reluctant to admit their true level of consumption.

> *"Older adults are less likely to be recommended for alcohol treatment than younger patients."*

(2) Standard cutoff scores used for defining heavy consumption may be inappropriate for older adults because of that group's increased sensitivity to alcohol. Older persons experience higher levels of peak alcohol concentrations for similar doses because, with age, a person loses lean body mass. Therefore, there is less area in which to distribute water-soluble alcohol. In other words, due to physiological changes, older persons can experience the same effects of alcohol with less consumption. Of particular concern is the fact that the first drug of choice among the elderly is alcohol to "numb the pain" from psychological and physical problems.

(3) Traditional measurements of social, legal, and health problems (e.g., interpersonal problems, employment problems, legal or financial difficulties, drinking and driving, neglecting responsibilities) may not apply to the elderly who are usually retired, may not own a car, and may have few family or social contacts and few responsibilities. Better indicators for the older adult may include housing problems, falls or accidents, poor nutrition, inadequate self-care, lack of physical exercise, and social isolation.

(4) Alcohol-related illnesses may be difficult to separate from other chronic illness, mental problems such as dementia, and the side effects of medication.

(5) Older adults may swap their medications with friends and family members, leading to unexpected negative interactions with consumed alcohol.

(6) Denial is a highly difficult issue to address with both older adults and their family members. In addition, the elderly may not recognize the symptoms, or may wrongly interpret symptoms of alcohol abuse or alcohol interaction with prescription or over-the-counter drugs as simply the effects of aging.

(7) Most recovery halfway houses will not accept a person over the age of 65.

Under-reporting is a factor that contributes to masking the extent of this problem. Alcohol abuse and alcoholism must first be recognized by medical staff in hospitals to be listed in the hospital discharge records. Recent epidemiology studies show alcohol-related problems are not diagnosed in significant proportions of hospital patients. In one study, fewer than 50 percent of the medical staff detected alcoholism in patients who positively screened for alcoholism. The study also found that physicians were less likely to identify as alcoholic those patients with higher incomes, higher education, or private medical insurance.

The coexistence of dementia and alcohol use poses special diagnostic problems in older people. Dementia associated with alcohol disorders must be distinguished from the dual disorder of Alzheimer's disease and coexisting alcohol use disorders. Some apparent dementia in older adults is actually a form of drug-induced cognitive impairment reversible in the absence of the alcohol and/or other drugs. Erroneous stereotypes of older alcohol abusers can prevent physicians from recognizing alcohol abuse or misuse in their older patients. Lastly, medical residents and other health professionals also may have problems diagnosing alcohol use disorders in outpatient health settings.

When older adults under-report their alcohol abuse or alcoholism, chronic health problems may be falsely attributed to normal aging or age-prevalent illnesses. The symptoms of alcohol abuse or misuse can include repeated falls, accidents, gaps in memory, trembling, weight loss, fatigue, insomnia, incontinence, aggression, depression, cognitive impairment, general debility, malnutrition, self-neglect, and increased problems with the control of certain diseases such as diabetes, gout, or angina. These and other problems may be caused and/or aggravated by alcohol abuse.

Even with this significant under-reporting of alcohol abuse and misuse by older adults, hospital discharge data for the period 1979-1985 show that the over-65 age group consistently had the highest proportion (60 percent) of alcohol-related diagnoses that were not primary diagnoses. More alcohol-related morbidity was found in older patients than in the younger age groups after they had been hospitalized for other, non-alcohol related reasons.

The Causes

What are the causes of alcohol abuse and misuse in the elderly? In most cases, loneliness and depression preceded the first drink. This is a common denominator to both the early- and late-onset drinker. The loss of productive social roles and status, loneliness, boredom, the loss of those close to them, and the absence of supportive social relationships are identified as the major causes of problem drinking among the elderly.

> *"Denial is a highly difficult issue to address with both older adults and their family members."*

Depression is the most prevalent non-organic mental disorder in later life. Approximately 15 percent of community-based older adults have symptoms of depression. One in two nursing home residents who are not severely cognitively impaired have some form of depression. There is a strong relationship between depression and physical illness and/or disability at all ages. Depression may coexist with alcohol and other substance abuse. Older adults take as many as eight or more prescription medicines a day that are prescribed by two or more physicians. The interactions of alcohol and other drugs can cause an even more serious negative response to the alcohol.

The Consequences

What are the consequences of alcohol abuse in the elderly? The older adult will experience depression, malnutrition, insomnia, cognitive problems, and loss of interest in life. The failure of practitioners to determine alcohol problems in the elderly may lead to unwanted interaction between the alcohol and properly prescribed medication.Unrecognized alcohol problems may also interfere with treatment of health problems unrelated to alcohol abuse or alcoholism. The older depressed alcoholic or alcohol abuser is the person at highest risk for committing suicide in this country today. The suicide rate among alcoholics is extremely high. Because of this, the diagnosis of primary depression in treating alcohol abusers must receive special attention.

> *"Older adults . . . have a better treatment prognosis than any other age group."*

The elderly are more at risk to the deleterious effects of alcohol because their bodies are weaker and they are usually on prescription drugs. We must remember that this problem is hidden because the elderly typically live alone. Also many older adults believe that alcoholism is a moral problem which makes it hard for them to seek help. Some older adults were raised in a tradition that discouraged sharing problems outside the family, and thus they may not be as comfortable sharing at a personal level with a therapist, or participating in group process. Alcohol abuse and alcoholism are not easily diagnosed in the elderly. Given the "hidden" nature of alcohol abuse for this group, conservative opinion would suggest there is an even greater prevalence of alcohol abuse and alcoholism among the elderly in the general population.

Treatment

Older adults, especially those with late-onset alcoholism, have a better treatment prognosis than any other age group. Research has shown that older alcoholics are more likely to complete their treatment and have a higher one-year sobriety rate than their younger counterparts. For this reason, alcoholism treatment among the elderly is cost-effective.

Prevention is the first means of treatment. Education of older adults regarding the hazards of a "quick fix" to deal with life's problems, and the availability of other resources to help them when in need, is essential. Educating nurses, physicians, and other service providers to the signs and symptoms of alcohol abuse and alcoholism, as well as appropriate follow-up, is critical. These professionals and others in the natural support system (for example, family members and the clergy) are equally important. Outreach and intervention are clearly the most cost-effective means of dealing with alcohol abuse and alcoholism in the elderly.

> *"Outreach and intervention are clearly the most cost-effective means of dealing with alcohol abuse and alcoholism in the elderly."*

Effective treatment for older alcohol abusers or alcoholics is responsive to age-specific considerations of biological sensitivities (such as that of alcohol concentrations) and psychosocial stressors (such as multiple losses). In addition to alcohol abuse, older adults often have health problems that need treatment. Alcohol can precipitate or worsen problems already compromising the well-being of an older person. Interaction of prescribed medications with alcohol can initiate additional health problems such as major depression, decreased or increased metabolism, additive sedation, reversible drug-induced dementia, sensory deficits, or short-term memory impairment.

Older alcohol abusers or alcoholics require the same range of services needed by younger alcoholics or alcohol abusers, such as detoxification facilities, residential or outpatient care, alcohol education, and individual and group therapies. However, the focus of treatment can differ:

Younger Alcoholics	Older Alcoholics
peer pressure	loss
work-related conflict	depression
marital difficulties	boredom
parental responsibilities	loneliness
	negative self-esteem
	decreased socialization

Late-onset alcohol abusers who drink as a reaction to the losses associated with aging benefit from group therapy which is supportive and deals with reaction to loss rather than being confrontational and dealing with the issues of younger adults. A necessarily broad range of treatment should include providing the means to cope with the problems of later life: adjustment to loss of income, spouse, or health; rebuilding social support networks; and general problem-solving. Involvement in formal community networks, especially voluntary organizations and religious involvement, can be helpful. Early-onset alcohol abusers or alcoholics may also need compulsory supervision, consistent aversive experiences related to drinking (for example, the medication disulfiram), or substitute social dependency. . . .

Given the rapidly growing number of older Americans in coming years and the increasing incidence of alcoholism in later life, it is incumbent upon the

Congress to legislate a plan for treating alcohol abuse and alcoholism among the elderly, which in addition to its costs in human terms exacts such a high financial toll.

The high institutional and treatment costs connected with alcohol abuse continue to be of monumental concern. Therefore, mechanisms of prevention and early identification of alcohol abuse in older adults must be devised to curtail later expensive institutionalization.

Studies support the cost-effectiveness of alcohol treatment. Even when only a small minority of alcohol abusers recover, cost savings remain considerable.

More longitudinal and prospective research is needed from the general population, as opposed to generalizations from data obtained from institutionalized populations.

Research for population-specific characteristics is urgently needed. Populations with specific treatment needs include older adults, women, minorities, adolescents, the homeless, and the mentally ill.

Less than 3 percent of NIAAA's [National Institute on Alcohol Abuse and Alcoholism] research funds in 1991 went toward study of alcoholism and the elderly. Given the growing number of older adults today, and in the future, more funds for research, as with prevention and treatment, must be made available.

Bibliography

Books

Al-Anon	*Youth and the Alcoholic Parent.* New York: Al-Anon Family Group Headquarters, Inc., 1991.
Margaret Bean-Bayog and Barry Stimmel, eds.	*Children of Alcoholics.* New York: Haworth Press, 1987.
Melody Beattie	*Co-Dependent No More: How to Stop Controlling Others and Start Caring for Yourself.* Revised edition. San Francisco: Harper, 1992.
Don Cahalan	*Understanding America's Drinking Problem: How to Combat the Hazards of Alcohol.* San Francisco: Jossey-Bass, 1987.
Timmen Cermak	*A Time to Heal: The Road to Recovery for Adult Children of Alcoholics.* New York: Avon Books, 1989.
Peter R. Cohen	*Helping Your Chemically Dependent Teenager Recover: A Guide for Parents and Other Concerned Adults.* Minneapolis: Johnson Institute, 1991.
Sidney Cohen	*The Alcoholism Problems.* Binghamton, NY: Haworth Press, 1983.
John C. Crabbe Jr. and R. Adron Harris, eds.	*The Genetic Basis of Alcohol and Drug Actions.* New York: Plenum Press, 1991.
James Christopher	*How to Stay Sober: Recovery Without Religion.* Buffalo: Prometheus Books, 1988.
James Christopher	*Unhooked: Staying Sober and Drug Free.* Buffalo: Prometheus Books, 1989.
Norman K. Denzin	*The Alcoholic Society: Addiction and Recovery of the Self.* New Brunswick, NJ: Transaction Publishers, 1993.
Jerry Dorsman	*How to Quit Drinking Without AA: A Complete Self-Help Guide.* Newark, DE: New Dawn, 1993.
Michael Dorris	*The Broken Cord.* New York: Harper & Row, 1989.
Herbert Fingarette	*Heavy Drinking: The Myth of Alcoholism as a Disease.* Berkeley: University of California Press, 1988.
Institute of Medicine	*Broadening the Base of Treatment for Alcohol Problems.* Washington, DC: National Academy Press, 1989.

E.M. Jellinek	*The Disease Concept of Alcoholism.* New Haven, CT: College and University Press, 1960.
Vernon E. Johnson	*I'll Quit Tomorrow: A Practical Guide to Alcoholism Treatment.* San Francisco: Harper & Row, 1980.
Jerry Johnston	*It's Killing Our Kids.* Irving, TX: Word, 1993.
Thomas H. Kelly, Richard W. Foltin, and Marian W. Fischman	"Effects of Alcohol on Human Behavior: Implications for the Workplace," in *Drugs in the Workplace.* Rockville, MD: National Institute on Drug Abuse, 1990.
Wayne Kritsberg	*The Adult Children of Alcoholics Syndrome: From Discovery to Recovery.* Pompano Beach, FL: Health Communications, Inc., 1985.
Emily Martin	*Relationships in Recovery: Healing Strategies for Couples and Families.* New York: Harper & Row, 1989.
Milton A. Maxwell	*The A.A. Experience: A Close-Up View for Professionals.* New York: McGraw-Hill, 1984.
Christina B. Parker	*When Someone You Love Drinks Too Much.* New York: Harper & Row, 1990.
Stanton Peele	*Diseasing of America: Addiction Treatment Out of Control.* Lexington, MA: Lexington Books, 1989.
Ronald L. Rogers, Chandler Scott McMillin, and Morris A. Hill	*The Twelve Steps Revisited.* New York: Bantam Books, 1990.
Walter F. Scanlon	*Alcoholism and Drug Abuse in the Workplace: Managing Care and Costs Through Employee Assistance Programs.* Westport, CT: Praeger, 1991.
Charles Sell	*Unfinished Business: Helping Adult Children Resolve Their Past.* Portland, OR: Multnomah Press, 1989.
Tina Tessina	*The Real Thirteenth Step: Discovering Confidence, Self-Reliance, and Autonomy Beyond the 12-Step Programs.* Los Angeles: Jeremy P. Tarcher, Inc., 1991.
U.S House of Representatives	*Confronting the Impact of Alcohol Labeling & Marketing on Native American Health & Culture.* Washington, DC: Government Printing Office, 1992.
U.S Senate, Committee on Labor and Human Resources, Subcommittee on Children, Family, Alcohol, and Drugs	*Breaking the Cycle: The Effects of Alcohol on Families.* Washington, DC: Government Printing Office, 1991.
Michael Windle and John Searles, eds.	*Children of Alcoholics: Critical Perspectives.* New York: The Guilford Press, 1990.
Steven J. Wolin and Sybil Wolin	*The Resilient Self.* Washington, DC: Project Resilience, 1993.

Bibliography

Bob Wright and Deborah George Wright	*Dare to Confront! How to Intervene When Someone You Care About Has an Alcohol or Drug Problem*. New York: Master-Media Limited, 1990.

Periodicals

Jill Abramson	"Alcohol Industry Is at Forefront of Efforts to Curb Drunkenness," *The Wall Street Journal*, May 21, 1991.
Sandra J. Ackerman	"Research on the Genetics of Alcoholism Is Still in Ferment," *Journal of NIH Research*, January 1992. Available from 1444 Eye St. NW, Washington, DC 20005.
Sandra R. Arbetter	"Children of Alcoholics Don't Talk, Don't Trust, Don't Feel," *Current Health 2*, February 1990. Available from 60 Revere Dr., Northbrook, IL 60062.
Judi Bailey	"The Spirituality of Twelve-Step Programs," *St. Anthony Messenger*, September 1991. Available from 1615 Republic St., Cincinnati, OH 45210.
Robert Bazell	"The Drink Link," *The New Republic*, May 7, 1990.
Kenneth Blum et al.	"Allelic Association of Human Dopamine D2 Receptor Gene in Alcoholism," *JAMA*, vol. 263, no. 15, April 18, 1990. Available from the American Medical Association, 535 N. Dearborn, Chicago, IL 60610.
David Gelman	"Clean and Sober—and Agnostic," *Newsweek*, July 8, 1991.
Boyd Gibbons	"Alcohol: The Legal Drug," *National Geographic*, February 1992.
Daniel Goleman	"Study Ties Genes to Alcoholism in Women," *The New York Times*, October 14, 1992.
Steve Hamilton	"Getting with the Program," *Crossroads*, April 1993. Available from PO Box 2809, Oakland, CA 94609.
Tom Hernandez	"Members of SOS Abandon the AA Ship and Save Themselves," *Sober Times*, February 1993, Available from PO Box 40259, San Diego, CA 92164.
Journal of Offender Rehabilitation	Entire issue on alcohol and drug rehabilitation, vol. 19, nos. 3 & 4, 1993.
Allen S. Kerr and E. Wayne Hill	"An Exploratory Study Comparing ACoAs to Non-ACoAs on Current Family Relationships," *Alcoholism Treatment Quarterly*, vol. 9, no. 1, 1992. Available from the Haworth Press, 10 Alice St. , Binghamton, NY 13904-1580.
Joanne Lipman	"Foes Claim Ad Bans Are Bad Business," *The Wall Street Journal*, February 27, 1990.
Lisa Mahon and Philip Flores	"Group Psychotherapy as the Treatment of Choice for Individuals Who Grew Up with Alcoholic Parents," *Alcoholism Treatment Quarterly*, vol. 9, nos. 3 & 4, 1992.

Joseph Martin

"The Growing Problem of Alcoholism and the Aged," *Origins*, vol. 21, no. 40, March 12, 1992. Available from National Catholic News Service, 1312 Massachusetts Ave. NW, Washington, DC 20005.

Michael Massing

"Mixed Messages," *Modern Maturity*, February/March 1992.

Media & Values

Spring/Summer 1991. Several articles on alcohol and advertising. Available from 1962 Shenandoah St. , Los Angeles, CA 90034.

National Institute on Alcohol Abuse and Alcoholism

"Finding the Gene (s) for Alcoholism," *JAMA*, vol. 263, no. 15, April 18, 1990.

Robert V. O'Brien

"The First Step: Therapy for Repression," *Alcoholism Treatment Quarterly*, vol. 9, nos. 3 & 4, 1992.

Prevention File

Spring 1991, vol. 6, no.2. Several articles on alcohol. Available from Alcohol and Other Drug Studies, UCSD Extension, X-001, La Jolla, CA 92093.

Andrew Purvis

"DNA and the Desire to Drink," *Time*, April 30, 1990.

David Rieff

"Victims All? Recovery, Co-Dependency, and the Art of Blaming Somebody Else," *Harper's*, October 1991.

Marc A. Schuckit

Drug Abuse & Alcoholism Newsletter. Available from Vista Hill Foundation, 2355 Northside Dr. , 3d Fl. , San Diego, CA 92108.

Ben Sherwood

"Wine and Poses," *The Washington Monthly*, May 1993.

Ron Winslow

"New Study Shows Inpatient Treatment May Be Best Course for Problem Drinkers," *The Wall Street Journal*, September 12, 1991.

Joshua Zimmerman

"Blitzed: Alcoholics Anonymous and Me," *The New Republic*, April 22, 1991.

Organizations to Contact

The editors have compiled the following list of organizations that are concerned with the issues debated in this book. All have publications or information available for interested readers. For best results, allow as much time as possible for the organizations to respond. The descriptions below are derived from materials provided by the organizations. This list was compiled at the date of publication. Names, addresses, and phone numbers of organizations are subject to change.

Al-Anon Family Group Headquarters
PO Box 862, Midtown Station
New York, NY 10018
(800) 344-2666 outside New York
(800) 245-4656 within New York

Al-Anon is a fellowship of men, women, and children whose lives have been affected by an alcoholic family member or friend. Members share their experiences, strength, and hope to help each other and perhaps to aid in the recovery of the alcoholic. Al-Anon Family Group Headquarters provides information on its local chapters and on its affiliated organization, Alateen. Its publications include the semiannual *Al-Anon Speaks Out* and the bimonthly *Alateen Talk*.

Alcoholics Anonymous (AA)
General Service Office
PO Box 459, Grand Central Station
New York, NY 10163
(212) 870-3400
fax: (212) 870-3003

Alcoholics Anonymous is an international fellowship of people who are recovering from alcoholism. Because AA's primary goal is to help alcoholics, it does not sponsor research or engage in education about alcoholism. AA does, however, publish pamphlets and a catalog of literature concerning the organization.

American Council on Alcohol Problems (ACAP)
3426 Bridgeland Dr.
Bridgeton, MO 63044
(314) 739-5944
fax: (314) 739-0848

ACAP is the successor organization to temperance organizations such as the American Temperance League and the Anti-Saloon League. It is composed of state temperance organizations, religious bodies, and fraternal organizations that support ACAP's philosophy of abstinence. ACAP works to restrict the availability of alcohol in the United

States by controlling alcohol advertising and educating the public concerning the harmfulness of alcohol. It serves as a clearinghouse for information and research materials and publishes the monthlies *ACAP Recap* and *The American Issue*.

Children of Alcoholics Foundation, Inc.
PO Box 4185, Grand Central Station
New York, NY 10163-4185
(800) 359-2623
(212) 754-0656

Children of Alcoholics Foundation, Inc. is a nonprofit organization devoted to helping both young and adult children of alcoholics. It develops educational programs and special materials for children of alcoholics, professionals, and the public to help break the intergenerational cycle of alcoholism. The foundation publishes information packets, brochures, reports, educational courses and materials, and distributes videos.

Hazelden Educational Materials
PO Box 176
Center City, MN 55012
(800) 328-9000
(612) 257-4010

Hazelden is a treatment center for alcoholism and drug addiction. Hazelden Educational Materials publishes and distributes a broad variety of materials on chemical dependency and recovery. A free catalog of these materials can be obtained by calling the toll-free number.

Licensed Beverage Information Council (LBIC)
1225 Eye St. NW, Suite 500
Washington, DC 20005
(202) 682-4776
fax: (202) 682-4707

LBIC is a coalition of organizations, including the Beer Institute and the Distilled Spirits Council of the United States, that represent producers of alcoholic beverages. LBIC provides grants for research on underage drinking, alcohol abuse and pregnancy, drunk driving, and alcoholism. It also distributes literature on these issues.

National Council on Alcoholism and Drug Dependence (NCADD)
12 W. 21st St.
New York, NY 10010
(800) 622-2255
(212) 206-6770

NCADD is a nonprofit organization whose goal is to educate Americans about alcohol abuse and drug addiction. Through its many local affiliates, NCADD provides community-based prevention and education programs as well as information and service referrals. NCADD publishes numerous pamphlets, brochures, and fact sheets.

Office for Substance Abuse Prevention (OSAP)
National Clearinghouse for Alcohol and Drug Information (NCADI)
PO Box 2345
Rockville, MD 20847-2345
(800) 729-6686

(301) 468-2600
TDD: (800) 487-4889 or (301) 230-2867

OSAP leads the U.S government efforts to prevent alcoholism and other drug problems among Americans. Through NCADI, OSAP provides the public with a wide variety of information on alcoholism and other addictions. NCADI answers more than fourteen thousand inquiries a month and distributes eleven million printed items annually. NCADI provides the public with scientific findings, data bases, the bimonthly *Prevention Pipeline*, videotapes, fact sheets, brochures, monographs, pamphlets, and posters.

Rational Recovery Systems (RRS)
Box 800
Lotus, CA 95651
(916) 621-2667

RRS is a national self-help organization that provides a rational way of recovery for alcoholics. Its philosophy is that alcoholics can attain sobriety on their own without depending on other people or a higher power. Rational Recovery Systems publishes materials about the organization and its method of rational-emotive therapy.

Rutgers Center of Alcoholic Studies
Smithers Hall, Busch Campus
Piscataway, NJ 08854
(201) 932-2190

The center is an international source of information of alcohol studies. Its international research focuses on the causes and treatment of alcoholism, the effects of alcohol on the human body, ways to prevent alcohol abuse, and alcohol consumption. The center offers courses on the study and treatment of alcoholism and provides information to the public through its library and its publications, which include the bimonthly *Journal of Studies on Alcohol*, books, monographs, and pamphlets.

Secular Organizations for Sobriety (SOS)
PO Box 5
Buffalo, NY 14215
(716) 834-2922

SOS is a nonprofit network of groups dedicated to helping individuals achieve and maintain sobriety. The organization believes that alcoholics can best recover by rationally choosing to make sobriety rather than alcohol a priority. Most members of SOS reject the religious basis of Alcoholics Anonymous and other similar self-help groups. SOS publishes the quarterly *SOS National Newsletter* and distributes the books *Unhooked: Staying Sober and Drug Free*, and *How to Stay Sober: Recovery Without Religion*, written by SOS founder James Christopher.

Index